# Building People, Building Programs

A PRACTITIONER'S GUIDE FOR INTRODUCING

THE MBTI® TO INDIVIDUALS AND ORGANIZATIONS

**GORDON LAWRENCE & CHARLES MARTIN**

CAPT
GAINESVILLE, FLORIDA

i

Published by
Center for Applications of Psychological Type
2815 NW 13 Street, Suite 401
Gainesville, FL 32609
352/375-0160

Center for Applications of Psychological Type, CAPT, and the CAPT logo, are trademarks of the Center for Applications of Psychological Type, Inc., in the United States and other countries.

*Looking at Type* is a trademark of the Center for Applications of Psychological Type, Inc., in the United States and other countries.

*CAPT Atlas of Type Tables* is a trademark of the Center for Applications of Psychological Type, Inc., in the United States and other countries.

Myers-Briggs Type Indicator, Myers-Briggs, and MBTI are trademarks or registered trademarks of the Myers-Briggs Type Indicator Trust in the United States and other countries.

*Introduction to Type* is a registered trademark of the Myers-Briggs Type Indicator Trust in the United States and other countries.

Printed in the United States of America.

ISBN 0-935652-54-X


Library of Congress Cataloging-in-Publication Data

Lawrence, Gordon, 1930–
Building people, building programs: a practitioner's guide for introducing the MBTI® to individuals and organizations/Gordon D. Lawrence, Charles R. Martin.

    p. cm.

    Includes bibliographical references.

    ISBN 0-935652-54-X

    1. Myers-Briggs Type Indicator. 2. Typology (Psychology) I. Martin, Charles R. II. Title.

BF698.8.M94 L39 2000

155.2'64—dc21                                  00-026200

# Acknowledgements

MANY PEOPLE have come to CAPT for training to become MBTI practitioners. Responding to their needs over the years prompted us to write this book. We are very grateful to workshop participants for the questions they brought, the issues and problems they shared with us, and the reactions and advice they gave us in our attempts to meet their needs. Their contributions were the sparks that lit the writing process, and the result is a book that we hope will meet the needs of both new and experienced practitioners in the type community.

We want to thank all of the friends and colleagues who helped make this book happen—there are too many to thank individually. Three people were closely involved with the manuscript, and we want to give them a hearty thank you. Keven Ward and Heather Curry helped nurture the book into reality through patient and brilliant editing and suggestions. Our appreciation also goes to Tom Thompson for his excellent and constructive feedback on the manuscript.

FROM CHARLES MARTIN—A book of this nature can only come into being through the concerted efforts, caring, experiences, input and vision of a number of people. Thank you to all of the people in my personal and professional life who have supported and contributed to this project. My deep appreciation goes to Gordon Lawrence who continues to teach me and talk with me about type in all of its subtlety and variations. He has been a mentor and a friend, and I have a deep and abiding respect for him and his work. Thank you as always to Mary McCaulley for her warm support and wisdom and for the opportunities she provides every day to learn about type. My wife and daughter are constant lights in my life and, well, how can I ever thank them enough?

Thank you Tamara and Alex for supporting who I am and what I do. And finally, thank you to all the individuals and groups who let me know in words and behaviors what they needed when learning about type. I hope in the end this book will serve teachers as well as students of psychological type.

FROM GORDON LAWRENCE—For over 25 years I have had the great blessing of working with a group of scholars of psychological type and expert users of the MBTI. We were drawn to this extraordinary instrument because of the brilliant lifetime of work of its author, Isabel Briggs Myers. We came together as a small community mainly through the initiatives of Mary McCaulley and through the forming and nurturing of the Association for Psychological Type. Our deep respect for the MBTI fired our efforts to promote and develop MBTI training programs of the highest quality we could collectively accomplish. This book draws on those collective efforts. They shaped much of what I know and have written about here. I am very grateful for the rich experiences I have had with these colleagues.

Two members of the group died this past year—John DiTiberio and Susan Brock. I miss them very much. My work on this book is dedicated to them and to their families who shared them with our community of MBTI workers.

Working with Charles Martin, on the book and in other respects, has been a treat for me. His knowledge of type and his skills as a trainer and writer are exceptional.

Finally, this book has been written because my wife, through her love and support, her belief in me and in the power of psychological type, helped to build into our lives the time to do the writing. Thank you, Carolyn.

**BUILDING PEOPLE**
**BUILDING PROGRAMS**

# Contents

*This guide is for people who have been introduced to the Myers-Briggs Type Indicator (MBTI), who see its potential for use in their own work, and who want to learn what is needed to start using it in their work with individuals and organizations.*

# Chapter 1

**WHY THIS GUIDE?** This practitioner's guide contains:

- the background information you will need before using the MBTI
- specific techniques and language to use with clients when explaining the ideas behind the MBTI
- suggestions you can give clients for using the MBTI in their lives
- what experienced MBTI users have learned about effective uses of the Indicator in organizations
- what the beginning MBTI practitioner needs to get from the *MBTI Manual*, including useful summaries of data from the *Manual*
- an introduction to exercises you can use with client groups, and frameworks for building and delivering MBTI training programs

Each chapter begins by orienting you with a list of the kinds of client questions that chapter will help you answer—as well as a list of topics to be covered. A glance at the table of contents of this practitioner's guide will also give you the specifics of the topics covered in each chapter. In addition, in each chapter you will find helpful boxes with summaries and hints for type users and trainers. In short, this book will help you introduce the MBTI and psychological type to individuals and organizations—to help you begin building people and building training programs.

**IS THIS THE MBTI MANUAL?** No. This practitioner's guide is not the *MBTI Manual*. Every user of a psychological instrument should own and use the manual prepared by the instrument's developer or publisher. For the MBTI, the publisher is Consulting Psychologists Press. The manual is the *MBTI Manual: A Guide to the Development and Use of the Myers-Briggs Type Indicator* (1998, Third Edition). Because the *Manual* is a comprehensive document—written for researchers, psychometricians and experienced users of the MBTI as well as beginning users—it contains more than you will need to get started. Part of our job in writing this practitioner's guide was to point out the parts of the *Manual* a beginning user of the MBTI needs to understand.

**HOW MUCH PREPARATION DO I NEED?** When first encountering the MBTI instrument and the descriptions of the personality types it indicates, many people see it as a fairly simple and straightforward system that one could start using without much preparation. That is a false impression. It is a sophisticated instrument developed over decades, and its ethical and effective use requires careful and continuing study. Its potential for helping clients is very great, but its incautious use can be hurtful—not only to clients, but to the reputation of the user as well. In short, it is unethical to use the MBTI without following the essential guidelines given in the *Manual* and presented in this book. This guide will help you begin well and avoid the mistakes we have seen happen all too often. Because of the potential for misuse, the sale of the MBTI is limited to qualified purchasers.

**WHO CAN BUY AND USE THE MBTI?** The MBTI is classified by the American Psychological Association as a controlled instrument, with its use limited to people who are qualified. To be qualified, a person has to have a professional use for the Indicator and have completed a college course in psychological tests and measurement. Someone who has taken a course in tests and measurement has learned about the pitfalls of using an instrument without first studying its manual and finding out how to use the instrument effectively and ethically.

The publisher of a controlled instrument has the responsibility of deciding who is qualified to purchase it. If you have had such a course, you can contact Consulting Psychologists Press (CPP) at 800-624-1765 and obtain a Professional Qualifications form to complete and return. CPP assigns a purchaser number to those they qualify and informs them by mail. The purchaser number is used when ordering the MBTI materials that are controlled: the question booklets, answer sheets and templates used for scoring. A similar process is followed when purchasing controlled materials through the Center for Applications of Psychological Type (CAPT). CPP and other organizations also publish and distribute many non-controlled materials related to use of the MBTI. We have included a fairly wide sampling of them in our resources sections at the end of each chapter.

**IS THERE ANOTHER WAY TO BECOME A QUALIFIED PURCHASER AND USER OF THE MBTI?** Yes. The MBTI is used in a number of professions. In some of them, coursework in psychological tests and measurement may not have been part of the professional training. To fill this gap, MBTI experts have designed qualifying training that combines the basics of tests and measurement with the MBTI essentials one needs to start using the Indicator. Consulting

Psychologists Press has authorized six organizations to conduct MBTI qualifying programs. Participants who pass the written exam given at the end of the training—the same exam is used in all the programs—are regarded by CPP as having sufficient work in tests and measurement to qualify to purchase the MBTI. The programs vary in approach and duration, but all include an on-site workshop of four days or more, preceded by home study. The workshops are offered in all regions of the United States and southern Canada, and in other English-speaking countries. The following organizations are licensed to conduct MBTI qualifying programs:

- Association for Psychological Type (APT)
  847-375-4717
- Center for Applications of Psychological Type (CAPT)
  800-777-2278
- Otto Kroeger Associates
  703-591-6284
- Temperament Research Institute (TRI)
  800-700-4874
- Type Resources
  800-456-6284
- Zeisset Associates
  402-435-0933

**WHAT IF MY STATISTICS AND MEASUREMENT SKILLS ARE RUSTY?** You may want to attend one of the qualifying programs. Program providers have found that about 25% of their participants have already completed college coursework in tests and measurement and choose to attend to get their skills refreshed in the context of learning about the MBTI as an instrument.

If you plan to use this book to guide your starting with the MBTI and want to sharpen your statistics skills as they are needed to understand the Indicator and its uses, there is a short, user-friendly book you can get: *Statistics and Measurement: An Introduction for MBTI Users,* (2000, Third Edition) by R. M. Zeisset, published by the Center for Applications of Psychological Type (CAPT) (800-777-2278). The MBTI has measurement features unlike nearly all other psychological instruments. These are well explained in the Zeisset book, and several of the qualifying programs use it.

**TO USE THIS GUIDE DO I NEED ANY OTHER RESOURCES?** Yes. You need a copy of the *MBTI Manual*, Third Edition. As you use the rest of this guide you will encounter other publications you may want to use with clients or for your own study.

**WHAT KIND OF MATERIAL DOES THIS GUIDE INCLUDE?** Our purpose was to make this book an interactive and practical resource for learning about and using the MBTI. For each topic, we have included—to the extent possible—exercises for you and materials you can use with clients. And each of these is accompanied by relevant supporting concepts, explanations, reasons and research.

| YOU WILL FIND: | ACCOMPANIED BY: |
|---|---|
| • presentation materials you may copy and use | • explanations of the presentations and reasons for them |
| • appropriate language to use in introducing the MBTI and the ideas that underlie it | • the concepts underlying the MBTI and reasons for the choices of the recommended language |
| • procedures to use in scoring the MBTI, and ways to report results | • the rationale for the MBTI scoring and reporting processes |
| • examples of questions clients ask and our suggestions for answering them | • the reasons why some answers are good and some answers are not |
| • sample handout materials that can be purchased from various sources | • rationale and guidelines for using these and similar handouts |
| • steps in setting conditions for using the MBTI in an organization | • reasons for the steps, and pitfalls you can avoid by using them |
| • ethical issues in using the MBTI | • suggestions for dealing with them |
| • steps in applying the MBTI ideas in various settings | • reasons for the steps, matching the various settings |
| • sample exercises you may use with individuals or client groups, such as teams | • rationales behind the exercises and guidelines for setting them up and debriefing them |
| • suggestions for summaries of research you may want to use with clients in particular settings | • samples of research data, and explanations of them |

Throughout this guide you will find references to source documents and other resources you may want to obtain. The end of each chapter lists the resources noted in that chapter. We recommend that you follow the order of the chapters in using this guide. The information in each builds on the information from preceding ones. We have also included exercises, checklists and self-tests in the chapters, to help you check your understanding and to summarize the important points. We hope you have fun as you continue to learn and teach about type!

**Resources**

Myers, I. B., McCaulley, M. H., Quenk, N. L., & Hammer, A. L. (1998). *Manual: A guide to the development and use of the Myers-Briggs Type Indicator* (3rd ed.). Palo Alto, CA: Consulting Psychologists Press.

Zeisset, R. M. (2000). *Statistics and measurement: An introduction for MBTI users.* Gainesville, FL: Center for Applications of Psychological Type.

*Just what is the MBTI and where did it come from?*

*Why do I need to know about type theory?*
*It seems as though giving the Indicator*
*is straightforward.*

*Why can't I just give someone their results*
*and let them read about their type?*

*Why is it so important to "verify" their type?*

*Everyone says the MBTI isn't like other instruments.*
*What do they mean by that?*

*How did the MBTI know so much about*
*me when I told it so little?*

*I keep hearing that Myers had to face a number*
*of issues no one had faced before when she developed*
*the MBTI.*
*What kind of things did she face?*

THIS CHAPTER INCLUDES background information that will help you, the MBTI professional, better use the MBTI and type theory. You may wish to share some of this material with the people to whom you are giving feedback. However, the material is *crucial* to your understanding, and sets the context for appropriate use of the instrument and appropriate teaching of type theory.

This chapter is divided into two broad sections. In the first section there are readings on some general theoretical issues in the use of the MBTI. In this first section, we will cover:

- a brief history of the MBTI
- why understanding type theory is so important in using the MBTI
- the limits of psychological instruments in general
- how the MBTI is like and different from other psychological instruments

In the second section, there is a summary of the more specific nitty-gritty issues Isabel Myers faced in developing the MBTI. In this section, some of the key topics covered are:

- how and why items were selected
- how the MBTI differs from other instruments

- why people are forced to choose between two responses

**WHY DO I NEED TO KNOW ALL OF THIS BACKGROUND?** You may be asking, "Why do I need to know so much about the context of the MBTI's development and how it was constructed?"

The answer is that you need to know what the MBTI is, and what it is not. Anyone who explains and interprets MBTI results will be asked questions about the instrument, and some of them will be tough questions that go right to the heart of the construction issues. A sample of tough questions often asked: "Some items are about such trivial things; how can they measure anything important about psychological makeup?" "Where did the items come from, and how can you be sure they measure Jung's types?" "How accurate can a self-report instrument be?" Answers given to such questions reflect directly on the credibility of the MBTI and the theory it represents. Those who interpret the results of a psychological instrument to a client have an ethical responsibility to know—to the best of their ability—the strengths and limits of the instrument, and its features that bear on the subtleties of interpretation. Knowing what the MBTI *is* will help you use it in appropriate and helpful ways. Knowing what the MBTI *is not* will help you avoid using the Indicator and type in unethical ways, or ways that limit your clients.

**General Issues:**
**Brief history**
**of the MBTI**

Isabel Briggs Myers and her mother, Katharine Cook Briggs, developed the Myers-Briggs Type Indicator. Their aim was to create a tool to indicate, validate and put to practical use C. G. Jung's work on psychological types. Jung (1875–1961) was a Swiss psychiatrist whose book *Psychological Types* was an outgrowth of his efforts to understand individual differences among people. Jung observed people over many years and developed a model that helped describe the patterns in people's behavior.

Katharine Cook Briggs (1875–1968) and her daughter, Isabel Briggs Myers (1897–1980), encountered Jung's ideas in 1923. They decided his ideas were so powerful that if only the public could learn about them, then people could make better life choices and use individual differences in constructive ways. Thus began two decades of "type watching." After several years of adding her own observations to those of Jung, Myers began creating a paper-and-pencil questionnaire to assess type. The Indicator was developed over the next three decades as research was collected on thousands of people. Research on the Indicator has continued into the present, with dozens of articles published each year.

The important piece of information here is that the MBTI is based on a *theory* developed by Jung. Jung's and Myers' descriptions captured the essence of the types, and the MBTI was developed to try to help people identify the type that was the best fit for them—that is, it was intended to point people to a description to "try on for size." The power was, and is, in the theory and the descriptions themselves, and the Indicator was so named because its intent was to direct people to a type description to read. This was the first step in helping people determine their best-fit type.

In 1975, Consulting Psychologists Press began publishing the MBTI for applied uses. In that same year, Isabel Myers and Mary McCaulley founded the Center for Applications of Psychological Type (CAPT), a nonprofit organization created to continue research on the Indicator and to provide training and education on type and the MBTI.

Since the MBTI's publication, applications of and research on type have expanded nationally and internationally. The MBTI has been translated into almost thirty languages. Since type describes some fundamental differences in the way people approach the world, take in information and make decisions, it relates to the multitude of situations people encounter every day. Thus, publications about type have appeared in the areas of education, careers, management, leadership, intimate relationships, counseling, parenting, children, teamwork, spirituality and life-long development.

==The intent behind the development and applications of psychological type in all cases is the belief that understanding your type can help you appreciate your own strengths, gifts and potential developmental needs, and also help you understand and appreciate how and why others may differ from you.==

## The limits of psychological instruments

PSYCHOLOGICAL INSTRUMENTS designed to measure personality have limits.

What we are saying here is that the MBTI is not a perfectly accurate measure of personality—of your particular type, or of type in general. ==*No* measure of personality is perfectly accurate.== Neither does the MBTI measure, nor purport to measure, all the components of personality.

Unlike measurement in the physical world, measurement in the psychological world is a bit more slippery and inaccurate. When you use a ruler to measure a length of shelf one day, you should get the same length if you measure it again the next day. That's because the shelf is solid and stable (OK, no comments from the physicists out there), and so is the ruler. You get accuracy and consistency.

However, when you attempt to measure personality, you are faced with a variety of difficulties in assessing it accurately and consistently. In personality assessment, these difficulties are referred to as measurement error. We'll talk about these issues more in later chapters, but for now, let's look at the highlights.

- Personality is not directly observable and measurable; that is, we can only extrapolate someone's personality type from his or her responses on the MBTI.
- The theory used to describe the personality may not be exactly right (the map is not the territory).
- The theory won't fit every individual exactly (people are more than their type).
- The MBTI is a tool for self-understanding, not for assessing others to pigeonhole them.
- Many things can influence someone's results on the MBTI, including:

**Type development:** Some may be unclear about their preferences because they are not yet well developed.

**Social expectation:** Some might have trouble distinguishing their true preferences from the expectations or preferences of their parents, family or friends.

**Work-home differences:** Respondents might have difficulty seeing their true preferences if their work asks them to behave in ways that are very different from their best-fit type. Or some might respond in a way that is the perceived "best" type for their jobs. This may be particularly likely if the respondent believes someone in authority will see the results.

**Development of nonpreferences:** Some might be "working on" a function, say Feeling, even though they are a Thinking type, and this work could lead to unclear responses.

**Beliefs:** Some might have beliefs about which is the "best" type to be, or what they "wish" they were. People can have greater or lesser levels of awareness that they are responding in this way.

**Stress:** People may respond under stress or in times of crisis in ways that are not typical of their behavior.

These are all reasons why we take such care to help people verify their results from the MBTI, rather than just giving them their results and "telling them" what their type is. The goal is to help people assess and verify their *true* type. The MBTI is *one tool* in the process of helping someone discover his or her best-fit type.

Another very important issue is that type is *just a theory*. It is a mental model developed to try to explain differences observed in people's behaviors and experiences of themselves. Type is a *very good* model of personality—it captures and explains many differences among individuals. However, type cannot (and does not purport to) explain all behaviors. Sometimes other personality theories may explain a person's behavior better than does type theory. Type theory is always up for revision if the revision better captures and explains individual differences.

In short, there are many reasons why someone may not be the type reported by the MBTI. Thus, it is important to help people read their MBTI results with the above issues in mind. The Indicator is an excellent tool for pointing people to a type that may be a good fit for them. Again, remember: the MBTI is based on a set of observations about people and a theory based on those observations. The instrument was designed to help people find the type that is the best fit *for them*. The instrument should not be used to "insist" a person is the type reported by the Indicator, because there are many factors that can influence results on the MBTI. Certainly, taking the Indicator can help one narrow down where to start reading the type descriptions, but it is the individual who ultimately decides which type description fits him or her best.

**How the MBTI is like and different from other psychological instruments**

THE MBTI IS A PSYCHOLOGICAL INSTRUMENT. Make no mistake. It was developed and is used in a fashion consistent with criteria described by professionals who create and use such instruments. In general though, as MBTI practitioners, we often prefer not to call it a psychological instrument, because the public often has negative associations with the use of the term "psychological." And we certainly never call it a "test." The word "test" often suggests that there can be right or wrong answers. Professionals who use the MBTI will often refer to it as the Indicator, or a personality indicator, inventory or questionnaire.

**THE MBTI IS SIMILAR TO OTHER PSYCHOLOGICAL INSTRUMENTS IN THAT:**

- it is a paper-and-pencil instrument designed to assess some qualities of one's personality
- people are asked to respond to questions about their preferences in various situations, and the result is an indicated "type" of personality
- knowing one's type gives insight into one's motives, behaviors and interactions with others

**THE MBTI IS UNLIKE MANY OTHER PSYCHOLOGICAL INSTRUMENTS IN THAT IT:**

- makes no assessment of mental health; there is no bad or unhealthy way to come out on the MBTI
- sorts personalities into different types rather than measuring personality in terms of amounts of qualities (that is, it identifies *types* rather than *traits*)
- assesses a person only in terms of their own responses rather than comparing that person's responses to the responses of others
- is built on a theory of dynamic interactions among preferences
- leaves the final assessment of the accuracy of the results in the hands of the respondent

Let's look at each of these for a moment.

**Mental health.** Many other psychological instruments (though by no means all) are designed to assess the level of one's functioning. They measure such things as aptitude, stress, depression, intelligence, shyness, and so on. The MBTI is different. There is no bad or unhealthy way to come out on the Indicator, because all of the types described in type theory are good types. The different types simply have different ways of taking in information and making decisions. No matter how you answer the MBTI, you can't come out in an *unhealthy* way. The MBTI's primary intent is for self-discovery—what is *right* with you.

**Type vs. trait.** Most personality instruments measure the *amount* of a particular quality that a person has. For example, people can be viewed as more or less happy, more or less sociable, more or less conscientious. That is, *conscientiousness* is a personality trait, the amount of which can be measured on a continuum. The MBTI and type theory differ from this way of assessing personality. In type theory, the different personality types are *qualitatively* different from each other, not in terms of amount, but in terms of being entirely different *kinds* of personality. In type theory, Extraverts are believed to be different from Introverts in the same way that apples are different from oranges—they are fundamentally different things. Trait theory would be more interested in the amount of "orangeness" one had, which from a type perspective doesn't make much sense.

In trait theory, the amount of a personality quality is often associated with a value judgment of some kind. For example, too little sociability might not be good. Neither would too much sociability. In type theory, one cannot have too much or too little of a type—one is either an Extravert or an Introvert. The value comes from knowing which one is, and knowing the consequences of being one or the other.

**Responses are not compared to those of others.** The type vs. trait issue also speaks to one other way in which the MBTI differs from many other instruments. In responding to the MBTI, one repeatedly chooses between phrases or word-pair questions. Your indicated type is determined by comparing your own responses to your own responses—to which side did you cast more votes? Other instruments, based on trait models, would compare your responses to those of other people to see "how much" of a certain trait you had relative to others. For example, how conscientious you are compared to other people your age, in your school, in your profession, and so on. On the MBTI and in type theory, whether you are an Extravert *or* an Introvert is the important issue, and that is determined by looking only at your responses. Once you have cast your votes, you are pointed to a description to read, a description that captures some of the qualities of your whole *type*—the nature of your appleness or orangeness.

**A dynamic model.** Another dramatic way in which the MBTI differs from other instruments is that it is built on a model of personality that involves the dynamic interaction among various mental functions. Thus, although the preference categories of the MBTI were designed to be statistically uncorrelated (independent of one another), within type theory the preferences are seen to interact in dynamic and complex ways. For example, one does not get a full description of a type by combining descriptors from each of the four separate preferences (e.g., E, N, T and P). Rather, a full description of a type comes from knowing that someone of that type orients some functions to the outer world, and some to the inner world, and that persons of that type prefer the mental functions in a certain order. For example, ENTPs extravert their favored Intuition and introvert their Thinking, while Sensing is their least preferred function. The import of this interaction will become clearer in Chapter Three, where we explain type dynamics. Knowing the dynamic theory also helps us as professionals to help our clients clarify their best-fit type.

**The respondent decides the accuracy.** This leads into the final issue. On the MBTI, the type that a person reports on the Indicator is considered a hypothesis that needs to be verified by the respondent as he or she tries on different type descriptions to determine which is the best fit. On many other psychological instruments, the assumption is that you get a result, and that is your result. The assumption with the MBTI is that it is a tool for self-discovery, and that the respondent weighs his or her reported type with other information to determine his or her best-fit type—which may or may not be the type reported on the MBTI. The other information weighed in the decision typically includes informal self-assessment, various readings, talking with others and self-observation. The degree to which someone's reported type is treated as a hypothesis can also vary greatly depending on the skill, experience and sensitivity of the MBTI user.

THIS NEXT SECTION moves into more of the specifics of the Indicator's development. We recommend reading this section before you use the MBTI with your clients. It will help answer a number of questions clients often ask about the rigor of the instrument's development.

## Specific key issues in the development of the Indicator*

Form M of the Indicator was developed after Isabel Myers' death. Although Form M and Form G of the MBTI are scored differently, the topics discussed in this section reflect issues that are relevant to both forms. Your understanding of all of these issues will give you deeper knowledge of the context and nature of the Indicator—and will make you a more informed user of the instrument today, whichever form you use. Those readers who want to understand the specific differences between the earlier forms of the MBTI (Forms A, B, C, D, E, F and G) are referred to Chapter Seven of the *MBTI Manual*, Third Edition.

The scope of the task of creating the Type Indicator was far broader and more complex than Isabel Myers or anyone else realized at the beginning. She was aware of some of the special conditions and needs of the project, but many more emerged as she proceeded. Following are some of the specific issues Myers faced as she developed the Indicator.

**1) ATTITUDES AMONG PSYCHOLOGY PROFESSIONALS.** In the 1940s, psychological testing was still new, and personality testing even newer. Norms and standards were uncertain, and exemplary tests were few. Isabel Myers knew that the psychological community would give a skeptical critique to any new instrument. In addition, Carl Jung's work was not well accepted in academic psychology at the time, and the instrument was based on Jung's theory of types. Today, the MBTI is one of the most widely used assessments in the world, but many researchers and practitioners in the social sciences still have trouble accepting the measurement assumptions of the instrument. Often this lack of acceptance is due to a misunderstanding of the theoretical underpinnings of the instrument (e.g., how type assessment differs from trait assessment).

**2) TYPE VARIABLES DO NOT FIT THE NORMAL CURVE.** One of the difficulties researchers have had with the MBTI is that statistics typically used in doing research with other instruments do not apply in the same way to the Indicator. Observations over many years suggested that the American population would not be evenly distributed among the sixteen types. If Sensing types do indeed outnumber Intuitive types, and if S–N scores were put on a single continuum with a mid-point of zero, the distribution of scores along the "scale" would certainly not be the normal, bell-shaped curve with which

*Adapted and extended from Lawrence, G. D. (1986). Issues in the development of the MBTI. *Journal of Psychological Type*, 12, 2–7.

psychological test makers and other researchers are accustomed to working. How would non-normal distribution affect the selection of statistics to be used with the Indicator? If Sensing and Intuition were examined as separate "scales," should the distribution of scores on each show a normal curve relevant at all to the Indicator's construction?

**3) CONSTRAINTS OF A SELF-REPORT FORMAT.** Those of us familiar with the MBTI take for granted the self-report form of questions used in it. Her many years of observing type-related behaviors convinced Isabel Myers that type preferences do exist and can manifest themselves in behavior. Whether people could self-report the preferences accurately was unknown. Briggs and Myers observed behavior patterns through eyes that had become expert. People taking the Indicator would know nothing about type theory and have no experience in looking for type-related behaviors. Therefore, the questions needed to be very carefully constructed to elicit true self-reports without the respondents having any knowledge of the ideas underlying the questions.

**4) FINDING NON-THEORETICAL AND NON-THREATENING LANGUAGE.** The theory of psychological type is complex, but the language of the Indicator items needed to be simple and non-theoretical. It had to be familiar and free of psychological jargon that might make people hesitant to respond. Questions had to be written that dealt with "seemingly simple surface behaviors in the hope that they would provide reliable clues to the complex and profound patterns that could not otherwise be reached in a self-report instrument…The strategy was to use observable 'straws in the wind' to make inferences about the direction of the wind itself" (Myers & McCaulley, 1985, page 141).

**5) REPRESENTING THE DICHOTOMOUS NATURE OF JUNG'S THEORY.** Jung and Myers believed that opposite types (e.g., Extraverts and Introverts) were *qualitatively different from each other*—that is, opposite types live in qualitatively different worlds, and are as different as the front and back of a coin. Because the theory is concerned with people's preferences between desirable opposites, the Indicator items needed to force them to choose between two answers that both have value. If people were presented each choice of a pair separately, both could be chosen as favored, and the preference of one over the other could not be identified. The need to have a forced-choice format brought about problems described in later paragraphs. This next issue is closely related to the idea that type is about qualitatively different categories of people.

**6) CREATING AN INSTRUMENT THAT SORTS RATHER THAN MEASURES.** Personality and educational instruments most commonly identify the quantity of a trait or skill that the respondent has. Isabel Myers was faced with the task of devising a means of *sorting* people into the theoretical categories of type. Most of the literature on test construction was concerned with *measuring* the skillfulness of a performance or the strength of a trait. She had to break new ground in instrument development and justify her innovations. While she was concerned with measuring the clarity of a preference, for example, of Intuition over Sensing, her purpose was not to measure whether someone had more or better Intuition than someone else. Moreover, the measurement of clarity of preference was subordinate to sorting the person into the "true" type category. There was considerable risk that the Indicator would be misunderstood, and she recognized the need for a carefully prepared *Manual* to minimize the risks.

**7) IDENTIFYING THE DOMINANT AND AUXILIARY FUNCTIONS.** In *Psychological Types*, Jung explained the concepts of dominant and auxiliary functions, but did not address the problem of identifying which preferred function is dominant and which is auxiliary. For example, if a person favors Introversion, Sensing and Thinking, how does one identify whether Sensing or Thinking is the dominant (most-favored) function? Briggs and Myers had to solve that problem as they approached the construction of the Indicator.

In her own research prior to the publication of Jung's book, Katharine Briggs identified people she called "spontaneous" and "executive" types. In merging her work into Jung's more complete theory, she realized that "spontaneous" described the *outward appearance* of people who used a perceiving function (Sensing or Intuition) mainly to run their outer lives.

Thus one useful way to distinguish the types was by the outward appearance of a Judging or Perceiving preference. If a J–P preference could be identified, then each type's dominant preference could be identified. The J–P preference, indicating the function most used outwardly, would be showing the dominant function for Extraverts, who prefer the outer world. For Introverts, who by definition reserve the dominant function for the inner world, the J–P index would point to the auxiliary function. As we know, the J–P index was developed successfully. A fuller explanation of the dominant and auxiliary functions and how to identify the dominant in each type can be found later in this guide, as well as in the *Manual,* Third Edition (Myers, McCaulley, Quenk, & Hammer, 1998).

**8) DEVELOPING BALANCED AND UNBIASED ITEMS.** People of different types reacted very differently to particular items that Isabel Myers wrote. It seemed vital that the choices in each item be made to appeal to type differences without one choice appearing to be more legitimate than the other. Both had to seem reasonable and responsible while at the same time differentiating people by type. How does one begin to know that an item is not biased and unbalanced, even for a minority of people? Briggs and Myers, through years of observation, developed a *criterion group* of relatives and friends, about twenty people "whose type preferences seemed to the authors to be clearly evident from long acquaintance" (Myers, McCaulley, Quenk, & Hammer, 1998, page 128).

A new Thinking–Feeling item, for example, on a three-by-five card, would be tried with those people in the criterion group whose preferences for Thinking or Feeling could be seen clearly enough to be manifest consistently in observable behavior. Items were kept if a greater than average number of the criterion group of Thinking types agreed with the T choice, and fewer than half of the Feeling types agreed with it. A similar process was used for the items for all four dimensions. Some people close to Briggs and Myers knew about type theory and were asked to improve the wording of items so that the choices would appeal more to their own types. Many hundreds of items were eventually evaluated in this way.

Using the criterion group to evaluate possible items was Myers' first step in a long process of testing the *validity* of the Indicator; that is, testing how accurately and adequately it did what it was supposed to do. She had a set of items that were balanced and unbiased when tested on the criterion group, but would the items be adequate with people outside that small group? The next step was to transfer the acceptable items from three-by-five cards into the first version of the Indicator and administer it to a larger number of people—including many people that Myers and Briggs had not observed for type. Each item was then tested to see how well people's responses to it matched their results on the total index. Items that did not match well were eliminated. For example, on the E–I index, she examined the results of people who scored as Extraverts to see how many of them chose the responses that were supposed to be Extravert choices. In the development of Form M, old and new items were initially included in the research form if they met similar criteria. New statistical theories and methods (e.g., item response theory, factor analysis) were used to make final item selections for Form M.

**9) ACCOUNTING FOR WAYS THAT EACH TYPE MIGHT ANSWER.** What if different types approached the Indicator questions with different strategies or mind-sets of how to search their memory of experiences for an appropriate answer? How can the Indicator be made sensitive to such different strategies? One difference in mind-set that emerged was between Extraverts and Introverts. Myers found that Extraverts tended to respond to a question by recalling the last time they actually made such a choice and then answering as they acted in that situation. Introverts tended to pick the key words in choices A and B, compare them, and decide which were most generally like them. Myers, an Introvert, had supposed everyone would use the latter strategy. From this, she decided to construct the word-pairs section of the Indicator to add to its ability to distinguish between the types. The use of both phrase questions and word pairs has continued in the MBTI's most recent revision, Form M.

**10) GETTING PRECISION AT THE MIDPOINT.** Precision at the midpoint for the Indicator is extremely important. Since type theory describes dichotomous categories of people, determining which side of the "fence" you are on is *the* most important assessment issue. Thus, the objective of the Indicator bi-polar preference categories was to sort individuals as accurately as possible to the side of the dichotomy that was the best fit for them—with the least overlap. That is, the MBTI needed to put every person "*in the category he belongs to, even if only by one point.* This problem has little or no precedent in statistics. It is the problem of the shepherd in the parable who left the ninety-nine sheep that were in the right place, and went after the one that had gone astray. The chief concern in improving the scoring of the Indicator is to recover the people who have strayed across the line" (Myers, undated, page 8). Placing people on the correct side of the midpoint turned out to be a complex problem that has been addressed throughout the development of the Indicator.

**11) SETTING THE DIVISION POINT OF EACH INDEX.** How could one objectively determine whether the midpoint is set just where it should be to distinguish between the Extraverts and Introverts, the Sensing types and Intuitive types, etc.? This was a tough question, one that was ultimately answered by examining how Extraverts and Introverts, for example, differ on measures of other characteristics (e.g., measures of aptitude, grade point average, gregariousness). On page 133 of the *Manual*, Third Edition, there is a description of how grade point average (GPA) data were used to relocate the division point on the E–I index. Introverts as a group tend to get higher GPAs than Extraverts, regardless of preference clarity. In this study, there was a jump in average GPA near the midpoint, where those with a slight preference for Introversion had a higher average GPA than those who showed a slight preference for Extraversion. These data were used to set the division point. Myers, and later the Form M development team, accumulated data for each of the four dichotomies to confirm the placement of the midpoint for each index.

Similar results were found in a study reported in the second edition of the *Manual* (page 163). Students who had a slight preference for Extraversion were seen as having gregarious qualities (as rated by faculty) much more like the other Extraverts than like the students who scored Introvert just across the midpoint. When graphed along a base of E–I scores, the only discontinuity in the slope of the ratings occurred exactly at the established midpoint of the E–I index. In the development of Form M, although the scoring is based on item response theory (IRT)*, the division points were set in a similar fashion. Individuals' MBTI results on each dichotomy were compared to an external criterion—in this case, those individuals' assessments of their best-fit type category.

**12) WEIGHTING THE ITEMS.** Beginning with the first sample of people whose type was unknown, Myers was concerned with those who scored near the midpoint. She knew that psychological test developers do their item analyses leaving out the people who score in the middle range of a scale being developed. Thus their criterion groups contain people with clear, contrasting differences. She knew that would be the wrong strategy for the Indicator because it needed precision in the middle to place correctly the people whose preferences were slight. So she defined her criterion groups to include them.

"The Extravert criterion groups included everyone with as many as two or more answers for E than I, and the Introvert groups everyone with as many as two or more answers for I than for E, and so on…The decision to include nearly all of the sample in the criterion groups was of course hard on the questions. It is much easier for an item to discriminate between top and bottom tenths or even top and bottom quarters than between top and bottom almost-halves. But in scoring a dichotomy, a question valid only for the top and bottom quarters obscures the very cases you most want clarified, the ones in the middle." (Myers, undated, page 5).

Through Form G, extra weight was given to items that discriminated well. In Forms C through G, the weight was given using a prediction ratio to determine if item choices should be weighted zero, one or two. In Form M, scoring is based on IRT, which varies the weight of *each item for each individual respondent*. The complexity of this type of scoring requires computer

* IRT scoring is based in modern test theory and varies the weight of each item for each individual respondent. For example, IRT scoring asks: given this person's pattern of responses to the Sensing–Intuition items, what is the likelihood of his or her being a Sensing or Intuitive type?

scoring of the MBTI, although a "close enough" result may be had using Form M templates.

**13) INFLUENCE OF SOCIAL DESIRABILITY ON RESPONSES.** When responding to questions on psychological tests, respondents will often answer a question not because the answer fits them, but because the answer reflects some quality that is considered to be the "best," most popular, most culturally acceptable or most *socially desirable*. In Forms C through G, the prediction ratio formula that was used to determine the weight of each response was also a way of controlling for this tendency of individuals to select responses that did not fit their type but which were "popular" for all types. The responses that were more socially desirable (that is, they were often chosen by the opposite type) got a lesser weight because they did not discriminate between the types as well. The responses that were very good at discriminating between the types got a higher weighting in the results. Thus, for example, an Extravert answer that attracted too many people who otherwise scored as Introverts was given zero weight, while the Introvert side of the response was weighted one or two. The forced choice format in general helps protect against the influence of social desirability because individuals are choosing between two equally attractive options (see issue #8).

**14) THE INFLUENCE OF GENDER ON RESPONSES.** Early in the development of the Indicator, it became clear to Myers that some items were more popular for males and some were more popular for females. She found, for example, that on a given T–F item, the Feeling choice might be selected by 80% of the Feeling types in the criterion group, but that the Feeling choice unexpectedly appealed to the Thinking types as well, chosen by 60% of them. The explanation is that males in the U.S. are typically socialized for and supported in behaviors related to a Thinking preference, and females are socialized and supported in behaviors related to a Feeling preference. Thus, Thinking responses are popular for males (even Feeling type males) and Feeling responses are popular for females (even Thinking type females). To address this issue, separate item analyses were made for males and females on all four dichotomies in Forms C through G. Those items that were differentially effective in distinguishing type for males and for females were given different scoring weights for the two sexes. Thus, in template scoring of Form G, there were different templates for males and females on the T–F dichotomy. The items that functioned differently for males and females (i.e., those items that previously had different scoring weights for males and females) are not included in Form M of the MBTI. As a result, template scoring of Form M has only one template for males and females for the T–F scoring.

**15) THE INFLUENCE OF AGE AND TYPE DEVELOPMENT ON RESPONSES.** Although Myers initially tested and developed Indicator items on persons whose type development she considered to be good, she ultimately wanted the Indicator to work accurately for people with less type development, who were of lower general ability, or who had less education. Fortunately she found that some items were distinguishing types well in both the earlier and later groups— so at that time those items were given greater scoring weights. In the development of Form M, this issue was addressed through an item-by-item examination of an item's ability to accurately distinguish type regardless of age or educational level. The items that performed best across all groups were retained. Some items still work better for older groups, but these were retained due to their efficacy in distinguishing the types.

**16) BREAKING TIES IN SCORING.** In the early stages of development, one could receive a tied score on an MBTI dichotomy and thus have an "x" as part of one's type formula (e.g., ENxP). In order to give respondents an initial description to read, a tie-breaking formula was adopted. In Form G of the MBTI, tied scores on any dichotomy were broken one point toward I, N, F and P. Myers reasoned that Introversion, Intuition and Perceiving were less represented in the general population and that if a person split his or her vote on the items of any of these dichotomies (in spite of social support for being an Extravert, Sensing and Judging type), then that person was likely to be an Introvert, Intuitive and Perceiving type. Her reasoning for tie breaking on the T–F dichotomy was different. Myers tried to compensate for gender role pressure (see issue #13) by weighting items on the T–F dichotomy differently for males and females. On the chance that she had overcompensated on the T–F items, she reasoned that if a male was unclear, then she scored him a Thinking type. If a female was unclear, then she was scored as a Feeling type. On Forms F and G, Myers added an extra point to the male hand-scoring template (males got one more point toward Thinking) to simplify the tie-breaking formula—males *and* females broke ties toward Feeling.

With Form M computer scoring using IRT, tied scores on a dichotomy are rare, but in template scoring of Form M, tied scores can be more common. For Form M scoring, ties are still broken toward I, N, F and P.

**17) KEEPING THE PREFERENCE DICHOTOMIES INDEPENDENT.** Indicator items were written for particular dichotomies, and Myers wanted each item to relate only to one dichotomy. Her purpose was to keep the dichotomies as uncorrelated with each other as possible, so that a person's preference on one dichotomy wouldn't distort the evidence on another. Consider, for example, an item that is good at indicating Sensing but is also answered by most Extraverts. One would not know whether Extraversion or Sensing most influenced how a person answered the question. To solve the problem, she calculated the correlation of every item with each of the four dichotomies, and eliminated those items that correlated well on more than one dichotomy. Each time she tried new items and the composition of the dichotomies changed, the calculations were redone!

## Conclusion

NO ONE WHO picks up the MBTI question booklet could get from it any notion of the complex issues Isabel Myers faced in its construction. Even developers of psychological instruments have expressed their awe at the comprehensive and meticulous research she conducted. The MBTI is certainly more valuable and useful because of the care she took in developing it. Those of us who use the Indicator share a legacy—the gift of a tool that carries with it a responsibility to use it ethically and in the manner Myers visualized.

**References**

Myers, I. B. (undated). *Construction of the Type Indicator, forms Zero to F.* Unpublished Manuscript.

Myers, I. B., & McCaulley, M. H. (1985). *Manual: A guide to the development and use of the Myers-Briggs Type Indicator* (2nd ed.). Palo Alto, CA: Consulting Psychologists Press.

Myers, I. B., McCaulley, M. H., Quenk, N. L., & Hammer, A. L. (1998). *Manual: A guide to the development and use of the Myers-Briggs Type Indicator* (3rd ed.). Palo Alto, CA: Consulting Psychologists Press.

**Resources**

Myers, I. B., McCaulley, M. H., Quenk, N. L., & Hammer, A. L. (1998). *Manual: A guide to the development and use of the Myers-Briggs Type Indicator* (3rd ed.). Palo Alto, CA: Consulting Psychologists Press.

Myers, I. B. with Myers, P. B. (1995). *Gifts differing: Understanding personality type.* Palo Alto, CA: Davies-Black Publishing. (Original work published 1980)

Jung, C. G. (1971). *Psychological types* (H. G. Baynes, Trans., revised by R. F. C. Hull). Collected Works, Vol. 6. Princeton, NJ: Princeton University. (Original work published in 1921)

Saunders, F. W. (1991). *Katharine and Isabel: Mother's light, daughter's journey.* Palo Alto, CA: Consulting Psychologists Press.

Watkins, C. E., & Campbell, V. L. (Eds.) (1990). *Testing in counseling practice.* Hillsdale, NJ: Lawrence Erlbaum Associates, Inc.—Includes a chapter by Mary McCaulley on the MBTI.

Zeisset, R. M. (2000). *Statistics and measurement: An introduction for MBTI users.* Gainesville, FL: Center for Applications of Psychological Type.

*Jung only talked about eight types, but Myers talked about sixteen. Why?*

*Now what's a good way to describe Thinking and Feeling again?*

*What do people mean when they say someone has good type development?*

*How do you tell which are the dominant and auxiliary functions from looking at the four-letter type?*

# Chapter 3

IN THIS CHAPTER, you will be (re)introduced to the basics of type theory, including type development and dynamics*. All of the information in this chapter is for you, the type professional. You may decide to communicate some or all of the content of these first sections to the person(s) taking the MBTI. The descriptions of the basic preferences and the discussion of development and dynamics may also be well used when explaining type to others. In this chapter, we cover:

- Jung, Myers and type theory: the background
- Descriptions of the preferences
- Understanding type development and type dynamics
- How to figure out the dynamics from the four-letter type formula

**JUNG, MYERS AND TYPE THEORY: THE BACKGROUND.** Carl Jung's initial work on psychological types focused on the differences between *extraverts* and *introverts*. Jung described how extraverts naturally orient to and draw energy from the outer world of people and activities, while introverts naturally orient to and draw energy from the inner world of images and ideas. He referred to extraversion and introversion as *attitudes*, and in fact spent most of his book *Psychological Types* describing the differences between these two types of people. After initially identifying these two attitudes, Jung discovered that the constructs of extraversion and introversion were not adequate to describe all of the differences he was observing in people's behavior.

Over a period of time, Jung identified four different kinds of extraverts and four different kinds of introverts: eight types in all. What distinguished the different types of extraverts and introverts was their emphasis on one of *four mental functions*, functions which could be understood as pairs of opposites: two perceiving mental functions (*sensing* vs. *intuition*), and two judging mental functions (*thinking* vs. *feeling*). Perceiving functions take in information, while judging functions weigh information and decide. Isabel Myers made it clear that psychological type is a result of the differences in the kind of perception and judgment that people prefer to use.

*The descriptions of the preferences, type development and type dynamics used in this chapter were adapted and used by permission from *Looking at Type: The Fundamentals*, © 1997 Charles Martin.

Each of the eight types identified by Jung used their favorite of the four mental functions (sensing, intuition, thinking or feeling) in a particular attitude—that is, they used that favored function in either an extraverted or introverted way. This favored function, called the dominant function, was the individual's most well developed function—the one that led the personality. Thus, the eight (dominant) types described by Jung were:

| | |
|---|---|
| Extraverted sensing types | Introverted sensing types |
| Extraverted intuitive types | Introverted intuitive types |
| Extraverted thinking types | Introverted thinking types |
| Extraverted feeling types | Introverted feeling types |

JUNG'S ORIGINAL DESCRIPTIONS of these eight types focused on the pure (and one-sided) expression of these mental functions. The following gives a description of these eight Jungian function-attitudes.

---

### THE EIGHT JUNGIAN FUNCTION—ATTITUDES

**Extraverted Sensing:** Outward and active focus on the objective world and on gathering factual data and sensuous experiences.

**Introverted Sensing:** Inward and reflective focus on subjective sensuous experiences and on the storing of factual historical data.

**Extraverted Intuition:** Outward and active focus on the new, the possibilities and meanings/patterns in the objective world.

**Introverted Intuition:** Inward and reflective focus on the subjective world of symbols, meanings, insight and patterns that come up from the unconscious.

**Extraverted Thinking:** Outward and active focus on applying logical order to the objective world through building structure, organizing and making decisions.

**Introverted Thinking:** Inward and reflective focus on the subjective world of reason that seeks understanding through finding the logical principles behind phenomena.

**Extraverted Feeling:** Outward and active focus on bringing order to the objective world through building and seeking harmony with others and alignment with openly expressed values.

**Introverted Feeling:** Inward and reflective focus on the subjective world of deeply felt values that seeks harmony through alignment of personal behavior with those values and evaluation of phenomena in light of those values.

Everyone uses all eight of these function-attitudes. What makes someone a type is that one of them is the dominant function—thus the characteristics of that function show significantly in that person's life.

ISABEL MYERS AND KATHARINE BRIGGS DEVELOPED fuller and healthier descriptions of the types by making explicit what was implicit in much of Jung's work—the balancing effect of a second favorite mental function: the auxiliary. Thus, Myers and Briggs built on and extended Jung's model of types by providing a way of determining which is the dominant and which is the auxiliary function for each type. They did this through the creation of a *judgment-perception* (J–P) dichotomy. We'll see later in this chapter how the four letters, and the J–P preference in particular, tell us what is dominant and auxiliary for each type. For now, it's simply important to understand that Myers and Briggs further subdivided Jung's eight types into sixteen types— each of the original eight dominant types having two variations:

Extraverted Sensing types with auxiliary Introverted Thinking (ESTP)
Extraverted Sensing types with auxiliary Introverted Feeling (ESFP)

Introverted Sensing types with auxiliary Extraverted Thinking (ISTJ)
Introverted Sensing types with auxiliary Extraverted Feeling (ISFJ)

Extraverted Intuitive types with auxiliary Introverted Thinking (ENTP)
Extraverted Intuitive types with auxiliary Introverted Feeling (ENFP)

Introverted Intuitive types with auxiliary Extraverted Thinking (INTJ)
Introverted Intuitive types with auxiliary Extraverted Feeling (INFJ)

Extraverted Thinking types with auxiliary Introverted Sensing (ESTJ)
Extraverted Thinking types with auxiliary Introverted Intuition (ENTJ)

Introverted Thinking types with auxiliary Extraverted Sensing (ISTP)
Introverted Thinking types with auxiliary Extraverted Intuition (INTP)

Extraverted Feeling types with auxiliary Introverted Sensing (ESFJ)
Extraverted Feeling types with auxiliary Introverted Intuition (ENFJ)

Introverted Feeling types with auxiliary Extraverted Sensing (ISFP)
Introverted Feeling types with auxiliary Extraverted Intuition (INFP)

In short, the MBTI identifies individuals as having preferences on four dichotomies—the E–I, S–N, T–F and J–P dichotomies. It is important to understand, however, that the types described by Jung and Myers all have a *dynamic* character. That is, the different preferences that people have on each of these four dichotomies interact to yield a very complex description of an individual's experience and behavior. The type descriptions go far beyond simply adding up descriptors from each of the four preference categories. Later in this chapter, for example, you will see how an Extraverted Intuitive type with auxiliary Introverted Feeling (ENFP) is very different from an Extraverted Feeling type with auxiliary Introverted Intuition (ENFJ), even though they have in common three of the four preferences.

## Descriptions of the preferences

WHEN WE INTRODUCE PEOPLE to type and the MBTI, we have several options of how to do so. Many practitioners choose to explain the four preference categories first, as separate categories. That is, they will describe the four pairs of opposites E–I, S–N, T–F and J–P, giving examples of how, say, Extraverts differ from Introverts, and how Sensing types differ from Intuitive types. This is the most basic level of presentation and understanding, and *may be all that is necessary* for some individuals and groups. However, the true power of type lies in understanding and appreciating the dynamic interactions of the preferences. As the practitioner, you will have to decide how you will introduce type, and in what depth (e.g., you may choose to introduce the basics in one session, and dynamics in another). The following section describes the four preference pairs as separate dichotomies. In the sections that follow, you will be introduced to type development and type dynamics, the complex way in which the mental attitudes and functions interact.

**TRAINERS:** The sections and text that follow were adapted from *Looking at Type: The Fundamentals,* and may be used as a model for introducing type to either individuals or groups. For further information on guidelines and frameworks for actually introducing type to individuals or groups, see Chapter Six, *Explaining Type and Helping Clients Choose a Best-Fit Type.*

## What are type preferences?

*Hint:*
*This is a useful exercise when introducing people to type*

To begin making use of type, one must understand a basic concept: type preferences. These preferences are the building blocks for the sixteen types that will be discussed later.

Type is about *psychological* preferences. These preferences, however, are not as simple as whether we prefer the color red or the color blue. Rather, they represent consistent and enduring patterns of how we use our minds. The preferences can also be understood as opposite but related ways of using our minds, with the opposites being two halves that make up a whole—like front and back, for example. In the type system, you report preferences on four dichotomies.

To better grasp the idea of preferences, try the following exercise. On a separate piece of paper or in the margin of this book, write your name. Now, put the pen or pencil in your other hand and write your name again. How would you describe the differences between the two experiences? Did they *feel* different? Are there differences in the *quality* of the writing?

Some adjectives people use to contrast the two experiences are: easy–hard, comfortable–awkward, effortless–concentrated, natural–unnatural and fast–slow. Others report differences in quality. Many people say that writing with the non-dominant hand looks very childlike and immature. Some people report that it was an interesting challenge, but not a challenge they would like to take on all day, every day. You certainly *could* give more attention to writing with your non-dominant hand, but it would take time and effort to become as comfortable with it as you are with your dominant hand.

There are important parallels to the psychological type preferences here. When people engage in everyday behaviors that call on their type preferences, they tend to feel natural, comfortable, confident and competent. In contrast, when people engage in behaviors that call on their non-preferences, they tend to feel unnatural, uncomfortable, less confident and less competent. Often people will try to find ways around or avoid doing things that call on their non-preferences. Everyone uses both sides of any given preference, but they tend to rely on one side more than the other. Since we do not use both preferences of a pair at the same time, we get in the habit of using one more often and are usually much better at one than the other. As a result, our non-preferences tend to be less developed and less trusted, although we still have and use them.

With practice, people can develop greater confidence and competence in their type non-preferences. However, it does take energy and effort to learn to use them, just as it would to learn to write with your non-dominant hand. Also, because people tend to feel so much more comfortable, natural and confident when they use their preferences, they typically do not like to use their non-preferences for extended periods! As a result, they always tend to have more comfort and skill in their preferences.

The exercise of preferences leads to differences among individuals. As we act on our type preferences, our behavior and personality come to reflect our unique approach to the world and to relationships. In short, our personality type grows out of exercising our type preferences. From a type perspective, there are no good or bad preferences; having different preferences simply leads to having different interests, different ways of behaving, and different ways of viewing the world. People who have different type preferences also tend to have different strengths and potential areas of needed growth. Knowing this can help us appreciate the unique contributions each of us brings to the world.

From *Looking at Type: The Fundamentals*

IN THE FOLLOWING SECTIONS, you will find descriptions of the basic type preferences.

---

### THE FOUR PREFERENCE DICHOTOMIES

| | |
|---|---|
| **Attitudes** | Extraversion (E) or Introversion (I) |
| | How do you direct your energy and attention? |
| **Perceiving mental functions** | Sensing (S) or Intuition (N*) |
| | How do you prefer to take in information? |
| **Judging mental functions** | Thinking (T) or Feeling (F) |
| | How do you prefer to make decisions? |
| **Orientation to outer world, or Lifestyle, or Attitude** | Judging (J) or Perceiving (P) |
| | How do you orient to the outer world? |

*N is used to represent Intuition so it is not confused with Introversion

## The Preferences

IN THE FOLLOWING DESCRIPTIONS of the preferences, you as the professional may wish to include more or less in what you say to the individuals or groups to whom you give feedback. Guidelines for presenting type to individuals and groups can be found later in this chapter. For now, it is *crucial* to understand that everyone has and uses each of the preferences. What makes each person a type is that each person uses some preferences more than others.

### Two attitudes (or orientations)
### Extraversion
### Introversion

THE FIRST TYPE PREFERENCE PAIR ASKS: what is the direction of your energy and attention? Do you more naturally turn to the outer world of people and things (Extraversion), or to the inner world of ideas and images (Introversion)? As we noted earlier, Jung gave the most attention to these attitudes, which are seen as complementary but opposing orientations to life. Everyone turns outward as well as inward, but people tend to orient one way or the other as a rule, which leads to dramatic differences in world views and behaviors for Extraverts and Introverts.

> **TRAINERS:** Although we often teach the four dichotomies separately, when it comes time to teach about type dynamics, we sometimes need to shift gears. That is, once we teach the four dichotomies as separate, we come back to teach the preferences on the four dichotomies that in fact are related dynamically, and that there are four kinds of Extraverts (e.g., Extraverted Sensing types, Extraverted Intuitive types, Extraverted Thinking types and Extraverted Feeling types), and four corresponding kinds of Introverts.
>
> Many trainers prefer to teach the four dichotomies separately, and then come back later to teach about dynamics if and when it is needed. The final section in this chapter offers an alternative way to teach about type dynamics through teaching about the eight function-attitudes directly. At that point, you can see some of the advantages and disadvantages of both approaches.
>
> As the professional, it will be up to you to determine how much you want to "stick to the basics" of the four dichotomies when you describe the mental functions, and the degree to which you want to talk about dynamics—that is, the forms of the eight function-attitudes. When you get to the descriptions of Sensing–Intuition and Thinking–Feeling in this chapter, there are *Reminder* boxes after each preference description to help you recall the differences between the extraverted and introverted forms of each function.

### THE EXTRAVERTED ATTITUDE (E)

**Key words:**

outer world • people • action • breadth

People who prefer Extraversion are energized by active involvement in events, and they like to be immersed in a breadth of activities. Their energy and attention are drawn magnetically to the outer world and to events around them. Extraverts are most excited when they are around people, and they often have an energizing effect on those around them. When you are extraverting, you like to move into action and make things happen—Extraverts usually feel very at home in the world. With their orientation to the outer world, Extraverts often find their understanding of a problem becomes clearer if they can talk out loud about it and hear what others have to say. People who use the extraverted attitude extensively will demonstrate more of the characteristics associated with Extraversion.

**People who prefer Extraversion may:**

- be seen as "go-getters" or "people-persons"
- feel comfortable with and like working in groups
- have a wide range of acquaintances and friends
- *sometimes* jump too quickly into activity and not allow enough time for reflection
- *sometimes* forget to pause to clarify the ideas that give aim or meaning to their activities

### THE INTROVERTED ATTITUDE (I)

**Key words:**

inner world • ideas • reflection • depth

People who prefer Introversion are energized and excited when they are involved with the ideas, images, memories and reactions that are a part of their inner world. Their energy and attention are drawn magnetically to what is going on inside them—their inner experiences. Introverts often prefer solitary activities or spending time with one or two others with whom they feel an affinity, and they often have a calming effect on those around them. When you are introverting, you take time to reflect on ideas that explain the outer world—Introverts like to have a clear idea of what they will be doing when they move into action. With their orientation to the inner world, Introverts truly like the *idea* of something, often better than the something itself, and ideas are almost solid things for them. People who use the introverted attitude extensively will demonstrate more of the characteristics associated with Introversion.

**People who prefer Introversion may:**

- be seen as calm and "centered" or reserved
- feel comfortable alone and like solitary activities
- prefer fewer, more intense relationships
- *sometimes* spend too much time reflecting and not move into action quickly enough
- *sometimes* forget to check with the outside world to see if their ideas really fit their experience

**THE MEANING OF EXTRAVERSION AND INTROVERSION IN TYPOLOGY**

As we've discussed, Jung created the words *Extraversion* and *Introversion* that are so widely used in our language today. As they are popularly used, the term *extraverted* is understood to mean *sociable* or *outgoing*, while the term *introverted* is understood to mean *shy* or *withdrawn.* Jung originally intended the words to have an entirely different meaning—the words described a preferred focus of one's energy on either the outer or the inner world. Extraverts orient their energy to the outer world, while Introverts orient theirs to the inner world. Both styles can be healthy, although different. It is the excessive attention to either world that leads to the one-sided and unhealthy descriptions of both Extraverts and Introverts. One of Jung's and Myers' great contributions to the field of psychology was their understanding that Introversion *and* Extraversion are both healthy variations in personality style.

## The four mental functions

### Sensing
### Intuition
### Thinking
### Feeling

As noted earlier, Jung went beyond his initial classification of people as Extraverts and Introverts by identifying four *mental functions* or *processes* into which most mental activity falls. To get through the day, every individual needs and uses all four functions: Sensing (S), Intuition (N), Thinking (T) and Feeling (F). Much of one's conscious mental activity falls into one of these four mental functions. What characterizes the different types is the relative emphasis each type gives to each of the mental functions and the attitudes in which they prefer to use them.

In type theory, perception means becoming aware of, taking in or gathering information. There are two different perceiving mental functions—Sensing and Intuition. Judgment means coming to conclusions, making decisions, weighing and evaluating. There are two different judging mental functions—Thinking and Feeling.

> **TRAINERS:** Remember, as we have already seen, each of the four mental functions is used in both an extraverted and introverted way (these are the eight function-attitudes described earlier). In practice, however, these dichotomies are often described without reference to the differences between, say, Extraverted Sensing and Introverted Sensing. Again, as the professional, it will be up to you to determine which approach to use. Do you want to describe the four dichotomies separately, without reference to the extraverted or introverted forms of the functions? Or do you want to "plant the seed" of dynamics from the beginning by talking about the forms of the eight function-attitudes? The *Reminder* boxes after each preference description can help you recall the differences between the extraverted and introverted forms of Sensing and Intuition.

## Two perceiving mental functions

### Sensing
### Intuition

The second type preference pair describes the way you like to take in information and what kind of information you tend to trust the most. In other words, what kind of perception do you prefer to use? Do you give more weight to information that comes in through your five senses (Sensing), or do you give more weight to information that comes into your awareness by way of insight and imagination (Intuition)? Jung called these the *irrational* mental functions in that they simply are in tune with the ongoing flow of events and are not concerned with ordering that experience through *reason*.

## SENSING PERCEPTION (S)

**Key words:**

facts • details • experience • present

People who have a preference for Sensing are immersed in the ongoing richness of sensory experience and thus seem more grounded in everyday physical reality. They tend to be concerned with what is actual, present, current and real. As they exercise their preference for Sensing, they approach situations with an eye to the facts. Thus, they often develop a good memory for detail, become accurate in working with data, and remember facts or aspects of events that did not even seem relevant at the time they occurred. Sensing types are often good at seeing the practical applications of ideas and things, and may learn best when they can first see the pragmatic side of what is being taught. For Sensing types, experience speaks louder than words or theory.

**People who prefer Sensing may:**

- recall events as snapshots of what literally happened
- solve problems by working through things thoroughly for a precise understanding
- be pragmatic and look to the "bottom line"
- work from the facts to the big picture
- put experience first and place less trust in words and symbols
- *sometimes* focus so much on the facts of the present or past that they miss new possibilities

## INTUITION (INTUITIVE PERCEPTION) (N)

**Key words:**

symbols • pattern • theory • future

People who have a preference for Intuition are immersed in their impressions of the meanings or patterns in their experiences. They would rather gain understanding through insight than through hands-on experience. Intuitive types tend to be concerned with what is possible and new, and they have an orientation to the future. They are often interested in the abstract and in theory, and may enjoy activities where they can use symbols or be creative. Their memory of things is often an impression of what they thought was the essence of an event, rather than a memory of the literal words or experiences associated with the event. They often like concepts in and of themselves, even ones that do not have an immediate application, and they learn best when they have an impression of the overall idea first.

**People who prefer Intuition may:**

- recall events by what they read "between the lines" at the time
- solve problems through quick insight and through making leaps
- be interested in doing things that are new and different
- work from the big picture to the facts
- place great trust in insights, symbols and metaphors and less in what is literally experienced
- *sometimes* focus so much on new possibilities that they miss the practicalities of bringing them into reality

## WHAT DO YOU MEAN IRRATIONAL?

Jung called Sensing and Intuition irrational functions to distinguish them from the rational (reasoning) functions, Thinking and Feeling. Some MBTI users believe the term "non-rational" serves better than "irrational" to carry Jung's meaning.

When we talk about Sensing and Intuition being irrational functions, we are saying that when they are used, an individual is not evaluating, weighing, judging or in any way directing the Sensing or Intuitive data that are presenting themselves to awareness. Someone using Sensing *purely* (without applying Thinking or Feeling) would allow himself or herself to respond to one sensory experience after another, without directing or judging those experiences. Someone using Intuition *purely* (again, without applying Thinking or Feeling) would allow the stream of associations, hunches and insights to flow freely without direction or judgment. A Sensing type asked to write about "a leaf" will often freely describe the physical characteristics of a leaf (e.g., green, yellow, veins, crinkly). An Intuitive type asked to write about "a leaf" will often write the many different associations they have to a leaf (e.g., a book leaf, Halloween, photosynthesis).

## Two judging mental functions

### Thinking
### Feeling

THIS THIRD PREFERENCE PAIR describes how you like to make decisions or come to closure about the information you have taken in using your Sensing or Intuition. In other words, what kind of judgment do you prefer to use? A person of good judgment is able to make distinctions among a variety of choices and settle on a course of action that demonstrates excellence of understanding. You can make these rational ordered judgments in two ways: by giving more weight to objective principles and the impersonal facts (Thinking), or by giving more weight to personal and human concerns and people issues (Feeling). Jung called these the *rational* mental functions because they are concerned with bringing information into order using reason—that is, characterized by the processes of weighing, discriminating, evaluating, deciding and constraining.

**TRAINERS:** Remember that the appearance and experience of Thinking and Feeling will differ depending on whether a person extraverts or introverts that function. That is, Extraverted Thinking differs markedly from Introverted Thinking. Again, it is up to you how much you distinguish between the two forms of Thinking and two forms of Feeling when you are doing a basic introduction.

Use the *Reminder* box after each preference description to help you distinguish between the extraverted and introverted forms of Thinking and Feeling.

### THINKING JUDGMENT (T)

Key words:

impersonal • truth • cool • tough-minded

People who have a preference for Thinking judgment are concerned with determining the objective truth in a situation. More impersonal in approach, Thinking types believe they can make the best decisions by removing personal concerns that may lead to biased analysis and decision making. Thinking types seek to act based on the *truth* in a situation, a truth or principle that is independent of what they or others might want to believe or wish were true. The Thinking function is concerned with logical consistency and analysis of cause and effect. As they use and develop their Thinking function, Thinking types often appear analytical, cool and tough-minded.

**People who prefer Thinking may:**

- have a technical or scientific orientation
- be concerned with truth and notice inconsistencies
- look for logical explanations or solutions to most everything
- make decisions with their heads and want to be fair
- believe telling the whole truth is more important than being tactful
- *sometimes* miss seeing or valuing the "people" part of situations, so they might be viewed by others as too task-oriented, uncaring or indifferent

### FEELING JUDGMENT (F)

Key words:

personal • value • warm • tender-hearted

People who have a preference for Feeling judgment are concerned with whether decisions and actions are worthwhile. More personal in approach, Feeling types believe they can make the best decisions by weighing what people care about and the points-of-view of persons involved in a situation. Feeling types are concerned with personal values and with making decisions based on a ranking of greater to lesser importance—what is *best* for the people involved. The Feeling function places high value on relatedness between people, and Feeling types are often concerned with establishing or maintaining harmony in their relationships. As they use and develop their Feeling function, Feeling types often come to appear caring, warm and tactful. Remember, in type language, Feeling does *not* mean being "emotional." Rather, it is a way of reasoning.

**People who prefer Feeling may:**

- have a people or communications orientation
- be concerned with harmony and be aware when it is missing
- look for what is important to others and express concern for others
- make decisions with their hearts and want to be compassionate
- believe being tactful is more important than telling the "cold" truth
- *sometimes* miss seeing or communicating about the "hard truth" of situations, so they might be viewed by others as too idealistic, mushy or indirect

**REMINDER:**

**Differences between
extraverted and introverted forms of Thinking**

- Extraverted Thinking: Outward and active focus on applying logical order to the objective world through building structure, organizing and making decisions.

- Introverted Thinking: Inward and reflective focus on the subjective world of reason that seeks understanding through finding the logical principles behind phenomena.

**REMINDER:**

**Differences between
extraverted and introverted forms of Feeling**

- Extraverted Feeling: Outward and active focus on bringing order to the objective world through building and seeking harmony with others and alignment with openly expressed values.

- Introverted Feeling: Inward and reflective focus on the subjective world of deeply felt values that seeks harmony through alignment of personal behavior with those values, and evaluation of phenomena in light of those values.

**TRAINERS:** It is very important to help others understand that *Feeling* as it is used in type language is to be distinguished from *emotions*. For Jung, Thinking and Feeling are both rational functions—used to weigh, discriminate, evaluate and decide. Both Thinking and Feeling types have emotions. As a rule, Feeling types are more willing to weigh emotions as important factors in decision-making, while Thinking types are more inclined to try to make decisions with as much detachment from emotions as possible. Remember, both Thinking and Feeling are *rational* functions—they are used to weigh, evaluate and order data perceived using Sensing and Intuition, and to come to conclusions. Thinking wants to bring things (ideas or the environment) into logical order. Feeling wants to bring things (again, ideas or the environment) into harmonious order with a set of values.

## The two orientations to the outer world

### Judging
### Perceiving

THIS FOURTH PREFERENCE PAIR describes how you like to live your outer life—what are the behaviors that others tend to see? Do you prefer a more structured and decided lifestyle (Judging) or a more flexible and adaptable lifestyle (Perceiving)? This preference may be thought of as your *orientation to the outer world*, and is also referred to as an *attitude* by some type users. Everyone uses the processes of judgment and perception all of the time. In fact, that is the basis for type. You need both perception *and* judgment. However, when it comes to dealing with the outer world, people tend to stay either more in the structured/decided/closure mode or more in the flexible/adaptable/curiosity mode.

## JUDGING (J) ORIENTATION

**Key words:**

structured • decided • organized • scheduled

People who have a preference for Judging use their preferred judging function (whether it is Thinking or Feeling) in their outer life. What this often looks like is that they prefer a planned or orderly way of life, like to have things settled and organized, feel more comfortable when decisions are made, and like to bring life under control to the degree that it is possible. Since they are using either their Thinking or Feeling in their outer world, they want to make decisions to bring things in their outer life to closure. Remember, though, this only describes how their outer life looks. Inside, they may *feel* flexible and open to new information (which they are). Remember, in type language, Judging means "preferring to make decisions." It does *not* mean "judgmental" in the sense of constantly making negative evaluations about people and events.

### People who prefer Judging may:

- like to make decisions, or at least like to have things decided
- look task oriented
- like to make lists of things to do
- like to get their work done before playing
- plan work to avoid rushing just before deadlines
- *sometimes* make decisions too quickly without enough information
- *sometimes* focus so much on the goal or plan that they miss the need to change directions at times

## PERCEIVING (P) ORIENTATION

**Key words:**

flexible • open • adaptable • spontaneous

People who have a preference for Perceiving use their preferred perceiving function (whether it is Sensing or Intuition) in their outer life. What this often looks like is that they prefer a more flexible and spontaneous way of life, like to understand and adapt to the world, and like to stay open to new experiences. Since they are using either their Sensing or Intuition in their outer world, they want to continue to take in new information. Remember again that this only describes how the person's outer life looks. Inside, they may *feel* very planful or decisive (which they are). Remember, in type language, Perceiving means "preferring to take in information." It does *not* mean "perceptive" in the sense of having quick and accurate perceptions about people and events.

### People who prefer Perceiving may:

- like staying open to respond to whatever happens
- look more loose and casual
- like to keep laid-out plans to a minimum
- like to approach work as play or mix work and play
- work in bursts of energy, and enjoy rushing just before deadlines
- *sometimes* stay open to new information so long that they miss making decisions that need to be made
- *sometimes* focus so much on adapting in the moment that they do not settle on a direction or plan

**HISTORY OF THE JUDGING—PERCEIVING (J-P) PREFERENCE PAIR**

Jung did not directly describe a Judging or Perceiving orientation to the outer world—although he did write about the judging and perceiving *functions*. In developing the Indicator, Myers realized that she would be able to tell if someone were an S or N, and whether they were a T or F. However, she wondered how she would tell which of the two favored mental functions was dominant and which was auxiliary.

Isabel Myers built on Katharine Briggs' observations and on Jung's work to conclude that some people demonstrate clearly in their outwardly observable behavior a preference for structure and decisiveness. Others demonstrate in their outwardly observable behavior a preference for flexibility and adaptability.

People who deal with the outer world in a structured way are using a judging function to interact with the outer world—and that function could be either Thinking or Feeling. Both functions seek closure and structure. People who deal with the outer world in an adapting way are using a perceiving function to interact with the outer world—and that function could be either Sensing or Intuition.

Another way of saying this is that the Judging–Perceiving preference describes the nature of our extraversion, because we all extravert at times, even Introverts, and all Extraverts introvert at times. The items on the J–P dichotomy ask us when we *do* extravert, do we extravert a judging (J) function (our favorite of Thinking or Feeling), or do we extravert a perceiving (P) function (our favorite of Sensing or Intuition)?

People who extravert their Sensing function or their Intuition function share certain characteristics in common. They extravert a *perceiving* function, and thus they are more in the curiosity mode or the information-gathering mode when dealing with the outer world.

People who extravert their Thinking function or their Feeling function share certain characteristics in common. They extravert a *judging* function, and thus they are more in the closure-seeking mode or the decision-making mode when dealing with the outer world.

The J–P dichotomy is also a reminder to us that *all types* extravert at times. Extraverts by nature prefer extraverting over introverting—but they also introvert at times. Introverts by nature prefer introverting over extraverting—but they also extravert at times.

**Your type is the combination of your preferences on the four dichotomies**

THE PREFERENCES YOU HAVE ON EACH OF THE FOUR DICHOTOMIES combine to yield a four-letter type pattern which is your *psychological type*. For example, preferences for Introversion (I), Sensing (S), Thinking (T) and Judging (J) combine to yield the four-letter type pattern: ISTJ. There are sixteen different ways the preferences on the four dichotomies can go together (e.g., INFP, ESFJ, ENTP). These four preferences interact in dynamic and complex ways that can tell you much about who you are and how you approach the world. Brief descriptions of the sixteen types can be found on the next two pages of this guide. Full-length descriptions of the sixteen types can be found in the Appendix.

The next section, *Type Development and Type Dynamics*, explains just *how* the type preferences interact to yield the pattern of personality we call "type." That section also describes how your type can show up in your lifelong development, and how your environment can affect the development of your type. Those having difficulty clarifying their preferences may find that section especially helpful.

**ISTJ**

For ISTJs the dominant quality in their lives is an abiding sense of responsibility for doing what needs to be done in the here-and-now. Their realism, organizing abilities, and command of the facts lead to their completing tasks thoroughly and with great attention to detail. Logical pragmatists at heart, ISTJs make decisions based on their experience and with an eye to efficiency in all things. ISTJs are intensely committed to people and to the organizations of which they are a part; they take their work seriously and believe others should do so as well.

**ISFJ**

For ISFJs the dominant quality in their lives is an abiding respect and sense of personal responsibility for doing what needs to be done in the here-and-now. Actions that are of practical help to others are of particular importance to ISFJs. Their realism, organizing abilities, and command of the facts lead to their thorough attention in completing tasks. ISFJs bring an aura of quiet warmth, caring, and dependability to all that they do; they take their work seriously and believe others should do so as well.

**ISTP**

For ISTPs the driving force in their lives is to understand how things and phenomena in the real world work so they can make the best and most effective use of them. They are logical and realistic people, and they are natural troubleshooters. When not actively solving a problem, ISTPs are quiet and analytical observers of their environment, and they naturally look for the underlying sense to any facts they have gathered. ISTPs often pursue variety and even excitement in their hands-on experiences. Although they do have a spontaneous, even playful side, what people often first encounter with them is their detached pragmatism.

**ISFP**

For ISFPs the dominant quality in their lives is a deep-felt caring for living things, combined with a quietly playful and sometimes adventurous approach to life and all its experiences. ISFPs typically show their caring in very practical ways, since they often prefer action to words. Their warmth and concern are generally not expressed openly, and what people often first encounter with ISFPs is their quiet adaptability, realism, and "free spirit" spontaneity.

**ESTP**

For ESTPs the dominant quality in their lives is their enthusiastic attention to the outer world of hands-on and real-life experiences. ESTPs are excited by continuous involvement in new activities and in the pursuit of new challenges. They tend to be logical and analytical in their approach to life, and they have an acute sense of how objects, events, and people in the world work. ESTPs are typically energetic and adaptable realists, who prefer to experience and accept life rather than to judge or organize it.

**ESFP**

For ESFPs the dominant quality in their lives is their enthusiastic attention to the outer world of hands-on and real-life experiences. ESFPs are excited by continuous involvement in new activities and new relationships. They also have a deep concern for people, and they show their caring in warm and pragmatic gestures of helping. ESFPs are typically energetic and adaptable realists, who prefer to experience and accept life rather than to judge or organize it.

**ESTJ**

For ESTJs the driving force in their lives is their need to analyze and bring into logical order the outer world of events, people, and things. ESTJs like to organize anything that comes into their domain, and they will work energetically to complete tasks so they can quickly move from one to the next. Sensing orients their thinking to current facts and realities, and thus gives their thinking a pragmatic quality. ESTJs take their responsibilities seriously and believe others should do so as well.

**ESFJ**

For ESFJs the dominant quality in their lives is an active and intense caring about people and a strong desire to bring harmony into their relationships. ESFJs bring an aura of warmth to all that they do, and they naturally move into action to help others, to organize the world around them, and to get things done. Sensing orients their feeling to current facts and realities, and thus gives their feeling a hands-on pragmatic quality. ESFJs take their work seriously and believe others should do so as well.

## INFJ

For INFJs the dominant quality in their lives is their attention to the inner world of possibilities, ideas, and symbols. Knowing by way of insight is paramount for them, and they often manifest a deep concern for people and relationships as well. INFJs often have deep interests in creative expression as well as issues of spirituality and human development. While their energy and attention are naturally drawn to the inner world of ideas and insights, what people often first encounter with INFJs is their drive for closure and for the application of their ideas to people's concerns.

## INTJ

For INTJs the dominant force in their lives is their attention to the inner world of possibilities, symbols, abstractions, images, and thoughts. Insight in conjunction with logical analysis is the essence of their approach to the world; they think systemically. Ideas are the substance of life for INTJs and they have a driving need to understand, to know, and to demonstrate competence in their areas of interest. INTJs inherently trust their insights, and with their task-orientation will work intensely to make their visions into realities.

## INFP

For INFPs the dominant quality in their lives is a deep-felt caring and idealism about people. They experience this intense caring most often in their relationships with others, but they may also experience it around ideas, projects, or any involvement they see as important. INFPs are often skilled communicators, and they are naturally drawn to ideas that embody a concern for human potential. INFPs live in the inner world of values and ideals, but what people often first encounter with them in the outer world is their adaptability and concern for possibilities.

## INTP

For INTPs the driving force in their lives is to understand whatever phenomenon is the focus of their attention. They want to make sense of the world—as a concept—and they often enjoy opportunities to be creative. INTPs are logical, analytical, and detached in their approach to the world; they naturally question and critique ideas and events as they strive for understanding. INTPs usually have little need to control the outer world, or to bring order to it, and they often appear very flexible and adaptable in their lifestyle.

## ENFP

For ENFPs the dominant quality in their lives is their attention to the outer world of possibilities; they are excited by continuous involvement in anything new, whether it be new ideas, new people, or new activities. Though ENFPs thrive on what is possible and what is new, they also experience a deep concern for people as well. Thus, they are especially interested in possibilities for people. ENFPs are typically energetic, enthusiastic people who lead spontaneous and adaptable lives.

## ENTP

For ENTPs the dominant quality in their lives is their attention to the outer world of possibilities; they are excited by continuous involvement in anything new, whether it be new ideas, new people, or new activities. They look for patterns and meaning in the world, and they often have a deep need to analyze, to understand, and to know the nature of things. ENTPs are typically energetic, enthusiastic people who lead spontaneous and adaptable lives.

## ENFJ

For ENFJs the dominant quality in their lives is an active and intense caring about people and a strong desire to bring harmony into their relationships. ENFJs are openly expressive and empathic people who bring an aura of warmth to all that they do. Intuition orients their feeling to the new and to the possible, thus they often enjoy working to manifest a humanitarian vision, or helping others develop their potential. ENFJs naturally and conscientiously move into action to care for others, to organize the world around them, and to get things done.

## ENTJ

For ENTJs the driving force in their lives is their need to analyze and bring into logical order the outer world of events, people, and things. ENTJs are natural leaders who build conceptual models that serve as plans for strategic action. Intuition orients their thinking to the future, and gives their thinking an abstract quality. ENTJs will actively pursue and direct others in the pursuit of goals they have set, and they prefer a world that is structured and organized.

## Understanding type development and type dynamics:
## Theory and Mechanics

WE HAVE ALREADY BEGUN TO DISCUSS the dynamic nature of type in the descriptions of the basic four dichotomies. As a type user, when introducing others to type you may decide you want to "plant the seeds" of dynamics as you describe the four basic pairs of opposites. For example, you can describe how Extraverts extravert a particular mental function, describe how Sensing and Intuition are perceiving mental functions and how Thinking and Feeling are judging mental functions, or tell people how the J–P preference describes which kind of function is oriented to the outer world.

In this section, you will get a quick overview of the basic principles behind the theory of type dynamics and type development. In the following section, you will learn how to mechanically "figure out" the dominant, auxiliary, tertiary and inferior functions for each type.

### Developmental dynamics:
### The theory

THE MBTI AND THE THEORY of psychological type are based in a model of human nature that is developmental. Though on the face of it the type *letters* appear static, in fact, Jung and Myers believed that people develop continuously throughout their lives. (By the way, one needn't necessarily subscribe to all of Jungian type theory to use type or the MBTI. However, knowing type theory is critical to understanding and explaining type dynamics, and adds immeasurably to the power of using type.)

The model of type development and type dynamics demonstrates how your type is more than just the combination of your four letters; it is in fact a dynamic and complex interrelated system of personality. In the following sections, we will see how type develops throughout a person's life, how the different parts of your type work with each other to make you a balanced and effective person, and how people can sometimes get pushed off their natural path of development.

### The mental functions

EVERYONE HAS AND USES ALL FOUR mental functions (in both attitudes), but the different types prefer and develop them in a different sequence throughout their lives.

Everyone has and uses the four mental functions: Sensing, Intuition, Thinking and Feeling. In fact, you couldn't get through the day without using all of them to some degree! People just differ in the order in which they prefer to use them and the order in which they develop them as they grow. For example, for some people logical closure (T) is the most important thing, then secondarily they attend to the facts and details (S). They give less weight to the possibilities (N), and the least weight to the people-impact of decisions (F). For someone else the order might be just the reverse, or some other order entirely. In type theory, the order in which we prefer these processes is inborn.

Two functions are for gathering information—that is, they are used for perceiving:

**Perceiving functions**

➤ Sensing—perception of details and current realities

➤ Intuition—perception of patterns and future possibilities

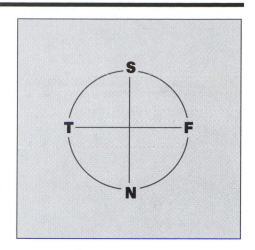

Two functions are for organizing information and making decisions—that is, they are used for judging:

**Judging functions**

➤ Thinking—decisions based on principles and logical consequences

➤ Feeling—decisions based on values and consequences for people

Everyone has a favored way of perceiving and a favored way of judging. At the most basic level, type development is the process of gaining greater development and command of your preferred way of perceiving and your preferred way of judging (the two middle letters of your four-letter type). Developing a mental function involves consciously differentiating a function from the others, exercising it, and becoming more skillful with it.

From Jung's point of view, we are born predisposed toward some functions over others, but all of the functions are largely unconscious and undifferentiated in the infant. As we grow and develop, the different functions become more differentiated and available to use in a conscious way. Those functions will also tend to develop in a particular order (assuming our environment supports us in our natural inclinations), and are referred to as the dominant (first-preferred), auxiliary (second-preferred), tertiary (third-preferred), and inferior (fourth-preferred).

From a Jungian perspective, your mind and personality are dynamically pushing for development. Imagine that an ocean of water is the unconscious mind, that the air above that water is the conscious mind, and that a beach ball represents the mental functions. A beach ball held beneath the water will *press* to reach the surface—in a similar fashion, the different functions *press* for conscious attention and development. That development, however, may be supported or thwarted, allowed or resisted.

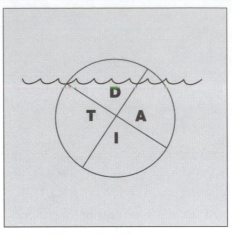

**The auxiliary balances
judging and perceiving**

D = dominant  A = auxiliary  T = tertiary  I = inferior

Let's look now at how the dominant, auxiliary, tertiary and inferior functions develop throughout an individual's life. As we move through the following section, remember *the four-letter type formula is a shorthand way of telling us about the order in which a person prefers to use the four mental functions.* The following table shows the order in which each type prefers the mental functions. You may wish to refer to it, and the table—*The eight function-attitudes and their characteristics*—on page 61 in this chapter to see how the developmental model makes sense for any given type.

## PRIORITIES OF FUNCTIONS

| **ISTJ** | **ISFJ** | **INFJ** | **INTJ** |
|---|---|---|---|
| 1) Sensing (Dominant) – I | 1) Sensing (Dominant) – I | 1) Intuition (Dominant) – I | 1) Intuition (Dominant) – I |
| 2) Thinking (Auxiliary) – E | 2) Feeling (Auxiliary) – E | 2) Feeling (Auxiliary) – E | 2) Thinking (Auxiliary) – E |
| 3) Feeling (Tertiary) – E/I | 3) Thinking (Tertiary) – E/I | 3) Thinking (Tertiary) – E/I | 3) Feeling (Tertiary) – E/I |
| 4) Intuition (Inferior) – E | 4) Intuition (Inferior) – E | 4) Sensing (Inferior) – E | 4) Sensing (Inferior) – E |

| **ISTP** | **ISFP** | **INFP** | **INTP** |
|---|---|---|---|
| 1) Thinking (Dominant) – I | 1) Feeling (Dominant) – I | 1) Feeling (Dominant) – I | 1) Thinking (Dominant) – I |
| 2) Sensing (Auxiliary) – E | 2) Sensing (Auxiliary) – E | 2) Intuition (Auxiliary) – E | 2) Intuition (Auxiliary) – E |
| 3) Intuition (Tertiary) – E/I | 3) Intuition (Tertiary) – E/I | 3) Sensing (Tertiary) – E/I | 3) Sensing (Tertiary) – E/I |
| 4) Feeling (Inferior) – E | 4) Thinking (Inferior) – E | 4) Thinking (Inferior) – E | 4) Feeling (Inferior) – E |

| **ESTP** | **ESFP** | **ENFP** | **ENTP** |
|---|---|---|---|
| 1) Sensing (Dominant) – E | 1) Sensing (Dominant) – E | 1) Intuition (Dominant) – E | 1) Intuition (Dominant) – E |
| 2) Thinking (Auxiliary) – I | 2) Feeling (Auxiliary) – I | 2) Feeling (Auxiliary) – I | 2) Thinking (Auxiliary) – I |
| 3) Feeling (Tertiary) – E/I | 3) Thinking (Tertiary) – E/I | 3) Thinking (Tertiary) – E/I | 3) Feeling (Tertiary) – E/I |
| 4) Intuition (Inferior) – I | 4) Intuition (Inferior) – I | 4) Sensing (Inferior) – I | 4) Sensing (Inferior) – I |

| **ESTJ** | **ESFJ** | **ENFJ** | **ENTJ** |
|---|---|---|---|
| 1) Thinking (Dominant) – E | 1) Feeling (Dominant) – E | 1) Feeling (Dominant) – E | 1) Thinking (Dominant) – E |
| 2) Sensing (Auxiliary) – I | 2) Sensing (Auxiliary) – I | 2) Intuition (Auxiliary) – I | 2) Intuition (Auxiliary) – I |
| 3) Intuition (Tertiary) – E/I | 3) Intuition (Tertiary) – E/I | 3) Sensing (Tertiary) – E/I | 3) Sensing (Tertiary) – E/I |
| 4) Feeling (Inferior) – I | 4) Thinking (Inferior) – I | 4) Thinking (Inferior) – I | 4) Feeling (Inferior) – I |

| E = Extraverted | I = Introverted | E/I = Theorists differ on the orientation of the tertiary |
|---|---|---|

## The dominant function

OF THE FOUR FUNCTIONS, everyone has a favorite which they use in their favorite (extraverted or introverted) world.

We develop one of these four mental functions to a greater degree than any of the other three. This first-preferred or favorite function is like the captain of a ship, having the most important role in guiding us, and it becomes the type core of our conscious personality. This mental function is called the *dominant* function. If parents and conditions support the infant and growing child, then the dominant function will tend to develop first. Thus, during the first years of your life, you come to rely on your dominant function, and you tend to develop the most skills with it.

Functions develop by being used consciously and purposefully for things that matter. As the dominant function is used, it becomes strengthened and differentiated from the other functions. We *tend* to have the most skills with—and conscious use of—this function, and we tend to trust it the most. By relative neglect, the function opposite the dominant tends to get less attention, conscious energy and development.

Some people, for example, give the most weight to their Intuition. They trust that function the most and they are the most energized when they use it. As children, they probably tended to focus on Intuition (assuming their family supported it), and they probably became involved in activities where they could use their imagination and focus on possibilities. Sensing, the function opposite Intuition, will get less attention and tend to have less development. With other children, exactly the reverse will be true.

---

### EXTRAVERTED INTUITIVES AND INTROVERTED INTUITIVES: HOW ARE THEY DIFFERENT?

For Extraverted infants, the dominant function will differentiate and grow in extraverted activity. Extraverts by definition prefer to live in the outer world. Therefore they use their dominant function in the outer world. They put their best foot forward. Thus, dominant Intuitives who are Extraverts turn their Intuition to the outer world. You are likely to see their Intuition in their outward behavior when you meet them. They would likely be actively involved in an ongoing stream of new ideas, projects and activities.

For Introverted infants, the dominant grows in introverted activity and is less visible to the world. Introverts by definition prefer to live in their inner world. Therefore, they use their dominant function in their inner world. Thus, dominant Intuitives who are Introverts turn their Intuition to their inner world. They would most likely be interested in reflecting on new ideas and on new ways images, concepts and symbols fit together. You are likely to see their Intuition only after getting to know them, and then only if they tell you what is going on in their inner world.

The extraverted and introverted forms of the mental functions are described for you in detail in the final section of this chapter—*The "function-attitude" way of teaching type and type dynamics.*

You will likely want to trust your dominant function in your life and be sure you have plenty of opportunities to use it, though you will still need to use your other functions as well.

**The auxiliary function**

EVERYONE HAS A SECOND FAVORITE function that gives balance to the dominant function.

If individuals used only the dominant function all of the time, they would be too one-sided. Their second-preferred function is called the *auxiliary* function because it helps give *balance* to the dominant function. It can be thought of as the first mate on the ship where the captain is the dominant function. If parents and conditions support the growing child and adolescent, then the auxiliary function tends to develop after, and then along with, the dominant function. During adolescence and early adulthood, individuals come to develop skills in and rely upon their dominant and auxiliary functions, while giving less attention to the opposite functions.

It is critical to understand *the basis for good type development is a well-developed dominant function and a well-developed auxiliary function that can support the dominant function*. The auxiliary function is very important in life, and in adults it tends also to have some conscious development. However, it is usually less developed than the dominant function, and always tends to rank second in importance to that function.

There are two ways your auxiliary function gives balance to your dominant function.

**1) The auxiliary helps you balance judging and perceiving.** For good type development, everyone needs to be reasonably comfortable and skillful with a judging function (T or F) and with a perceiving function (S or N). *Everyone* needs to be able to take in new information, and *everyone* needs to be able to come to closure or make decisions about that information. The auxiliary helps ensure you do both.

If a person were all perception, he or she would be blown around like a small boat with an oversized sail and a small keel—driven by any and every change in wind direction. Such a person would be constantly drawn by new perceptions (whether Sensing or Intuition) but have difficulty making decisions or coming to conclusions. In contrast, if a person were all judgment, he or she would be like a boat with a very large keel and a small sail—very sure and stable, but not open to new input from the wind. Such a person would be sure of his or her decisions (whether using Thinking or Feeling), but would not be able to take in new and needed information to modify his or

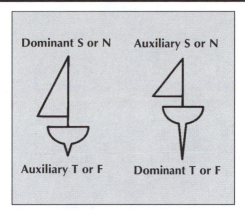

Dominant S or N    Auxiliary S or N

Auxiliary T or F    Dominant T or F

**The auxiliary balances
judging and perceiving**

her behavior as conditions changed.

If someone's dominant function is a perceiving function (S or N), a well-developed auxiliary function (T or F) helps that individual make judgments (decisions). The reverse is also true.

If someone's dominant function is a judging function, a well-developed auxiliary function helps that individual stay open to new perceptions.

In short, the auxiliary function provides needed judgment for dominant perceiving types (S or N dominant), and needed perception for dominant judging types (T or F dominant).

Sometimes when looking at the last dichotomy of the MBTI, the J–P preferences, people will express that they exhibit the characteristics of both. Remember, the J–P pair of opposites tells us the nature of a person's extraverting—do they extravert a judging function or a perceiving function? It may help to clarify that people need to and *do* exercise both judging and perceiving functions in their lives, but one tends to be exhibited more in their outer world, and the other more in their inner world. That is, they may feel very orderly/structured (J) on the inside, yet their outer life looks spontaneous and adaptable (P). Alternatively, they may feel very curious and open-ended in their inner world, yet their outer life looks more structured or decided. The J–P preference asks us to look at what we use *when we engage with the outer world.*

Dominant Intuitives, for example, have Thinking or Feeling as their auxiliary function. If they prefer Feeling, then we would typically find that the Feeling function developed next in their life after Intuition. They would still give the most weight to their Intuitive perceptions, but *then* they would make use of their Feeling to reason and to make decisions about those Intuitive perceptions.

**2) The auxiliary helps you balance extraversion and introversion.**
*Everyone* needs to be able to pay attention to the outer world and to move into action, and *everyone* needs to be able to pause for reflection and to pay attention to their inner world. Extraverts need to be able to turn to their inner world at times, and Introverts need to be able to turn to the outer world at times. The auxiliary function helps in this balancing act.

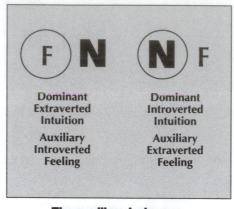

**The auxiliary balances extraversion and introversion**

As you saw before, if you are an Extravert, you use your dominant function in the outside world. For balance, you use your auxiliary function in the inner world. The outer world is of more importance to you, but your auxiliary is what you use mainly to be involved in your inner world. Without using their auxiliary, Extraverts would never stop to reflect.

If you are an Introvert, you use your dominant function in your inner world. For balance, you use your auxiliary function in the outer world. The inner world is of more interest to you, but your auxiliary is what you use to be involved in the outer world. Without using their auxiliary, Introverts would never move into action.

Thus, dominant Extraverted Intuitives who prefer Feeling use their Feeling function in their inner world. You are more likely to see their Intuition than their Feeling when you first meet them. Dominant Introverted Intuitives who prefer Feeling use their Feeling function in the outer world. You are more likely to encounter their Feeling when you first meet them.

> This answers the issue often raised in feedback sessions. Extraverts say, "but I want to be alone sometimes," and Introverts say, "but I like to be with other people." Type dynamics make it clear that *everyone* extraverts and *everyone* introverts at times—and needs to for good development. What leads to a type is the habitual use of one attitude over the other. The auxiliary function is, however, providing needed introversion for Extraverts, and needed extraversion for Introverts.

## The tertiary function

THE THIRD-PREFERRED FUNCTION tends to be less interesting to individuals and they tend to have fewer skills associated with it. Development of this function tends to come later in life.

The tertiary is the third-preferred function, tends to develop later in life (midlife), and tends to be much less conscious than the dominant and auxiliary functions. It is the opposite function from the auxiliary function. Later in life the neglected functions start getting more interesting. The individual has grown and done well with the dominant and auxiliary. Now the question arises, is this all there is? A Thinking type with tertiary Intuition starts taking literature courses. A Thinking type with tertiary Sensing starts taking carpentry or weaving.

In what attitude is the tertiary? Isabel Myers read Jung to say that the auxiliary, tertiary and inferior are all in the same attitude and opposite the dominant, which is in the preferred attitude. In other words, if the dominant function is extraverted, then the auxiliary, tertiary and inferior are all introverted. Others regard the tertiary as being in the same attitude as the dominant, while the auxiliary and the inferior are in the same attitude and in the opposite attitude from the dominant.

> **THAT DARNED TERTIARY FUNCTION!** If people ask the direction of the tertiary function, tell them there is disagreement in the type community and among Jungians. Ask people which they experience more consciously—the extraverted or introverted form of their tertiary? Refer to the table, *The eight function-attitudes and their characteristics,* on page 61 in this chapter to get some hints as to the extraverted and introverted forms of the functions.

Though you use all four mental functions, your third and fourth-preferred functions tend to be less interesting and less well-developed than your dominant and auxiliary functions. You tend to use them less consciously. As you grow and develop, you learn that there is a time and place to use your third and fourth functions as well. Your development of these functions tends to occur later in life, and you may experience great satisfaction in their development. However, because you have given less conscious attention to developing them, they tend to lag behind your dominant and auxiliary in skill level.

For example, if Intuition and Feeling are your two most favored functions, then you will probably be more inclined to focus on the future, the abstract, harmony, and especially "possibilities for people." You might also have some difficulty developing interests or skills in using your Sensing and Thinking, because these are the opposites of your natural preferences. For example, you would probably have less interest in developing skills in the impersonal analysis of technical data.

### The inferior function

THE FOURTH-PREFERRED FUNCTION tends to be the least interesting to individuals and they tend to have even fewer skills associated with it. Development of this function tends to come significantly later in life—and it can be the source of great stress and/or the seed for significant development.

The inferior function is the fourth-preferred function, and tends to be the least conscious and least differentiated for an individual. The dominant function has most of the conscious energy—so the function that will have the greatest difficulty coming into consciousness will be its opposite. The inferior is opposite of the dominant and in the opposite attitude of the dominant (e.g., for dominant Extraverted Thinking types, the opposite is Introverted Feeling).

This function generally provides you with clues about which areas of your life you tend to avoid, and involves skills you tend to have the hardest time developing. For example, if Thinking were your dominant function, Feeling would be your least-preferred function. You would probably have significantly less interest in and fewer skills with the Feeling function (e.g., attending to harmony in relationships, giving weight to the personal aspects of decision making).

"Inferior" simply means the function is inferior to the dominant function in conscious development for that individual, not that it is pathological. Opportunities for the conscious development of the inferior function tend to occur much later in life. Even with development, the inferior function will tend to remain largely unconscious and less developed than the dominant and auxiliary functions.

Extended use of your inferior function tends to require a great deal of energy, and ongoing use of it may leave you feeling stressed or tired. Excessive use of the inferior function can lead to an experience where a person is "in the grip" of his or her inferior function. The inferior may also manifest under stress, when resources of the dominant and auxiliary are exhausted.

When the inferior function manifests in someone's life, that person may say, "I don't know what got into me." It often feels like being out of control (outside the conscious ego). The inferior may manifest in negative, immature ways, *or* it may offer great gifts and insights. People often feel like a hero or a fool when they are "in the grip" of their inferior—that is, when their inferior function rather than the dominant is in control. For example, inferior Intuition may manifest not as creative possibilities, but rather worry over every possibility that can go wrong, *or* it may provide transcendent insight into the way the world is put together. An excellent resource for learning more about the inferior function may be found in the book *Beside Ourselves* by Naomi Quenk.

**True type and type falsification**

YOUR NATURAL PREFERENCES—your true type—interact with your environment as you grow. Your environment may or may not support your path of natural development.

As we have said, people tend to develop the functions in the order in which they prefer them. If family, school and environment support this natural path, individuals will come to use and trust most their dominant function, followed by increasing use and trust of their auxiliary function. Your *true type* is the type that represents your *natural* preferences.

Sometimes family, school and culture do not allow individuals to develop along their natural paths. For example, a child who tries to make logical and objective decisions using Thinking may be made to feel guilty for not attending enough to family harmony and other Feeling values. In this manner, an individual *may* be discouraged from developing his or her naturally preferred dominant and/or auxiliary functions, and may instead be pushed to develop another less-preferred function first. This kind of *type falsification* may lead to a person's not feeling comfortable with his or her ability to make good decisions or not knowing what is important information to attend to in his or her life. For these and other reasons, a person may feel tension between some preferences (between Thinking and Feeling, or between Sensing and Intuition) and not be sure which is his or her natural preference.

## Type dynamics: The mechanics

THE ISSUES DESCRIBED IN THE SECTION on type theory not only give you the context for understanding type dynamics and development, they also provide the framework for looking at a four-letter type formula and "figuring out" what is dominant, auxiliary, tertiary and inferior for someone with that type. For those who want to "check their work" as they go along, see the *Priorities of Functions* table on page 54 in this chapter. That table shows the dynamics of the functions for each of the sixteen types.

### THE "CLASSIC" WAY TO IDENTIFY DYNAMICS.

Remember:

- *Type formula* refers to the four letters used to designate an MBTI type.
- *Attitude* refers to Extraversion or Introversion (the first letter in the type formula); remember that the J–P dichotomy is sometimes called an attitude, but is more commonly referred to as an orientation.
- *Function* refers to Sensing, Intuition, Thinking and Feeling.
  Perceiving functions are Sensing and Intuition
  (the second letter in the type formula).
  Judging functions are Thinking and Feeling
  (the third letter in the type formula).
- *Opposite function* means opposite on the same dichotomy
  (S and N are opposites; T and F are opposites).

### POSITIONS OF THE LETTERS IN THE FOUR-LETTER TYPE FORMULA

| Attitude | Perceiving functions | Judging functions | Orientation (or attitude) |
|----------|---------------------|-------------------|---------------------------|
| E or I | S or N | T or F | J or P |

**RULE ONE.** Look at the last letter (J or P) in the four-letter type formula. This letter *always* tells you which function is extraverted—a judging function or a perceiving function. Remember, every type extraverts at times. Remember also that the J–P preference refers to orientation to the *outer world*. That is, it refers to the nature of that type's extraverting.

- If the letter is a J, the person extraverts their favored judging function (T or F), the third letter in their type formula.
- If the letter is a P, the person extraverts their favored perceiving function (S or N), the second letter in their type formula.

**Step One:** Write a subscript$_E$ beside the function that is extraverted.

Examples: $ENF_EJ$   $ISF_EJ$   $EN_ETP$   $IS_ETP$

**RULE TWO.** The dominant and the auxiliary functions (the two middle letters of the type formula) are in opposite attitudes. One function is extraverted and one is introverted. You just identified which is extraverted—therefore, the other is introverted. We haven't yet identified which of the two middle letters is dominant or auxiliary, but we do know they are oriented in opposite directions.

**Step Two:** Write a subscript $_I$ beside the function that is introverted (the function *other* than the one from Step One).

Examples: $EN_IF_EJ$    $IS_IF_EJ$    $EN_ET_IP$    $IS_ET_IP$

**RULE THREE.** Extraverts and Introverts use their dominant function in their favorite attitude. That's what makes them Extraverts or Introverts. Extraverts use their dominant in the extraverted attitude. Introverts use their dominant in the introverted attitude.

**Step Three:** Look at the first letter (E or I) of the type formula and match it to the function that has the same letter (E or I) beside it. Circle it—that's the dominant function. The auxiliary function is the one *not* circled. You know its attitude because you've already written a subscript $_E$ or $_I$ next to it.

Examples:   $EN_I\text{Ⓕ}_EJ$    $I\text{Ⓢ}_IF_EJ$    $E\text{Ⓝ}_ET_IP$    $IS_E\text{Ⓣ}_IP$

Examples:

In ENFJ, the dominant function is F and it is extraverted.
The auxiliary function is N and it is introverted.

In ISTP, the dominant function is T and it is introverted.
The auxiliary function is S and it is extraverted.

**RULE FOUR.** The tertiary function is opposite the auxiliary function. As noted earlier, the attitude of the tertiary is a point of debate—Myers said it is in the same attitude as the auxiliary.

**Step Four:** Just below the two mental functions, write the two remaining mental functions (e.g., under N and F write S and T). Choose the opposite function of the auxiliary and write a subscript next to it that is the same subscript that is next to the auxiliary.

Examples:

$EN_I\text{Ⓕ}_EJ$   $I\text{Ⓢ}_IF_EJ$   $E\text{Ⓝ}_ET_IP$    $IS_E\text{Ⓣ}_IP$<br>
$S_IT$       $NT_E$      $S \quad F_I$      $N_EF$

**Rule five.** The inferior function is opposite the dominant function, and in the opposite attitude.

**Step Five:** Choose the function opposite of the dominant and write a subscript next to it that is the opposite of the subscript next to the dominant.

Examples: $E\,N_I\,\widehat{F}_E\,J$  $I\,\widehat{S}_I\,F_E\,J$  $E\,\widehat{N}_E\,T_I\,P$  $I\,S_E\,\widehat{T}_I\,P$

$\phantom{Examples: E\,}S_I\;T_I\phantom{xxxx}N_E T_E\phantom{xxxx}S_I\;\;F_I\phantom{xxxx}N_E F_E$

---

**Bottom Line Rule:**

**The J–P preference points to the dominant of Extraverts and the auxiliary of Introverts.**

- **Extraverts:** J–P points to the extraverted function, which is dominant. The other function is auxiliary and introverted.
- **Introverts:** J–P points to the extraverted function, which is auxiliary. The other function is dominant and introverted.

---

The "classic" way to figure out the dynamics for each type works, *although* it may seem a bit slow in the beginning. You may ask, "Will I ever just *know* what is the dominant and auxiliary function for the different types, without having to figure it out?" Yes, absolutely. With time and practice, when you see the letters ISTP, you will naturally know that Introverted Thinking is the dominant function, and that Extraverted Sensing is the auxiliary function.

Actually working through the dynamics for the different types can give you a deeper understanding of how each type works. For example, "seeing" that Thinking is introverted for ENTPs helps us understand that they naturally brainstorm out loud (Extraverted Intuition), but they need to turn inward to give logical order (Introverted Thinking) to an issue on which they are working.

**The "function—attitude" way of teaching type and type dynamics.** Notice that we said the way of *teaching* dynamics—rather than *identifying* dynamics. This section describes another model for understanding and learning about the complexities of type dynamics. This approach is not really about "mechanically" figuring out what is the dominant and auxiliary function from the four-letter type formula. Rather, this way of teaching people about type and type dynamics actually *begins* with teaching the qualities of the extraverted and introverted forms of the mental functions. An understanding of dynamics naturally flows from this approach.

In this approach, when you first introduce type, you begin by describing for people the qualities of: Extraverted Sensing, Introverted Sensing, Extraverted Intuition, Introverted Intuition, Extraverted Thinking, Introverted Thinking, Extraverted Feeling and Introverted Feeling (see the box *The eight function-attitudes and their characteristics* on page 61). Instead of teaching the four preference pairs separately, and then identifying the dominant and auxiliary from the four-letter type formula, you actually talk first about the eight function-attitudes. From that point you can begin to teach about how the MBTI was designed to indicate which function was dominant (and in which attitude), and which function was auxiliary (and in which attitude).

**WHAT DOES THIS APPROACH LOOK LIKE?**

**Step One.** You can begin your teaching about type by walking clients through Jung's understanding of type (described earlier in this chapter in *Jung, Myers and Type Theory: The Background*). Note how Jung first identified the attitudes of Extraversion and Introversion, and then later determined that there were different kinds of Extraverts and different kinds of Introverts. What distinguished, say, the different types of Extraverts was their emphasis on one of the four mental functions (Sensing, Intuition, Thinking or Feeling). That is, some Extraverts used primarily Sensing when interacting with the outer world, others used Intuition, while others used Thinking and others used Feeling.

Someone who habitually prefers Extraversion and who habitually uses the mental function of Feeling in the outer world would be an Extraverted Feeling type—that is, Extraverted Feeling would be their dominant function. Jung also concluded that individuals have a second most favored function (the auxiliary) that provides balance to the first. Thus, someone with Extraverted Feeling as a dominant would likely have Introverted Sensing or Introverted Intuition as an auxiliary function. For further explanation of how the auxiliary function gives balance to the dominant function, see the section entitled *The auxiliary function* earlier in this chapter.

As you offer descriptions of the function-attitudes and associated behaviors, your clients can usually readily recognize the different forms of the mental functions.

**Step Two.** Recall from the discussion of the J–P dichotomy that it is intended to indicate whether a judging function or a perceiving function is extraverted. When teaching about the eight function-attitudes, remember that the Extraverted Thinking and Extraverted Feeling functions are judging functions. Thus, if someone has Extraverted Thinking or Extraverted Feeling as the dominant *or* auxiliary function, then the last letter of his or her four-letter type would be "J." Conversely, Extraverted Sensing and Extraverted Intuition are perceiving functions. If either of those are the dominant *or* auxiliary for a person, then the last letter of his or her four-letter type would be "P." Again, the last letter (J or P) of the four-letter type tells us what that person *extraverts*—whether they are an Extravert or Introvert.

The following diagram can help you and your clients visually grasp this way of talking about and teaching type and type dynamics—how functions are extraverted or introverted. From this diagram, we can see that the four preference pairs of the MBTI are not really separate from one another. That is, Extraverts *extravert* a particular function, and that function is either a judging (J) or perceiving (P) function. Introverts *introvert* a particular function, and when they extravert, they extravert either a judging (J) or perceiving (P) function.

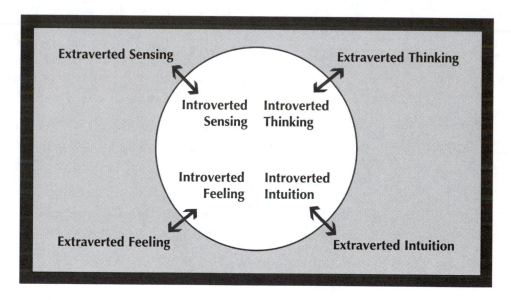

Remember, we use all of the eight function-attitudes every day. What makes us a type is that we more consciously use some over the others. The following descriptions of the function-attitudes build on the descriptions earlier in this chapter.

**THE EIGHT FUNCTION-ATTITUDES AND THEIR CHARACTERISTICS**

**Extraverted Sensing:** Outward and active focus on the objective world and on gathering factual data and sensuous experiences. Characterized by: quick responsiveness to the environment, realism, present-orientation, excitement of anything that stimulates the senses, concrete language and factual speech.

**Introverted Sensing:** Inward and reflective focus on subjective sensuous experiences and on the storing of factual historical data. Characterized by: clarifying of facts, attention to past associations and experiential memory, recall of physical world memories as "snapshots," and attention to bodily sensations.

**Extraverted Intuition:** Outward and active focus on the new, the possibilities and meanings/patterns in the objective world. Characterized by: attention to the world of ideas, symbols and possibilities, brainstorming activity, noticing and making "connections" while watching the world or by talking out loud, adaptability and an orientation to change.

**Introverted Intuition:** Inward and reflective focus on the subjective world of symbols, meanings, insight and patterns that come up from the unconscious. Characterized by: vision, attention to "psychic," even mystical realities, metaphor in thought and words, possibilities in the world of ideas, complexity, multiple perspectives and an orientation to the future.

**Extraverted Thinking:** Outward and active focus on applying logical order to the objective world through building structure, organizing and making decisions. Characterized by: cause-and-effect thinking, establishing objectively defining and ruling principles, planning, logical debate and critiquing, and analysis of pros and cons.

**Introverted Thinking:** Inward and reflective focus on the subjective world of reason that seeks understanding through finding the logical principles behind phenomena. Characterized by: giving order to ideas (rather than objects), seeking the "truth," tough-minded (and often categorical) analysis, logical precision, making conceptual linkages, and reliance on and trust in own logic that may go against the "norm."

**Extraverted Feeling:** Outward and active focus on bringing order to the objective world through building and seeking harmony with others and alignment with openly expressed values. Characterized by: expressing warmth and empathy, relationship-seeking, emotional responsiveness, sensitivity to social mores, harmony in relationships, attention to expectations in relationships, and consideration and acceptance of others.

**Introverted Feeling:** Inward and reflective focus on the subjective world of deeply felt values that seeks harmony through alignment of personal behavior with those values and evaluation of phenomena in light of those values. Characterized by: attention to ethical concerns, drive to fulfill deeply passionate ideals, seeking of abstract universal values, trust in one's own values and evaluations of right and wrong that may go against the "norm."

**TRAINERS:** Teaching about type using the eight function-attitudes can be a very helpful way of introducing people to type dynamics. The advantage is that this method quickly introduces people to dynamics and the differences between, say, an ESTP (Extraverted Sensing type) and an ESTJ (Extraverted Thinking type). The disadvantage is that people may have a bit more to learn than if you taught "just" the four preference pairs. When you teach the four pairs one at a time, you can move fairly quickly, but then your clients need to "shift gears" if and when you teach about dynamics. As the professional type user, you must decide which method fits with your way of understanding type, and which best serves the needs of the particular group with which you are working.

If you want to learn more about this way of understanding and teaching type, we recommend reading *Jung's Function-Attitudes Explained* by Henry Thompson.

## Conclusion

DON'T BE DISCOURAGED! Learning and teaching about type dynamics can be one of the trickier aspects of type. People will come up with their own ways to learn and teach about the subject. Keep going—dynamics are the core of type. Understanding and applying dynamics will serve you and your clients well. Pick a method that works for you, and don't get (overly) confused in the beginning by others. After you are thoroughly grounded in a method that works for you, you may want to try some different ways—if only for the sake of having options when teaching clients who may well have different learning styles from your own!

## Resources

Jung, C. G. (1971). *Psychological types* (H. G. Baynes, Trans., revised by R. F. C. Hull). Collected Works, Vol. 6. Princeton, NJ: Princeton University. (Original work published in 1921)

Martin, C. R. (1997). *Looking at type: The fundamental*s. Gainesville, FL: Center for Applications of Psychological Type.

Myers, I. B. with Myers, P. B. (1995). *Gifts differing: Understanding personality type.* Palo Alto, CA: Davies-Black Publishing. (Original work published 1980)

Myers, K. D., & Kirby, L. K. (1994). *Introduction to type dynamics and development: Exploring the next level of type.* Palo Alto, CA: Consulting Psychologists Press.

Quenk, N. L. (1993). *Beside ourselves: Our hidden personality in everyday life.* Palo Alto, CA: Davies-Black Publishing.

Thompson, H. L. (1996). *Jung's function-attitudes explained.* Watkinsville, GA: Wormhole Publishing.

How do I respond when clients ask:

*Why do I have to take this instrument?*
*Why do I suspect this is a waste of time?*

*Can I get out of taking this thing?*
*What are the consequences of saying "no"?*

*Is this psychobabble or something useful?*

*What benefit do I get out of it, or is it just for someone else's purposes? I'm a guinea pig, right?*

*Should I give straight answers or try to guess the "right" answers?*

*Is it going to reveal something about me I don't want others to know, or maybe I don't want to know about myself?*

Some clients will have these thoughts but not speak them. How do I plan to handle these concerns?

# Chapter 4

**WHAT DO I NEED TO ANTICIPATE?**
Suppose you have been asked to respond to a self-report instrument and you are just sitting down to look at it. No one has given you a clear explanation of what it is about. You aren't sure about the reasons for taking it, or what will be done with the results, or who will see the results. What's your attitude toward this instrument as you look at it? Some of the reactions on the preceding page are typical. These are not extreme reactions. They are natural responses to something strange that has not been adequately explained. And often your clients may not share their concerns with you as they take the Indicator.

When you approach clients to use the MBTI, even when you take care to assure the right conditions are in place, you always run the risk that some people will have negative reactions and suspect bad consequences. What are the chances of accomplishing anything valuable with the MBTI when such questions are in people's minds? Slight, at best.

You as a professional know the importance of keeping a client's trust. In this short chapter we focus on:

- the assumptions clients may have about tests and the MBTI in particular
- how to address those assumptions

You will learn about the precautions and planning needed to assure good conditions for clients to respond to the Indicator and to get results they value. The practices summarized here are those that experienced MBTI users have found to work well.

**WHAT ASSUMPTIONS DO CLIENTS HAVE ABOUT TESTS? HOW DO I DEAL WITH THEM?** Prospective respondents to the MBTI generally bring with them a mindset about psychological instruments that has to be overcome or countered by the MBTI practitioner. The MBTI has features that are *essentially* different from other apparently similar instruments. Your job is to proactively help prospective respondents understand the MBTI as being distinctly outside their image of psychological instruments. There are at least five assumptions they are likely to have about tests that do not apply to the MBTI.

## Inappropriate assumptions

**1)** THE PURPOSE FOR **taking the instrument is set by the test developer and the tester.**

This assumption is deeply held and pervasive. It is a correct assumption for many tests, but MBTI practitioners should not let it apply to the MBTI. It certainly is true for competency tests, the kind of tests used most often in schools and training programs. The test developers and testers (teachers) control the purpose of the test. It is also true for some aptitude and interest inventories. But practitioners who are not testing for competency must make that clear to clients. If their intention is to help clients find better self-understanding by using an instrument, the MBTI included, practitioners have an obligation to:

- tune in carefully to the clients' purposes, motives and mindset
- match the instrument and the interpretation of the instrument's outcome to each client

Consider the client's mindset as a stream of energy already focused on something, already moving toward some objectives, however vague or clear. Clients will buy into and use the ideas of psychological type only to the extent that they see type concepts as *useful* to help them better accomplish what they are *already* working on. Even if you see clients' purposes as wrong or in need of refinement, it is important to hook type into their existing purposes so that they commit to it as a tool in their own tool kit. Their growing understanding of type will help them refine their own purposes.

**2)** **Psychological tests probe into mental health, and they report good/bad profiles.**

Always tell clients at the outset that the MBTI has no right or wrong answers and no good/bad outcomes. One's MBTI type tells nothing about mental health, maturity, balance or imbalance. All sixteen profiles identified by the MBTI are positive, representing different ways of mental processing. Remind them again of these qualities of the MBTI when they are discussing their results with you. If they want to dwell on their type's blind spots, help them see that all types have strengths and blind spots.

**3)** **Self-report tests that aren't seriously about mental health are probably pop psychology and not worth taking.**

The MBTI items are about everyday choices and interests and, to some respondents, the items may appear to be about trivial matters. You will help most of your clients by telling them that the MBTI is the most widely used, research-based instrument of its kind, and that virtually everyone finds their MBTI results to be valuable.

**4)** Even though they tell you the test has no right or wrong answers, it really does. And it is going to compare me with someone else or some "norm."

Always tell clients, "The MBTI is not a test, scored right or wrong; it is an Indicator that points to one of sixteen profiles, all of which are positive. You are the only one given your MBTI results, and no one will be judging your results as right or wrong." There are no comparisons to norms. Scores do not tell you anything about skills, maturity or development.

**5)** You make yourself vulnerable when you take a psychological test—vulnerable to having the results used in ways you don't know about or want.

Tell clients who may have this concern, "The MBTI results are for your study and self-understanding. You are the *only* one given your results. No one sees them unless you choose to show them the results. There are no other ways that anyone can use them without your explicit permission." If clients are taking the Indicator along with other people—a spouse or work team members, for example—and they tell each other their types, their type differences become a means to mutual understanding and constructive use of their differences.

In summary, anticipate client concerns, check with the client about his or her perception of the MBTI, and get a sense of assurance that the client trusts you and feels positive about taking the Indicator. Here is a checklist you can use.

---

**GUIDE SHEET: ARE THE CONDITIONS RIGHT FOR USING THE MBTI?**

**Have I checked to see that the client:**

❑ **wants** to take the MBTI?

❑ sees the MBTI as potentially **useful for his or her purposes**?

❑ understands that the MBTI is **not a test**, scored right or wrong; it is an Indicator pointing to one of sixteen profiles, all of which are positive?

❑ understands that the MBTI is **about types of mental processing**, not about mental health?

❑ understands that **no one else** will get his or her MBTI results, "unless you choose to tell them your results"?

❑ *if concerned about the MBTI's credibility*, understands that it is the most widely used, research-based instrument of its kind?

❑ *if concerned about being compared with someone else or some "norm,"* knows that he or she alone will decide the uses of the MBTI results, and that the MBTI report does not involve norms?

### HOW MUCH DO I CHARGE?

A question we are often asked is: "How much do I charge for MBTI feedback or training?" Of course, there is no simple answer. If there were a simple answer, it would be this—charge what you are worth!

What you are worth depends on many things. It depends on your knowledge, background and experience. It depends on your self-evaluation. It depends on the going rate for that kind of service in your area. It depends on your values around the kind of work you do.

Professionals who have a "rate" will probably charge whatever their rate is for similar services. So if you are a counselor or therapist, you will probably charge at least your hourly rate for the amount of time you spend giving feedback. If you are doing individual feedback, this can range from free to $100 an hour. And you might use the same model for group feedback—a four-hour session is four times your hourly rate. Of course, that may vary by client, by what folks can afford, and how skilled you are with this particular instrument.

People who are beginning to give feedback will often start at a lower rate as they gain experience and charge more as their expertise builds.

When you charge for feedback, you should build in the costs of scoring and the materials that you give out. When working with groups, many people find it valuable to charge for their feedback or training time, plus the cost of scoring and materials per person in a group. Others wrap scoring, materials, and their own time into one training fee.

If you have experience in consulting or training in organizations, you probably already have a feel for what to charge for your time in that setting. Type is just one more tool in your toolbox, and you charge your going rate. But what is the rate for type training and MBTI feedback in organizations? This varies widely by region, size of city, by organization, and by your perceived expertise. Some people charge $250 for a full day of training, while others charge $3000 a day or more. For-profit organizations are often used to paying highly for expertise, while nonprofit organizations, educational institutions and volunteer groups are typically able to pay much less. Let your self-evaluation and your conscience be your guide.

One of the best ways to know what to charge is to talk to people in your area who do similar work with similar clients. Ask them what they would charge for training and feedback. This way you get a sense of the going rate for the kind of work you want to do.

**Resources**

Lawrence, G. D. (1993). *People types and tiger stripes* (3rd ed.). Gainesville, FL: Center for Applications of Psychological Type.

The Winter 1995 volume of the *Bulletin of Psychological Type* has several articles on ethical issues in the use of type, and the Association for Psychological Type's (APT) ethical principles are reproduced there. See specifically Ethics of type: APT's ethical principles. *Bulletin of Psychological Type*, 18(1), 7–8.

*There are so many different forms of the MBTI—
which do I choose?*

*Our company has bought a large number of Form Gs.
Is it obsolete now? And do I have to go buy Form M
right away?*

*Can I give the Indicator to a student in junior
high school?*

*What do I say when I hand the Indicator to clients?*

*I'm giving someone the MBTI and they ask me
what a word means—what do I say?*

# Chapter 5

THESE ARE NOT THE KINDS of questions our clients ask—they're the kind *we* ask as professionals. What do I need to know before, during and after the administration of the MBTI? What are the pragmatics and mechanics of choosing, administering and scoring it? In this chapter you will learn:

- what reading level is expected of respondents
- cross-cultural issues that relate to taking the MBTI
- which form to use
- the differences between Form M and Form G
- how to give instructions for people taking the MBTI
- how to hand-score with templates

**BEFORE ADMINISTERING THE MBTI.** Beyond the essentials identified in Chapter Four, what else do I need to know about the client and the situation before administering the MBTI? Three things: Can the client read the MBTI questions? Is culture an issue? And, what form of the MBTI is best suited to this situation?

**READING LEVEL.** At least an eighth grade reading level is required to answer the MBTI questions. Many adults do not read at or beyond the eighth grade level. However, among them are those whose listening vocabulary is considerably beyond their reading ability. If you suppose the client(s) might have difficulty with the reading, the *MBTI Manual* endorses your reading the questions aloud. You may ask, for example, "If you would like me to read the questions aloud while you fill in your answers, I'd be glad to do that." Just be careful when reading the items to take a neutral tone on all response options.

When administering the Indicator to *students below the college level,* be sure to tell them to consider the fact that the items were written with adults in mind. Children who are twelve and thirteen can take it if they read at the eighth grade level, but accuracy of the Indicator results may be lower. Factors such as level of development within one's type, self-knowledge, vocabulary, and conceptual level affect reliability. If any of these appear to be an issue, you need to take extra care in interpreting results and helping the young person find a best-fit type. As the professional user of the MBTI, you will need to use your best judgment to assess the suitability of using the Indicator with persons who are close to these minimums.

> Minimum appropriate requirements for taking the MBTI: Eighth-grade reading level and fourteen years of age. Form M may be used with twelve- and thirteen-year-olds with caution.

**CROSS CULTURAL FACTORS.** The Indicator's reliability and validity have been established primarily with literate English-speaking people who live in the United States. The items of the Indicator contain expressions that may not have the same meanings and connotations to people outside that cultural mainstream. If you are considering using the MBTI with people who speak English as a second language, or are from other English-speaking countries, you must carefully decide whether the MBTI is appropriate for your clients.

This means giving attention to both reading level and degree of acculturation. Again, at least an eighth-grade English reading level is needed, with the same age level issues noted above. A score of at least 500 on the TOEFL (Test of English as a Foreign Language) is needed. *More* importantly, you must consider the degree to which the words on the MBTI have the same meaning as they do for mainstream English-speaking people in the U.S. That is, how acculturated to U.S. culture is the individual—do the idioms and colloquial language hold the same meanings? As the professional, you must ethically concern yourself with such issues, and inform clients of any cautions you have in this regard.

The MBTI is available commercially in sixteen translations—in effect validated in fourteen cultures. An equal number of research translations are in the process of being validated. Contact Consulting Psychologists Press for information on availability of translations.

> In all cases where reading and cross-cultural factors may be a concern, you will want to consider carefully whether or not to use the MBTI, and if you choose to move forward, you should be especially careful in interpreting and verifying the results. Bear in mind the standard principle that type results are considered a hypothesis until verified by the client. Such administrations of the MBTI must be seen as "experimental"—and informing the client of these issues is the ethical approach.

**WHICH FORM OF THE MBTI?** Form M (which is replacing Form G) is the standard form. The publisher refers to it also as Step I. Its ninety-three items are scored for the basic report of one's type. As you can see in the table, *Forms of the MBTI*, this form can be obtained in four versions: a) for template scoring; b) for mail-in computer scoring; c) for on-site computer scoring using the publisher's software; and d) a self-scorable version that the respondent (or MBTI practitioner) scores without a template.

As you might suppose, the versions differ in features and cost. Through the years, template scoring has been by far the most used method, probably because the cost is considerably less than the other options. Its question booklets are reusable. Many trainers and consultants use the self-scorable version for its convenience. The computer-scored version of Form M has been shown to be somewhat better than Form M template scoring in reporting the type that respondents validate as their best-fit type. This is because the computer program is able to give more weight to the items that are better predictors of the individual's best-fit type. Template and self-scorable versions give each item the same weight.

Form Q of the MBTI (144 items) is used for obtaining Step II profiles. Besides giving the basic report of one's type, it reports results on sub-sets of traits within the four dimensions of type. For example, the Extraversion–Introversion dimension has five sub-sets, one of which is Expressive–Contained. Some MBTI practitioners, especially those whose work is individual counseling or coaching, find this expanded version useful. In contrast, when the MBTI is used with groups for understanding differences among group members, Step I is most often used. Step II is available to anyone who is qualified to purchase Step I; however, getting trained in its use is strongly advised.

Form J (290 items) is used for Step III. It is a clinical instrument, restricted to psychologists and other mental health practitioners, that reports possible problem areas for consideration in the counseling process.

The publisher of the MBTI, Consulting Psychologists Press, will be glad to send you its catalog, listing all the MBTI materials and their prices. Call 800-624-1765.

**Form M? Form G?** Because Form G was the standard for over twenty years, many MBTI users may have a large supply of Form G on hand. At the time of this writing, they are asking about the change of forms and how it affects them. If you work for an organization that has Form G materials on hand, you may have the same questions. If, as a new user of the MBTI, you have no MBTI materials, you should start with Form M. The table *Form M? Form G?* was written to answer current MBTI users' questions about the transition to Form M. If you are currently using Form G materials, rest assured that they have strong reliability and validity, and that you can continue to use them in good conscience until you decide to move to Form M.

**FORMS OF THE MBTI AND WHEN TO USE EACH**

**FORM M.** The current standard form of the MBTI. 93 items. Scored for the four-letter type. Computer or template scoring available. Computer scoring may be done through mail-in or through use of on-site scoring software. Use it when you are able to give the MBTI ahead of the feedback session.

**FORM M SELF-SCORABLE.** The current standard self-scorable form. 93 items. Scored for the four-letter type. It is hand-scored by the individual taking the MBTI, or by the professional. Use it when there isn't time to give participants the Indicator before the feedback session, or when everyone in the group feedback session may not be available to take the MBTI before the feedback session.

**FORM G.** The most recent standard form of the MBTI. 126 items. Scored for the four-letter type. Computer or template scoring available. Again, use it when you are able to give the MBTI ahead of the feedback session. Hint: If you use Form G and time is a concern, simply have respondents complete the first 95 items (items number 94 and 96–126 are actually research items). In this way, time to complete the MBTI does not differ for Form M and Form G.

**FORM G SELF-SCORABLE.** The most recent standard self-scorable form. 94 items. Scored for the four-letter type. It is hand-scored by the individual taking the MBTI, or by the professional. Again, use it when there isn't time to give participants the Indicator before the feedback session, or when everyone in the group feedback session may not be available to take the MBTI beforehand.

**FORM Q.** Used to generate a four-letter type and the Step II Interpretive Report. 144 items. The Step II report generates scores on twenty sub-sets (trait-like behavior patterns within each of the four primary MBTI dichotomies). Used when more in-depth individual feedback is given (e.g., coaching, counseling, executive development).

**FORM J.** The current research form of the MBTI. Used to generate the Step III Type Differentiation Indicator (TDI) profile. 290 items. Computer scored for TDI sub-sets, or can be template-scored with Form F templates (the old research form of the MBTI). The Step III report generates the twenty sub-sets of Step II plus seven Comfort-Discomfort set of scores. Also used when more in-depth individual feedback is given (e.g., coaching, counseling, executive development). The TDI gives information about issues of mental health and development, and thus to purchase Form J one must demonstrate extensive educational background in the administration and interpretation of tests.

If you are interested in using Form Q and Form J, it is highly recommended that you get training in their use.

## FORM M? FORM G? QUESTIONS AND ANSWERS FROM EXPERIENCED MBTI USERS

**Q: Form M replaces Form G, right?** Right. Form M is being phased in as the "standard" form of the MBTI, used for identifying the four basic type preferences. Introduced in mid-1998, Form M incorporates several improvements over Form G (1977). Form M is no longer considered an experimental form but is in a period where further data are being gathered on its performance, where larger samples can be used for validity studies (e.g., best-fit) and longer time periods can be used in test-retest reliability studies.

**Q: What happened to H, I, J, K and L?** That's another story. For basic scoring, M replaces G.

**Q: Is Form G obsolete? We have a lot of Form G booklets and answer sheets on hand and would use them if they are still considered valid and reliable.** Form G is not obsolete. It is just being phased out. Computer scoring will be available indefinitely. The validity and reliability of Form G have not changed; they are excellent.

**Q: If Form G has excellent reliability and validity, why have a new form?** Instrument makers always seek to improve reliability and validity. Of course, the MBTI's reliability and validity *for any particular respondent* depends heavily on your skill in administering it, explaining type concepts, and interpreting the MBTI results. That factor doesn't change with the new form.

**Q: We score with templates. Does that process change with Form M?** Form M requires its own templates; Form G templates won't work on Form M answer sheets. Template scoring has been simplified a little for Form M. The main difference is that Form M template scoring does not use item weights of zero, one and two as Form G does. All item responses have equal weight. You do not need to convert raw points into preference scores, as with Form G. In addition, since items that had different scoring weights for males and females were removed from Form M, there are not separate T–F scoring templates for men and women. Thus, Form M has four scoring templates instead of the five used with Form G.

**Q: Form M template scoring with no item weights is more accurate than Form G template scoring *with* item weights?** That isn't clear yet. The 1998 *MBTI Manual* reports comparisons of computer scoring of Form M and Form G—favoring Form M—but the *Manual* does not show any results of comparing template scoring for the two forms. Because most MBTIs are scored by template, this is an important question, and we can expect it to be answered soon.

**Q: Form M has fewer items than Form G. Does responding to Form M take less time?** Self-scorable Form G and self-scorable Form M have the same number of items and should take the same amount of time. Responding to template scored or computer scored Form G and Form M can take the same amount of time if respondents only answer questions 1–95 of Form G, the items that score for basic type. (The 32 items of Form G not scored for type yield other data beyond basic type.) If a respondent answers all 126 questions of Form G, more time is needed than answering the 93 items of Form M.

**Q: If I am qualified to use Form G, am I qualified to use Form M?** Yes. The third edition of the *MBTI Manual* highlights the process of developing Form M and explains its features. Except for the changes in scoring—which you can grasp easily—Form M does not change your work with the MBTI.

## When handing the MBTI to respondents

**RIGHT CONDITIONS.** Check your guide sheet in Chapter Four. If you have not covered all the points listed there, do it now.

**FRAME OF MIND.** Tell clients to respond to the items not as their job self or ideal self, but as they are naturally—when the world is not pulling on them to be or do something else. Many MBTI users have been using the phrase, "take it with your *shoes-off self* in mind."

**INDICATOR INSTRUCTIONS.** Tell respondents to read and follow the instructions on the first page of the MBTI question booklet. In a group administration, it is almost always best to read the instructions aloud to them. In either case, at a minimum, read to them three statements from the first page:

- "There are **no 'right' or 'wrong' answers**."
- "Do not spend too much time thinking about any one question." Tell them there is **no time limit**, but the items were written to get the first response that comes to mind.
- "If you cannot decide on an answer, skip that question."

**INDICATOR, NOT A TEST.** Remember to avoid referring to the MBTI as a test.

**ANSWER SHEET INSTRUCTIONS.** Remind respondents to read and follow the instructions on the answer sheet form. They need to put their name or identification number on the front of the sheet. The remainder of the front side and the left column of the back side contain spaces for entering demographic data that can be used for research. These data need not be filled in for obtaining the type report. Tell your clients whether to fill in these categories, three through fourteen. If you will use computer scoring, the respondents must be reminded to carefully blacken all their responses on the answer sheet, including those in the name field below the space where they print their name.

**INSTRUCTIONS FOR THE SELF-SCORABLE VERSION.** The guidelines above apply to the self-scorable version as well. The instructions to the respondent are the same. We strongly recommend telling respondents to stop after they finish answering the questions, and not to pull apart the scoring section until after you have given them an explanation of the concepts behind the MBTI. This approach follows the reasoning given in Chapter Two.

## While clients respond to the MBTI

IF YOU ARE PRESENT when clients are responding to the Indicator, and if you see someone struggling over the questions, it usually means one of two things: he or she did not understand the instructions or your explanation about the nature of the instrument and its uses; or the reading is too difficult. Ask the person if there is any concern. If needed, clarify the instructions. Suggest to the person who seems to be pondering each question a long time to try to respond on the basis of his or her first impression, rather than studying the questions. If the person asks the meaning of a word or a question, it is best to say, "Answer on the basis of your understanding. If you just can't decide, it's better to leave the response blank."

If reading ability or visual impairment appears to be a factor, say "If you'd rather, I'd be glad to read the questions aloud while you fill in the answers." Be sure to read the items in an even-handed and neutral way.

People will typically finish taking Form M of the MBTI in fifteen to twenty-five minutes, but some individuals may take longer. Remember though, there is no time limit.

## Scoring the MBTI

THERE ARE SEVERAL OPTIONS for scoring the MBTI: mail-in computer scoring (using pre-paid answer sheets), template scoring, and the self-scorable version. There are also local software licenses and web delivery scoring options available through CPP—contact them for more information on those methods.

> **Note:** Form G and earlier forms of the MBTI used a prediction ratio to determine if item choices should be weighted zero, one, or two, with higher weights given to items that discriminated well. In Form M, a new method of scoring based on item response theory (IRT) varies the weight of *each item for each individual respondent.* The complexity of this type of scoring requires computer scoring of the MBTI for the greatest accuracy, although a "close enough" result may be had using Form M template scoring.
>
> Since template-scoring and self-scorable versions of Form M only approximate the results that would come from computer scoring using IRT, it is possible for a template-scored Form M to yield a different result from the computer scoring of the same answer sheet. In reality there is a 94–98% agreement between the two methods. As a sensitive MBTI user, you will recognize the importance of verifying type *especially* where preference clarity is slight—whether the MBTI was computer or template scored. Much of the next chapter is devoted to helping clients clarify their best-fit type.

What we describe here is *standard template scoring of non-prepaid Form M answer sheets.* Pre-paid computer-scored Form M answer sheets can also be template-scored, but require a different set of templates, available through CPP. Template scoring of Form G has different instructions, which can be found in the second edition of the *MBTI Manual* (1985). Directions for scoring of the self-scorable version are very clearly written on the booklet itself.

**TEMPLATES.** Template scoring is simple once you have practiced the routine. If you have Form M templates available to you, put one in front of you as you follow these instructions. If you are reading this before you have the scoring materials, you can reread this section as you practice the scoring process. There are *four* templates, one each for E–I, S–N, T–F and J–P. They are plastic and opaque except for the small, clear windows used to position the templates over the filled-in answer sheet and to tally the responses. Each template is divided into three vertical panels, the left one containing instructions and the other two the windows for scoring. On the E–I template, for example, the middle panel contains the windows for scoring E responses and the right one is for scoring I responses.

**POSITIONING AND TALLYING.** The following instructions can help you with the mechanics of template scoring the MBTI.

- Each scoring panel of a template has two small, *square* windows on the left side of the panel, one at the top, one at the bottom. They are used for positioning the panel over the answer sheet so that the client's responses show through the correct *round* windows.

- If you have an MBTI Form M answer sheet, look at the item response area. In the right margin are two asterisks, one at the top and one at the bottom of the sheet.

- Start with the E–I template. The E panel of the template goes over the client's answers so that the asterisks show though the square windows of the E panel. The client's E responses will then show through the round windows so that you can count them. Each blackened spot is counted as one point.

- Slide the template off and write the total E points in the blue shaded box on the answer sheet marked *Points*, located to the left of the response section.

- Then put the template back over the answer sheet so that the I panel is on top of the responses, with the asterisks showing through the square windows of the I panel. Count the I responses as you did the E responses, and put the total in the I part of the blue shaded box.

- On the right side of the shaded box, write in E or I to indicate which had more points. If the points are equal, write in I. Ties on any dichotomy are scored as I, N, F or P. The rationale for breaking ties in this way was given in Chapter Three. The Third Edition, *MBTI Manual* cautions practitioners against over-interpreting the rationale for breaking ties. It reminds us that the reported type is a starting point for dialogue about what the best-fit type may be, especially with clients who score with slight preferences.

- Complete the scoring with the other templates. The blue box on the answer sheet will now show four preference categories, e.g., ENFJ. That is what you report to the respondent.

- Read "Section 6 Optional" on one of the templates, in the lower left corner. This paragraph concerns reporting preference clarity on the four MBTI dichotomies. MBTI practitioners differ on the issue of whether to report the preference clarity to the respondent. Isabel Myers made a clear recommendation that respondents not be given a numerical inter-pretation of MBTI results—that they be told the four letters but not the outcome of the four numerical tallies made to arrive at the letters of the type. The option given in Section 6 is not whether to give numbers; it is whether to report just the letters or to also tell the client the preference clarity category of each of the four dimensions.

- As you can see on each template, there are four preference clarity categories that could be reported to the client on each of the four dichotomies: slight, moderate, clear, or very clear—depending on the point count. The four categories indicate how confident we can be that the Indicator is reporting the type that fits the client best. You identify the correct category for each respondent by noting the larger of the two tallies made on each dichotomy. For example, if points for E were 16 and points for I were 5, the 16 tells you the category is Moderate. On the next page is a table to help in the conversion of raw points to prefer-ence clarity categories. In the next chapter, we discuss how to talk with clients about their MBTI results and whether to tell them the clarity categories of their preferences.

| Dichotomy | Greatest Raw Points | Preference Clarity Category |
|-----------|---------------------|----------------------------|
| E–I | 11–13<br>14–16<br>17–19<br>20–21 | Slight<br>Moderate<br>Clear<br>Very Clear |
| S–N | 13–15<br>16–20<br>21–24<br>25–26 | Slight<br>Moderate<br>Clear<br>Very Clear |
| T–F | 12–14<br>15–18<br>19–22<br>23–24 | Slight<br>Moderate<br>Clear<br>Very Clear |
| J–P | 11–13<br>14–17<br>18–20<br>21–22 | Slight<br>Moderate<br>Clear<br>Very Clear |

When items are omitted on a dichotomy, the highest raw points on that dichotomy may be lower than in the range listed for "slight." In that case, use "slight" as the preference clarity category.

- Transfer the four-letter MBTI result to a report form. See the next chapter for a discussion of the reporting process.

- Finally, look at the dark box in the upper left corner of each template. It tells the maximum number of points that can be tallied for the preference pair. For example, there are 21 E–I items. A person's responses may vary from 21 for E and 0 for I, to 0 for E and 21 for I. If the E and I tallies you made for the respondent do not add up to 21 total, the person skipped one or more items—or you counted wrong. It is a good practice to glance at your tallies to see that they add up to the maximum for that dichotomy.

- **Omissions** can affect reliability of the MBTI results. When more than four omitted items appear on either the E–I or J–P templates, or when more than five omissions appear on the S–N or T–F templates, the reported type may be affected. Flag the results, check over the answer sheet, and discuss with the client what prompted the omissions and whether the reported type seems right on the affected polarity.

**Reporting results**

FOR THOSE WHO COMPUTER SCORE, the method of reporting MBTI results varies depending on your needs. At the most basic level, you receive only your client's reported type preferences and preference clarity indices. You can then provide the type descriptions and other supporting materials as you see fit. For those who want narrative reports for particular applications, you can also get computer scoring reports in such domains as organizational or team behavior.

For those who template score, there are a number of options for reporting your client's results from the MBTI. You can transfer their results to a report form specifically designed for practitioners who template score (e.g., *Your Results from the MBTI* and *Profile of Your MBTI Results*), and then you can provide them with a type description. As a practitioner who template scores, you have a variety of options for providing clients with type descriptions (e.g., booklets, report generators, and reproducible masters). In the next chapter, we give guidelines for interpreting and verifying MBTI results with your clients. In addition, we list some sources for type descriptions and other supporting materials you might use in your feedback sessions.

**Resources**

Lawrence, G. D. (2000). *Your results from the Myers-Briggs Type Indicator.* Gainesville, FL: Center for Applications of Psychological Type.

Lawrence, G. D., & Martin, C. R. (1996). *Profile of your MBTI results.* [Includes *Your Results* and brief type descriptions]. Gainesville, FL: Center for Applications of Psychological Type.

Myers, I. B., McCaulley, M. H., Quenk, N. L., & Hammer, A. L. (1998). *MBTI Manual: A guide to the development and use of the Myers-Briggs Type Indicator* (3rd ed.). Palo Alto, CA: Consulting Psychologists Press.

*What kind of materials do I need when I explain type to others?*

*What do I do or say when I give someone an explanation of type?*

*A client is wrestling with two type descriptions. How do I help her decide which is her best-fit type?*

*When I was giving feedback, someone asked me if his type would change. What do I say?*

*What do the scores on the MBTI mean?*

*Help! I have a workshop on Monday. What do I do? How do I put it together?*

# Chapter 6

THIS CHAPTER deals with giving an MBTI explanation to any client. Giving a type explanation to people in an organization involves some additional factors—which are covered in Chapter Eight. In this chapter we will cover how to:

- plan for explaining type and reporting MBTI results
- give the type explanation, and provide some guidelines
- help the client choose a best-fit type
- help the client put type to use
- respond to questions clients commonly have about type
- explain type to groups

This chapter includes a framework that many practitioners have found useful when explaining type to groups. At the end of the chapter is a checklist you can use to remind yourself of the main points presented.

## PLAN FOR EXPLAINING TYPE AND REPORTING MBTI RESULTS.

**1) Plan for time and support materials needed.** An hour or more is usually necessary for a solid, initial introduction to type. There is always pressure to shorten the time, but you should resist it. We have found that many people don't automatically see how type differences play out in their lives, and it takes time to help them see that. And type concepts will not become tools for them until they have had some coaching in putting the tools to use. That takes time, often several sessions. Most likely you will be helping clients use the lenses of type to examine some aspect of their lives—relationships at work, in the family, etc.—and the timing and pacing of that examination will dictate the scheduling.

SUPPORT MATERIALS are essential to reporting MBTI results and explaining type. At a minimum, each client *should* have:

- A handout to look at while you explain the four dimensions—E–I, S–N, T–F and J–P—with terms to characterize the preference pairs. CAPT publishes several handouts for that purpose: *Verifying Your Type Preferences/ MBTI Vocabulary* and *Words to Help Understanding of Type Concepts* are two of them. They are reproduced here.

- A full-length type description for the type they reported on the MBTI and/or ultimately verify. If you computer score,

# Verifying Your Type Preferences

## Worksheet

| **E** Extraversion | | Introversion **I** |
|---|---|---|
| Energized by outer world | | Energized by inner world |

| **S** Sensing | | Intuition **N** |
|---|---|---|
| Work with known facts | | Look for possibilities and relationships |

| **T** Thinking | | Feeling **F** |
|---|---|---|
| Base decisions on impersonal analysis and logic | | Base decisions on personal values |

| **J** Judging | | Perceiving **P** |
|---|---|---|
| Prefer a planned, decided, orderly way of life | | Prefer a flexible, spontaneous way of life |

| VERY CLEAR | CLEAR | MODERATE | SLIGHT | SLIGHT | MODERATE | CLEAR | VERY CLEAR |
|---|---|---|---|---|---|---|---|

| | **E** or **I** | **S** or **N** | **T** or **F** | **J** or **P** |
|---|---|---|---|---|
| (1) Self-Assessment Type: | | | | |
| (2) Work-Situations Type: | | | | |
| (3) Indicator Type: | | | | |
| (4) Best-Fit Type: | | | | |

800.777.2278 toll-free USA • www.capt.org

# MBTI® Vocabulary

### ORIENTATION OF ENERGY: DIRECTION OF FOCUS, SOURCE OF ENERGY

**E  Extraversion**

Energized by outer world
Focus on people, things
Active
Breadth of interest
Live it, then understand it
Interaction
Outgoing

**Introversion  I**

Energized by inner world
Focus on thoughts, concepts
Reflective
Depth of interest
Understand it before live it
Concentration
Inwardly directed

### PERCEIVING FUNCTION: WAYS OF TAKING IN INFORMATION

**S  Sensing**

Facts
Data
Detail
Reality-based
Actuality
Here and now
Utility

**Intuition  N**

Meanings
Associations
Possibilities
Hunches, speculations
Theoretical
Future
Fantasy

### JUDGING FUNCTION: WAYS OF COMING TO CONCLUSION

**T  Thinking**

Analysis
Objective
Logic
Impersonal
Critique
Reason
Criteria

**Feeling  F**

Sympathy
Subjective
Humane
Personal
Appreciate
Values
Circumstances

### ORIENTATION TO OUTER LIFE: ATTITUDE TOWARD THE EXTERNAL WORLD

**J  Judging**

Organized
Settled
Planned
Decisive
Control one's life
Set goals
Systematic

**Perceiving  P**

Pending
Flexible
Spontaneous
Tentative
Let life happen
Undaunted by surprise
Open to change

Center for Applications of Psychological Type
2815 NW 13th Street • Suite 401
Gainesville Florida 32609 USA
www.capt.org • **800.777.2278** toll-free USA
352.375.0160 • 800.723.6284 toll-free fax

# WORDS TO HELP UNDERSTANDING OF TYPE CONCEPTS

### E: EXTRAVERSION

When extraverting, I am
- Oriented to the outer world
- Focusing on people and things
- Active
- Using trial and error with confidence
- Scanning the environment for stimulation

### I: INTROVERSION

When introverting, I am
- Oriented to the inner world
- Focusing on ideas, concepts, inner impressions
- Reflective
- Considering deeply before acting
- Probing inwardly for stimulation

### S: SENSING PERCEPTION

When using my sensing, I am
- Perceiving with the five senses
- Attending to practical and factual details
- In touch with the physical realities
- Attending to the present moment
- Confining attention to what is said and done
- Seeing "little things" in everyday life
- Attending to step-by-step experience
- Letting "the eyes tell the mind"

### N: INTUITIVE PERCEPTION

When using my intuition, I am
- Perceiving with memory and associations
- Seeing patterns and meanings
- Seeing possibilities
- Projecting possibilities for the future
- Imagining; "reading between the lines"
- Looking for the big picture
- Having hunches; "ideas out of nowhere"
- Letting "the mind tell the eyes"

### T: THINKING JUDGMENT

When reasoning with thinking, I am
- Using logical analysis
- Using objective and impersonal criteria
- Being firm-minded
- Prizing logical order
- Being skeptical

### F: FEELING JUDGMENT

When reasoning with feeling, I am
- Applying personal priorities
- Weighing human values and motives, my own and others
- Appreciating
- Valuing warmth in relationships
- Prizing harmony
- Trusting

### J: JUDGMENT

When I take a judging attitude, I am
- Using thinking or feeling judgment outwardly
- Deciding and planning
- Organizing and scheduling
- Controlling and regulating
- Goal oriented
- Wanting closure even when data are incomplete

### P: PERCEPTION

When I take a perceiving attitude, I am
- Using sensing or intuitive perception outwardly
- Taking in information
- Adapting and changing
- Curious and interested
- Open-minded
- Resisting closure in order to obtain more data

8/98

**Published by Center for Applications of Psychological Type, Inc.**

you may have already chosen a scoring option that generates a narrative report. If you computer score only for reported preferences or if you template score, you have a number of options for providing clients with full-length descriptions. You can use reproducible reports and report-generators (e.g., *Looking at Type: The Basic Report, Looking at Type: The Workplace Report*). These kinds of descriptions are an alternative to computer-scoring reports, and allow for unlimited reproduction of individual reports. You can also provide clients with a full-length type description through booklets that contain descriptions of all sixteen types.

- A booklet to take home containing descriptions of all sixteen types. Clients should *not* leave with just the description of one type or just a sheet of fifteen to twenty word sketches of each of the sixteen types. The reason is that clients usually want to talk about type with family or colleagues, and they will need a resource giving all sixteen descriptions. There are several to choose from, ranging in price from fifty cents to about $8.00. Your budget and the context will help you decide. The following are some of your options for booklets of type descriptions:

  - *Descriptions of the Sixteen Types.* This eight-page booklet contains condensed but full descriptions. *Profile of Your MBTI Results* is a slightly expanded version, containing the same descriptions. A sample of a page is reproduced on page 90. The bulleted format of the descriptions makes it easy for clients to read several or all of them. The descriptions are arranged on the pages so that opposite types are across from each other, to show contrasts in what the types value most.

  - *Looking at Type: The Fundamentals.* This sixty-page booklet gives full-length type descriptions and applications of type to daily life. It explains the basic nature of type and type dynamics, development within one's type, and gives an overview of the role of type in relationships, careers, education, organizations, and problem-solving. This book was written as an introductory text for individuals to learn about type, and is a particularly useful tool to give clients as an adjunct to getting feedback on their MBTI.

  - *Introduction to Type.* This thirty-page booklet, now in its sixth edition, is a revision of the booklet that Isabel Myers wrote in 1970 to put the sixteen descriptions into the hands of those who take the MBTI and to give them suggestions for using type in their lives.

There are also other booklets, focused on particular applications of type, that some MBTI users give clients at the initial explanation of type instead of or in addition to the ones listed above. The *Looking at Type* series published by CAPT includes *Looking at Type and Careers, Looking*

## ENTJ

Intuitive, innovative **ORGANIZERS**; analytical, systematic, confident; push to get action on new ideas and challenges. Having extraverted **THINKING** as their strongest mental process, ENTJs are at their best when they can take charge and set things in logical order. They value:

- Analyzing abstract problems, complex situations
- Foresight; pursuing a vision
- Changing, organizing things to fit their vision
- Putting theory into practice, ideas into action
- Working to a plan and schedule
- Initiating, then delegating
- Efficiency; removing obstacles and confusion
- Probing new possibilities
- Holding self and others to high standards
- Having things settled and closed
- Tough-mindedness, directness, task-focused behavior
- Objective principles; fairness, justice
- Assertive, direct action
- Intellectual resourcefulness
- Driving toward broad goals along a logical path
- Designing structures and strategies
- Seeking out logical flaws

## ESTJ

Fact-minded practical **ORGANIZERS**; assertive, analytical, systematic; push to get things done and working smoothly and efficiently. Having extraverted **THINKING** as their strongest mental process, they are at their best when they can take charge and set things in logical order. They value:

- Results; doing, acting
- Planned, organized work and play
- Common sense practicality
- Consistency; standard procedures
- Concrete, present-day usefulness
- Deciding quickly and logically
- Having things settled and closed
- Rules, objective standards, fairness by the rules
- Task-focused behavior
- Directness, tough-mindedness
- Orderliness; no loose ends
- Systematic structure; efficiency
- Categorizing aspects of their life
- Scheduling and monitoring
- Protecting what works

## ISFP

Observant, loyal **HELPERS**; reflective, realistic, empathic, patient with details. Shunning disagreements, they are gentle, reserved and modest. Having introverted **FEELING** as their strongest mental process, they are at their best when responding to the needs of others. They value:

- Personal loyalty; a close, loyal friend
- Finding delight in the moment
- Seeing what needs doing to improve the moment
- Freedom from organizational constraints
- Working individually
- Peacemaking behind the scenes
- Attentiveness to feelings
- Harmonious, cooperative work settings
- Spontaneous, hands-on exploration
- Gentle, respectful interactions
- Deeply held personal beliefs
- Reserved, reflective behavior
- Practical, useful skills and know-how
- Having their work life be fully consistent with deeply held values
- Showing and receiving appreciation

## INFP

Imaginative, independent **HELPERS**; reflective, inquisitive, empathic, loyal to ideals: more tuned to possibilities than practicalities. Having introverted **FEELING** as their strongest mental process, they are at their best when their inner ideals find expression in their helping of people. They value:

- Harmony in the inner life of ideas
- Harmonious work settings; working individually
- Seeing the big picture possibilities
- Creativity; curiosity, exploring
- Helping people find their potential
- Giving ample time to reflect on decisions
- Adaptability and openness
- Compassion and caring; attention to feelings
- Work that lets them express their idealism
- Gentle, respectful interactions
- An inner compass; being unique
- Showing appreciation and being appreciated
- Ideas, language and writing
- A close, loyal friend
- Perfecting what is important

**Published by Center for Applications of Psychological Type, Inc.**
Copyright 1995, 1998 Gordon Lawrence • Duplication or storage of this form, by any means, is strictly prohibited.

*at Type and Learning Styles, Looking at Type and Spirituality,* and *Looking at Type in the Workplace.* The *Introduction to Type* series published by Consulting Psychologists Press includes *Introduction to Type and Careers, Introduction to Type in College,* and *Introduction to Type in Organizations.* In all of these publications the type descriptions are presented in the context of the application—for example, in the workplace.

**2) Plan to focus the type explanation on the client's reason for taking the MBTI.** By the time you meet with the client to explain the MBTI results, you will be aware of the reason(s) he or she wants to learn about type. Be ready to bring to the dialogue some examples, anecdotes and questions that will help the client relate type concepts to his or her experiences—as a team member, manager, learner, marriage partner or whatever application the client has in mind. You may want to have on hand a book or two the client can use to explore type more fully.

**3) Plan to engage the client as a participant.** The type explanation is more effective when you plan to approach the client as a partner in finding the best-fit type. Explain that Myers called her instrument an Indicator because she saw it as a pointer to one of the sixteen types, inviting the respondent to try it on for size. Which type is the best fit is the client's responsibility to decide, not yours as the MBTI interpreter. As the *MBTI Manual*, Third Edition, indicates, "The interpreter's role is not to determine the accuracy of the MBTI personality inventory. The interpreter's task is to provide ways in which respondents can understand their best and most trustworthy way of functioning" (p. 123), that is, their best-fit type. That is best accomplished through dialogue at each step of the type explanation.

**4) Plan to adapt the type explanation to the client's reported type.** A type explanation generally is best received when you take into account the client's probable type as you conduct the dialogue. The type identified by the Indicator is referred to as the *reported type.* You can use it to plan some aspect of the dialogue. For example, an Extravert is more likely to want to talk out thoughts frequently in the session, and to prefer that the session move at a fairly rapid pace. An Introvert may want a slower pace, with more time for internal processing. ST types commonly want the facts that clarify the meaning and use of the MBTI, and want a linear, straight ahead explanation, with practical examples but not too much elaboration. Intuitive types want to start with the big picture, and so on. As you are just beginning to give type explanations, you can help yourself prepare by reading ahead of time the description of the reported type of the client and noting what he or she is likely to value as a participant in the dialogue.

When providing a type explanation to a group, adapting the style of explanation to the specific group is often as important as when you are working with an individual client. With a group, you make a type table of the MBTI reported results and identify the type or types most represented in the table. A session with a group composed mainly of ST types should be planned differently from a session for mainly NF types.

## Give the type explanation

1) EXPLAIN TYPE BEFORE giving the MBTI results to the client. While not all MBTI practitioners explain type concepts first, we recommend it. When clients are given their MBTI results first—"The MBTI reports an ESTJ profile for you. Let's talk about what that means…"—some of them are unduly influenced by the instrument's report. It makes them less likely to hear your explanation with an open mind.

As you begin, we suggest you say to the client something like this: "I want to explain the concepts behind the MBTI first and, as I go along, have you make an estimate of how your profile will come out. Then I'll give you the MBTI results to compare with your estimate. If they differ in some way, we can then talk about what that might mean." Again, we believe it is very important that clients do a self-assessment before getting their MBTI results.

2) **Follow a set of guidelines.** In time, you may want to make your own set of steps and prompts to follow as you give the explanation of type. To begin, we suggest you use the *Guidelines for explaining MBTI results* that appear here. They are arranged as a checklist that you can use to remind yourself what to say and ask. Have the checklist in your hand as you talk. Many experienced MBTI practitioners regularly use it or a similar list as a prompting device. As you can see in the checklist, the reporting of the client's MBTI results comes after the explanation. We recommend that you follow the items in the order that they appear on the checklist.

## GUIDELINES FOR EXPLAINING **MBTI** RESULTS

### ATTEND TO YOUR CLIENT

- ❑ Have **dialogue** with your client so you are clear about his/her reasons for taking the MBTI.
- ❑ **Plan to adapt** your explanation of type to his/her reasons for taking the MBTI.
- ❑ **Encourage questions** and dialogue during your explanation.

### EXPLAIN THE NATURE OF THE **MBTI**

- ❑ The MBTI shows useful **patterns of mental processing; all** the patterns are **OK**. There are no good or bad (or sick or well) profiles; **no right or wrong answers.**
- ❑ The MBTI is not a "test" but an **"indicator"** pointing to one of sixteen profiles. As I explain the concepts behind the MBTI, you estimate how your profile will come out. With the help of the MBTI results, **you decide** which profile fits you best.
- ❑ Your responses to the MBTI items are like votes on pairs of mental preferences. Type is a **shorthand** way of telling about the **four pairs of mental preferences.**

### EXPLAIN THE NATURE OF TYPOLOGY

- ❑ Use visual **support materials**. Use language and **examples** appropriate to the client. Use the **handedness exercise** to demonstrate "preference."
- ❑ **Avoid stereotyping**. Use: "When extraverting we…; when introverting we…" Avoid "This is how you are…" Use questioning approach: "Is this true for you…?"
- ❑ A type is **not a pigeonhole**, but a **dynamic** organization of mental energy. All types are valuable.
- ❑ Everyone **uses all four** processes and all four attitudes. But each of us is better at (and likes) some more than others.
- ❑ Describe the four preference pairs, using word pairs, such as in *Looking at Type.*

### HELP THE CLIENT TO INTERPRET THE RESULTS

- ❑ Show how **the four elements combine** to make up one's type.
- ❑ Guide the client through **type description(s)**. Point the client toward other resources.
- ❑ Help the client see **applications** in his or her own experience.
- ❑ Explain that MBTI scores indicate **clarity** of preference, **not skill level** or maturity.
- ❑ Help the client see that trusting one's favorite processes is key to personal development.

**3) Use visuals.** Many experienced MBTI practitioners use the illustrated 8½" by 11" booklet, *Looking at Type*, by Earle Page, as they give the explanation of type to an individual. We suggest you consider using it as you start to develop your own style of explanation. It was designed to carry the explainer and client through the key ideas, page by page. You can both look at the same copy, you can work from two copies, or you can have the client read it alone while asking you questions along the way. A few pages of it have been reduced in size and reproduced here so you can see how it looks. It is written in large print, with many helpful sketches. The booklet covers all the items in the *Guidelines* checklist. It can also be obtained as transparencies or in Power Point to be shown when giving a group explanation.

**4) Use well-planned words when describing the four preference pairs.** Choosing the right words to use when talking about type preferences is a challenge. We have been explaining type to people for many years, and we still have the occasional problem of someone taking the wrong meaning because of a word we used that misled him or her. There are **two rules** to follow that will help you get the right meanings across.

**First, always discuss the preference pairs as a set.** For example, whenever you use a term to describe the nature of Extraversion, always couple it with a corresponding word to go with Introversion. If you use the terms *outgoing* or *sociable* to go with Extraversion, always supply the polar opposite term you intend to go with Introversion, such as *reserved*. If you don't give the contrasting term *at the same time*, the client will supply whatever opposite comes to mind—in this case perhaps *shy* or *antisocial*. This response, of course, puts the wrong light on Introversion. Similarly, if you describe Introverts as *reflective*, and don't supply an appropriate contrast, the client may add the stereotyping opposite of *impulsive* or *unreflective*. To head off this kind of response, always give the contrasting terms in tandem—E: sociable, I: reserved.

Look again at the handout reproduced earlier in the chapter, "Words to Help Understanding of Type Concepts." Note the language: "When extraverting, I am…" and "When introverting, I am…" Describing the preferences as *actions* is another way of presenting the contrasts in pairs and minimizing the risk of stereotypes coming into the client's mind. Have the client read each line across, first the extraverting pole, then the introverting pole.

**Second, stick to tried and true words.** In the *Looking at Type* (Earle Page) booklet, there are lists of word pairs we recommend. The four lists

# EXTRAVERSION AND INTROVERSION
## ARE COMPLEMENTARY ATTITUDES
## TOWARD THE WORLD

**E**

An Extravert's Essential Stimulation Is From The
Environment—The Outer World Of People And Things.

**I**

An Introvert's Essential Stimulation Is From
Within—The Inner World Of Thoughts And Reflections.

• • • • • • • • • • • • • • • • • • • • • • • • • • • • • • • • • • • • • • • • • •

Both Attitudes Are Used By Everyone, But One Is
Usually Preferred And Better Developed

# EXTRAVERSION
### Tendencies & Characteristics

# INTROVERSION
### Tendencies & Characteristics

**Feels Pulled Outward By External Claims And Conditions**

**Feels Pushed Inward By External Claims And Intrusions**

**Energized By Other People, External Experiences**

**Energized By Inner Resources, Internal Experiences**

## EXTRAVERSION
### Tendencies & Characteristics

Acts, Then
(Maybe) Reflects

Is Often Friendly,
Talkative, Easy To Know

## INTROVERSION
### Tendencies & Characteristics

Reflects, Then
(Maybe) Acts

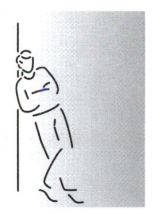

Is Often Reserved,
Quiet, Hard to Know

are shown here reduced in size. Over time you will discover other terms that work well, but begin with these pairs of words, and those on the handouts reproduced in this chapter. Having a copy of this list in front of you as you give feedback can be very helpful.

## Some key words

| E<br>Extraversion | I<br>Introversion | S<br>Sensing | N<br>Intuition |
|---|---|---|---|
| Active | Reflective | Details | Patterns |
| Outward | Inward | Present | Future |
| Sociable | Reserved | Practical | Imaginative |
| People | Privacy | Facts | Innovations |
| Many | Few | Sequential | Random |
| Expressive | Quiet | Directions | Hunches |
| Breadth | Depth | Repetition | Variety |
| | | Enjoyment | Anticipation |
| | | Perspiration | Inspiration |
| | | Conserve | Change |
| | | Literal | Figurative |

| T<br>Thinking | F<br>Feeling | J<br>Judgment | P<br>Perception |
|---|---|---|---|
| Head | Heart | Organized | Flexible |
| Objective | Subjective | Structure | Flow |
| Justice | Harmony | Control | Experience |
| Cool | Caring | Decisive | Curious |
| Impersonal | Personal | Deliberate | Spontaneous |
| Critique | Appreciate | Closure | Openness |
| Analyze | Empathize | Plan | Wait |
| Precise | Persuasive | Deadlines | Discovery |
| Principles | Values | Productive | Receptive |

From *Looking at Type*, Fourth Edition by E. C. Page. Copyright 1998, Center for Applications of Psychological Type. Reprinted with permission.

## Help the client choose a best-fit type

WHEN YOU HAVE COMPLETED THE DESCRIPTIONS of the four preference pairs, and after they have done a **self-assessment**, you and the client then **look at the MBTI reported type**. This can happen in several ways, depending on how the scoring was done. If the client responded to the self-scorable version, he or she will now tear the form open and hand score it. If you used computer scoring, show the client the output. If you used template scoring, hand the client the results. As we noted earlier, if you template scored, you have a number of options for reporting results.

Some practitioners report the results on a published template-scoring report form, such as *Your Results from the MBTI*. The front page of this form is reproduced here (the back has brief type descriptions). Some use the booklet, *Profile of Your MBTI Results*, and write the type on the report page. Others simply circle the brief description of the type in a type booklet (e.g., *Descriptions of the Sixteen Types, Looking at Type: The Fundamentals* or an *Introduction to Type* booklet). Remember, at some point the client will need at least a full-length description of their reported and/or best-fit type, and preferably descriptions of all sixteen types. These descriptions are available from a variety of sources (e.g., *Looking at Type* booklets, reproducible reports).

Have the client **compare his or her self-assessment with the MBTI reported type**. Good language to use would be, "Your type came out __ __ __ __ (ESTP, for example). Is that what you estimated?" Some practitioners prefer to report the MBTI results one preference at a time, after each preference pair has been explained to the client. For instance, "As you predicted, your results came out E on the E–I dimension."

If the client's self-assessment agrees with the type reported on the MBTI, have the client **read the full type description**. (Note: some practitioners will give the client the full-length description of the MBTI reported type *before* comparing the self-assessment with the Indicator assessment.) Allow the client as much time as needed to read the description. Ask how well it fits. In the discussion about the description, you may want to mention that not everyone who comes out, say, ESTP will agree with all aspects of the description; no two people of the same type are exactly alike, because a personality consists of a lot of things besides type. If the client sees the description as a good fit, move on to helping the client make use of type.

If the client does not agree with the results—the reported type and self-estimate type did *not* come out the same—you and your client have some

# Your Results from the Myers-Briggs Type Indicator® Instrument

Name _____  Date _____

The Myers-Briggs Type Indicator® instrument reports **a person's preferred ways of attending to the world and making decisions**. Each item you answered is counted on one side or the other of four scales. The scales are composed of pairs of opposite preferences represented by the letters E–I, S–N, T–F, and J–P, as shown in the diagram. The side of each scale that received more votes is reported as your preference.

| | | |
|---|---|---|
| **E** | Extraversion | Interest in the people and things around you |
| **I** | Introversion | Interest in ideas in your mind that explain the world |
| **S** | Sensing | Interest in what is real and can be seen, heard, touched |
| **N** | Intuition | Interest in what can be imagined, seen with the mind's eye |
| **T** | Thinking | Interest in what is logical and works by cause and effect |
| **F** | Feeling | Interest in knowing what is important and valuable |
| **J** | Judging | Interest in acting by organizing, planning, deciding |
| **P** | Perceiving | Interest in acting by watching, trying out, adapting |

The preferences combine in sixteen ways, representing sixteen types of mental processing. Each type has a distinctive way of attending to the world and making decisions. Everyone has interests in all the categories, but favors one from each pair. The preferences you showed when you completed the instrument indicate that you came out with a preference for:

| | | | | |
|---|---|---|---|---|
| **Extraversion** or **Introversion** | slight | moderate | clear | very clear |
| **Sensing** or **Intuition** | slight | moderate | clear | very clear |
| **Thinking** or **Feeling** | slight | moderate | clear | very clear |
| **Judging** or **Perceiving** | slight | moderate | clear | very clear |

**Your Reported Type:** ____  ____  ____  ____

800.777.2278 toll-free USA • www.capt.org

exploring to do. In the client's reading material (e.g., *Looking at Type* booklet, *Descriptions of the Sixteen Types*) **point out the alternate descriptions—** the one indicated by the MBTI and the one matching the client's self-estimate, and variations on the two. **Have the client read them to see which seems a better fit.** Depending on your client and your time, you can have the client read the brief or full-length descriptions for comparison. If they are reading more than two descriptions, it is valuable to have them first read the brief descriptions to narrow the choice down to two types (*Looking at Type: The Fundamentals,* for example, has brief descriptions on pages 14–15). If the client feels well-described by one of them, you can have the client read a longer description if they have not already done so, or you can go on to helping the client to make use of type. If he or she does not want to settle on either the reported or self-estimate type, and you want to suggest another type as a possibility, you will want to examine the preference clarity on the four preference pairs. If the client's preference clarity on one dichotomy is slight, he or she should read the type description that would be reported if the slight preference were toward the opposite pole. For example:

- if the reported type was ESTP,
- the client's estimate was ESFP,
- neither description seemed to be a good fit, and
- the preference for E was slight,

then have the client read the ISTP description, and possibly the ISFP description in their reading materials. If further exploring is still needed, have some discussion about which words and phrases in the descriptions are a good fit and which are not. That may lead to a choice that works. By the end of the session, you should try to **have the client settle on a type to take as a hypothesis for a while.** Don't push for a definite choice. Rather, show the client how to further explore through reading and reflection, and perhaps dialogue with colleagues and family members as to what type descriptions they see as a good fit.

> ### THE STEPS IN BRIEF
>
> - Describe the preferences and have the client do a self-estimate of his or her type.
> - Look at the type reported on the MBTI.
> - Have the client compare his or her self-assessment with the MBTI reported type.
> - If they match, have the client read the full-length type description (remember, some practitioners give out the full-length report first, and then note how it compares with the self-estimate).
> - If the self-estimate and MBTI assessment differ, point out the alternative descriptions.
> - Have the client read them to see which seems a better fit (can use brief or longer descriptions for comparison).
> - Have the client settle on a type to take as a hypothesis for a while—but don't push for a definite choice.

**WHAT TO SAY TO CLIENTS ABOUT "SCORES."** Clients sometimes ask about their MBTI scores and what they mean. For several years there has been a shift by many MBTI users to de-emphasize or simply not report the numerical part of the Indicator results—that is, to just report the four-letter type, or the four-letter type and the preference clarity category (pcc, which can be slight, moderate, clear, or very clear) associated with each letter. The third edition of the *MBTI Manual* lays out a clear position that the numbers should be referred to—if mentioned at all—as preference clarity indexes (pci) or preference clarity categories (pcc)—not scores. The term *scores* connotes, in ordinary usage, such qualitative comparisons as more or less desirable, stronger or weaker, more or less clear or confused. The only correct interpretation to be put on pci numbers is "the likelihood that the preference has been correctly reported… Any other interpretation of MBTI results is incorrect and leads to misunderstanding and misinterpretation" (page 121). As you can see in the example in the previous paragraph, we used the pci to identify an alternate type description for the client to read—in that case, a pci in the "slight" range for Extraversion suggested a reading of the ISTP description because the client did not find the ESTP to be a good fit.

Although the phrase "preference score" is used with Form G scoring, it is wise to interpret those numbers in the same light—that is, they are most accurately interpreted as the confidence that the preference has been correctly reported.

Research does show that the clearer a person's preference on a dichotomy the more confidence we can have that the person's true preferences were reported on the Indicator. Research does *not* show that having higher clarity on a preference means an individual is better at the skills of that preference than someone with lower clarity. The Indicator does not ask individuals to report on the quality with which they use a preference. It only asks people to vote between different but equally valuable choices.

Remember also that a slight clarity index is not bad or wrong result. We just have less confidence that an individual's true preference has been reported on the Indicator.

> **In summary:** It is your *preference* for one or the other side of the dichotomy that is important. The preference clarity index is best interpreted as the likelihood that the preference has been correctly reported. Do not over-interpret the preference clarity index (Form M), or the preference score (Form G).

**WHY MIGHT THE MBTI REPORTED TYPE NOT BE THE BEST-FIT TYPE?** Even when you do a good job setting up the conditions for someone to take the MBTI (Chapter Four), and you administer and score the MBTI correctly (Chapter Five), there will be times when the type reported by the MBTI will not be the type subsequently found to be the best fit. While following the guidelines in Chapters Four and Five will dramatically reduce the chances of an inaccurate report, there are other factors that play into self-report instruments such as the MBTI. As a result of these factors, the respondent may:

- be unclear or confused about his or her true preferences
- be consciously trying to improve the skills associated with a non-preferred mental process or one of the attitudes and thus be giving that process or attitude a disproportionate emphasis in answering the MBTI questions
- in growing up have developed a definition of self that reflects more the parents' desires and patterns than his or her true preferences
- have given responses to the MBTI that reflect other kinds of social pressure
- feel pressure to conform to expectations of the work environment
- believe he or she "should" be a certain type to get choice work assignments, or to get hired/promoted
- be in a situation of unusual stress
- have been unable to read some of the words of the MBTI questions
- not have followed instructions (even though you gave them clearly and correctly, of course!)

## Help the client put type to use

These are factors you generally cannot predict or control. In instances where these factors are affecting the MBTI responses, it is all the more important to take an adequate amount of time to help the client discover the best-fit type, or a good hypothesis type.

WHEN THE CLIENT feels at least fairly clear about one type being a good fit, you can go on, in this session or subsequent ones, to exploring how a knowledge of type can be helpful in the issues that prompted use of the MBTI—career decisions, personal relationships, improving teamwork, etc. Earlier in the chapter we mentioned booklets focused on these kinds of applications of type. They are a good place to start, since they were written for client use.

There are many rich resources for your own use as well. An excellent place to start is the last section of the *MBTI Manual*, Third Edition, "Part V: The Uses of Type." These chapters are devoted to uses of type in counseling and psychotherapy, education, career counseling, organizations, and multicultural settings. They each provide a review of research involving type, and reports of ways that type has been used effectively in these areas. Chapter Seven of this guide also provides you with a quick summary of issues and research related to these areas.

## Respond to the client's questions about type*

THROUGHOUT THE PROCESS of introducing people to type concepts, you will encounter questions. Clients will have questions even when you believe you have touched all the bases. Here are some questions commonly asked about type and our suggestions for answering them. Our suggested answers may include more than you want to say, but they are meant to give you ideas for forming your own answers.

We have listed the questions first, by themselves, in case you want to try your hand at answering them before you read our suggested answers.

- Doesn't type fence you in?
- How does a person get to be a type?
- About the four mental processes, how do you develop a mental process?
- Are types kinds of personalities?
- Are the types essentially different kinds of traits?
- Can you change your type?
- What is the best type to be?
- Is everyone of the same type alike?
- Can you guess someone's type, and is that a good thing to do?
- How frequent is my type?

*Adapted from *People Types and Tiger Stripes*, © 1993 Gordon Lawrence. Used by permission.

**DOESN'T TYPE FENCE YOU IN?** Some people say, "Being just one type feels very confining. Am I stuck with being just one?" This kind of question may come when someone reads several of the type descriptions and says, "I could do that, and that, and that. It seems to me that I shift from type to type, depending on the circumstances." One's type is a mental framework onto which you can hang many skills. Understanding your mental framework gives you important clues about developing whatever skills you want to have. You don't need to be an Extravert to have excellent extraverting skills. Introverts just go about developing extraverting skills differently. Knowing you are an Introvert, and what that means in Jung's sense of it, helps you to know how to get energized and focused for learning and doing the extraverting things you need to do. You can't simply imitate an Extravert to get the extraverting skills. And the fact of being an Extravert is no assurance of having good skills in extraverting.

No, you don't shift from type to type. That would mean dismantling your mental framework and reconstructing another. It doesn't happen.

Does type fence you in? Not if you understand it. An understanding of type frees you in several ways. It gives you confidence in your own direction of development—the areas in which you can become excellent with the most ease and pleasure. It can also reduce the guilt many people feel at not being able to do everything in life equally well. Acknowledging your own preferences opens the possibility of finding constructive values instead of conflicts in the differences you encounter with someone whose preferences are opposite yours.

**HOW DOES A PERSON GET TO BE A TYPE?** Jung and Myers believed that we are born with a predisposition for one type. Environmental factors are very important, since they can foster type development or get in its way. One of the four mental processes (S, N, T or F) and one attitude (E or I) are your natural bent, according to Jung, and these natural preferences make up the heart of type.

Type may not be clear in young people; that is, the dominant process may not yet be developed enough to organize and integrate the personality. The first task of a young person in type development is to have one of the processes emerge as leader in the personality. A later task is to gain balance by developing the auxiliary process. The other two processes also have to be developed, at least passably, because all four processes are needed every day of our lives. In middle life, some people begin to focus on their third and fourth processes and can become very skillful in them.

**ABOUT THE FOUR MENTAL PROCESSES, HOW DO YOU DEVELOP A MENTAL PROCESS?**
By using it purposefully to achieve something you think is important. A good example comes from the use of Sensing. Development of Sensing provides a direct and keen awareness of physical realities and excellent powers of observation. If you are sitting on a train watching the scenery go by, you are using your Sensing but not particularly developing it. If you are driving yourself around a strange city, you will probably concentrate your Sensing to notice and remember landmarks—this process develops your Sensing. Of course, this kind of focus and effort requires both perception and judgment, the dominant helping the auxiliary to develop, and vice versa.

**ARE TYPES KINDS OF PERSONALITIES?** Many things go into the makeup of a personality—genetics, family life, circumstances outside the family, society's expectations and requirements, and many learned traits. Psychological type is just one aspect of personality. Because people's types express themselves in so many parts of their lives, the types are often called personality types. But type is not synonymous with personality. With people who are likely to be put off by the term "psychological," we refer to the types as personality types.

**ARE THE TYPES ESSENTIALLY DIFFERENT SETS OF TRAITS?** No. Type and trait represent different ways of looking at our psychological natures. The type preference categories are not traits. Rather, they are mindsets, mental frameworks or distinct ways of processing experiences that become visible as traits. For example, Extraversion as a type preference is an either–or category, not a trait that is measured as more or less Extraversion, or degrees of skillfulness. One takes *either* an Extraverted *or* an Introverted approach in life. If someone talks about the *degree* or *extent* of Extraversion or Introversion, they have moved outside the approach taken by Jung and Myers.

**CAN YOU CHANGE YOUR TYPE?** Preferences as reported by the MBTI can be changed depending on how you answer the questions. Answering differently can result in a report of a different type. You can change your Indicator outcome, but that is not the same as changing your type. Jung seemed to believe that each person has a true type that he or she may not yet have discovered. The true type does not change, although it may seem to, as one focuses on developing different mental processes at different stages of one's life. Behaviors can change, of course, but the roots of them remain the same.

However, there are many reasons you might take the MBTI two different times and come out different types—even when you didn't intentionally skew your answers in one direction or another. The change of reported type might happen because you may still be discovering your preferences, and trying them on for size. Or, you might be working especially hard to develop one of the mental processes, so that you report it on the MBTI with stronger than usual emphasis. Or, you might take the MBTI one time as your "job self," responding as you see yourself acting on the job, and you might take it another time as your "home self," responding as you see yourself in your home environment. If your type differs in two reports, this fact may lead to interesting information about yourself. As you cast your thoughts back to your frame of mind when you were answering the questions, consider how it may have affected your reporting of yourself, and may or may not reflect your true type.

**HOW FREQUENT IS MY TYPE?** One of the common questions people ask after *determining* their type is: How *frequent* is my type? The table below shows estimates of the relative frequency of each of the sixteen types in the United States population. The symbols on the type table represent percentages of the general population. This means you can "eyeball" the table and detect the relative frequency of your type.

## ESTIMATED FREQUENCIES OF THE TYPES IN THE UNITED STATES POPULATION

| | | | |
|---|---|---|---|
| **ISTJ** 12–16% | **ISFJ** 10–13% | **INFJ** 2–3% | **INTJ** 3–4% |
| **ISTP** 5–7% | **ISFP** 5–7% | **INFP** 4–5% | **INTP** 5–6% |
| **ESTP** 5–7% | **ESFP** 6–9% | **ENFP** 6–8% | **ENTP** 4–7% |
| **ESTJ** 10–12% | **ESFJ** 10–12% | **ENFJ** 3–5% | **ENTJ** 3–5% |

| E | 50–55% | I | 45–50% |
|---|---|---|---|
| S | 65–70% | N | 30–35% |
| T | 45–55% | F | 45–55% |
| J | 55–60% | P | 40–45% |

■ = approximately one percent

Looking at this table, you can see that the weight of the population lies across the bottom two rows and in the left two columns. The intersection of these two rows and two columns in the bottom left quadrant represents the highest concentration of the general population. Most data suggest that Extraverted types and Sensing types are relatively more frequent than Introverted types and Intuitive types.

While most ES types probably found many other people like themselves as they grew up, their counterpart types, the Introverts with Intuition (INs), were less likely to find people like themselves.

One consequence of being a less frequent type, such as an IN type, is that these individuals report as young people having had more difficulty finding kindred spirits among their classmates. Interestingly, because of career choice patterns, the percentage of IN teachers increases as grade level increases. So the ES students, while in the majority, will find fewer and fewer teachers like themselves as they advance through the grades. In contrast, the less frequent IN students will find more teachers like themselves as they advance. Overall, the types least likely to find teachers who appreciate their adaptable hands-on learning style are the four SP types.

As each of the types leaves high school to work or to pursue higher education, we begin to see differences in the frequencies of the types that are attracted to work and to school. The practical and active ES types are much more likely to enter the world of work and pursue jobs in business and industry. In contrast, the reflective and theory-oriented IN types tend to pursue college and advanced degrees, and are more often found in careers in education, the sciences and the humanities. Although these patterns generally hold true, it is important to understand that every type is found at every level of education and in virtually every career. For more information on type and careers, see the section on career research in Chapter Seven.

**WHAT IS THE BEST TYPE TO BE?** For you, the type you really are. Jung's theory says your best satisfactions in life will be those that come through the strengths of your type.

**IS EVERYONE OF THE SAME TYPE ALIKE?** No. There are many individual differences within each type, because many things influence personality besides type. Some people are at a higher level of type development than others. Even in people of the same type who are well developed, there are big differences. Take an ESFJ, for example. You would expect all the ESFJs to share a wish for people around them to be happy, and to work to achieve harmony. Some ESFJs might be interested in education and become teachers, some might become family doctors, and others might become salespersons. Still others might find satisfaction in volunteer work or in being a good parent. All these activities offer effective ways of using Feeling in the outer world, as Extraverted Feeling types are predicted to do.

**CAN YOU GUESS SOMEONE'S TYPE, AND IS THAT A GOOD THING TO DO?** When we are trying to understand, influence, manage or teach someone else, we often do not know the person's type. As soon as we learn type concepts, we see the value of estimating people's types so as to reach them better. Making a wild guess about someone's type can be easy and fun, yet often inaccurate, and sometimes the guess seriously defeats its own purpose. If we make a wrong guess about a person's type and act as if it were a truth about that person, we may be increasing rather than closing the communication gap between us.

Accurately guessing someone's type is a skill that takes a long time to develop. Type concepts have been important in our lives for many years, and we are continually learning new ways to recognize characteristics of type, as well as correcting misconceptions we have been carrying. People who know type concepts well will tell you that the learning never ends.

When you do want to guess someone's type preferences to improve communication between the two of you, treat your guess as a hypothesis to be checked out, then listen carefully and be ready to change your guess. As you continue to learn about type, you will discover an endless number of behaviors to listen and watch for as indicators of type preferences.

## Explaining type to groups

**PRACTITIONERS SOMETIMES FIND** it helpful to know what models other type users have found useful as they work with groups, so we have included a framework for explaining type to groups. All of the material in this chapter up to this point applies to group explanations of type as well. You'll see that the components of this model are an expansion on the components of an individual explanation, allowing time for group exercises and with extra attention to follow-up.

Remember, this is a model for a type *explanation*. As a professional who uses the MBTI, you will need to clarify what purpose the group type explanation serves. For example, you may introduce type to a group (say, partners in a couples workshop) where the purpose is clearly to serve the needs of the individual participants in the workshop. Sometimes, however, you will be introducing type into an organization for the purpose of effecting a change in organizational functioning. When you introduce type into an organization, you need to be aware of particular issues that will arise. Chapter Eight introduces you to the issues and context of introducing type into an organization. Please read that chapter before giving a group explanation within an organization!

## Framework for a group explanation of type

How much you cover and the specifics of what you cover in a group explanation of type will depend on how much time you have and the needs of the particular group. When you will be introducing type in an organization, please see Chapter Eight of this book to clarify the issues discussed there.

What follows is a general framework for doing a feedback session on the MBTI. Remember, this is only one model!

**1) Introduction.** Introduce yourself. Begin a discussion of individual differences without reference to type, basing the discussion on the needs of the group (e.g., "We all know managers have different styles. Some do their best work when walking around, while others do their best work behind the closed door of their office.").

**2) Describe type and the MBTI.** Depending on the needs of the group you may give greater or lesser emphasis to the following: Jung's development of the theory, language for understanding individual differences in perception and judgment, Myers' development of the MBTI, the decades of research behind the Indicator, relevance of type for career choice, management style, etc. The box *Guidelines for explaining MBTI results* on page 93 describes the basic components of the type explanation itself.

**3) Handwriting exercise.** Have the group do the handwriting exercise or a related exercise to provide a basis for understanding preferences and skill development. The handwriting exercise is described on page 29 of this book.

**4) Description of the preferences.** Using appropriate visuals (e.g., *Looking at Type* overheads) and handouts (e.g., *Verifying Your Type Preferences*), walk participants through the four dichotomies (E–I, S–N, T–F, J–P) and have them self-assess their preferences. You can modify your examples and anecdotes to meet the needs of your specific group. For example, if you are working with managers, you can give examples of how Sensing and Intuitive managers might differ in their problem solving.

**5) Return MBTI results.** Hand out computer scoring or template scoring results. If you template score, participants need a record of their results (e.g., *Your Results from the MBTI*) and a full-length type description of the type they came out on the MBTI (e.g., *Looking at Type* booklet, *Introduction to Type* booklet, *Descriptions of the Sixteen Types*). Emphasize that their MBTI type is a hypothesis until they have verified their type.

**6) Verification of their type.** Discuss why self-assessment results may differ from Indicator results. If someone's self-assessment type is different from their Indicator type, they need a resource for reading alternative type descriptions (e.g., *Looking at Type* booklet. See the *Support Materials* section earlier in this chapter for options). For a list of possible reasons why someone may not agree with the type they came out on the MBTI, see the answer to the question "Why might the MBTI reported type not be the best-fit type?" posed earlier in this chapter. Further discussion of this topic can be found in Chapter Six (page 120) of the *Manual*—"Factors that influence accuracy of self-report."

**7) Exercises/applications.** Once participants have had a basic explanation of type, you may wish to use exercises to help the group see type in action and to see the application to their own setting. You can use the preference exercises (for E–I, S–N, T–F and J–P) presented in Chapter Ten of this book, which are easily modified for different settings. Often the exercise will be one of dividing the group into smaller type-alike groups (e.g., STs, SFs, NFs and NTs), and giving them some task to perform (e.g., define an ideal organization). One exercise may take anywhere from 30 minutes to an hour. A variety of handouts may also be relevant at this point—choose handouts relevant to this group's particular needs (e.g., management, leadership, communication).

It is critical that participants walk away with some sense of how to apply type after they leave the workshop. Building links from exercises to applications is the natural way to do this. After participants have done the exercise (e.g., clarifying for what Ts and Fs like to be appreciated), have them think of one person with whom they work and write down what they might say to that person in the next week to help him or her feel appreciated.

**Note:** Some practitioners prefer to do an exercise before or after the discussion of each preference. That is, they will describe the E–I preferences, then do a short E–I exercise, then describe the S–N preferences, then do a brief S–N exercise, and so forth.

**8) Closing.** The closing is not only a place for you to bring an end to the session, but to offer participants resources for follow-up as well. It is important to let participants know where and how you may be reached if they have follow-up questions or needs. You can also tell them the next steps for finding out more about type. You may even wish to leave resources for borrowing (e.g., copies of *Looking at Type in the Workplace*) with your contact person, so participants can have easy access to follow-up materials.

> **CHECKLIST: HELPING CLIENTS UNDERSTAND MBTI RESULTS AND CHOOSE A TYPE**
>
> ❑ **Have time allotted**
>
> - an hour or more
>
> ❑ **Have support materials**
>
> - handout of preference pairs
> - booklet of type descriptions for client to keep
> - visuals, such as *Looking at Type* booklet
> - loaner book(s) for client
>
> ❑ **Be aware of client's MBTI results**
>
> - have read type description
> - ready to adapt explanation of type to client's preferences
> - ready with strategy to engage client as participant in choosing a type
> - ready with a means of giving the MBTI outcome to client—report form or other means
>
> ❑ **Be aware of client's reasons for taking MBTI**
>
> - ready with examples, anecdotes, questions related to client's application of type
>
> ❑ **Have *Guidelines for explaining MBTI results* to use (see page 93)**
>
> ❑ **Have word lists of preference pairs to use**
>
> ❑ **Have in mind what's needed to help client choose best-fit type**
>
> ❑ **Have in mind what to say if client asks about MBTI "scores"**
>
> ❑ **Have ready questions and materials to help client put type to use**

**Resources**

Handouts for recording MBTI results with brief descriptions.

Lawrence, G. D. (1995). *Descriptions of the sixteen types.* Gainesville, FL: Center for Applications of Psychological Type.

Lawrence, G. D. (2000). *Your results from the Myers-Briggs Type Indicator.* Gainesville, FL: Center for Applications of Psychological Type.

Lawrence, G. D., & Martin, C. R. (1996). *Profile of your MBTI results.* Gainesville, FL: Center for Applications of Psychological Type.

**Useful handouts for giving basic MBTI explanations.**

Kummerow, J. M. (1985). *Talking in type.* Gainesville, FL: Center for Applications of Psychological Type.

Kummerow, J. M. (1997). *Verifying your type preferences.* Gainesville, FL: Center for Applications of Psychological Type.

Lawrence, G. D. (2000). *Words to help understanding of type concepts.* Gainesville, FL: Center for Applications of Psychological Type.

McCaulley, M. H. (1995). *Understanding the type table.* Gainesville, FL: Center for Applications of Psychological Type.

**Resources**

Introductory booklets and sources for full-length type descriptions.

The *Looking at Type* series published by CAPT (Gainesville, FL) includes:

*Looking at Type: The Fundamentals* (1997)—C. R. Martin
*Looking at Type and Careers* (1995)—C. R. Martin
*Looking at Type and Learning Styles* (1997)—G. D. Lawrence
*Looking at Type and Spirituality* (1997)—S. K. Hirsh & J .A. G. Kise
*Looking at Type in the Workplace* (1997)—L. Demarest

The *Introduction to Type* series published by Consulting Psychologists Press (Palo Alto, CA) includes:

*Introduction to Type* (1998, 6th ed.)—I. B. Myers, with L. K. Kirby & K. D. Myers
*Introduction to Type and Careers* (1993)—A. L. Hammer
*Introduction to Type in College* (1993)—J. K. DiTiberio & A. L. Hammer
*Introduction to Type in Organizations* (1998, 3rd ed.)—S. K. Hirsh & J. M. Kummerow

**Reproducible full-length type reports for those who template score, published by CAPT.** These products allow the practitioner to generate unlimited reproductions of each of sixteen different type reports:

*Looking at Type: Reproducible Masters*
*The Basic Report*
*The Career Report*
*The Learning Styles Report*
*The Workplace Report*

**Resources**

Visual supports for teaching about type.

Grant, C. (1995). *A visual invitation to type: Identifying decision-making styles*. Gainesville, FL: Center for Applications of Psychological Type. Available in overheads and slides.

Page, E. C. (1998). *Looking at type* (4th ed.). Gainesville, FL: Center for Applications of Psychological Type. Available in PowerPoint, overheads, slides, and as a booklet.

Thompson, H. L. (1996). *Type preference pro-set*. Watkinsville, GA: High Performing Systems, Inc. Available in PowerPoint and overheads.

How do I respond to clients' questions, such as these?

*I've taken the MBTI before. What is the likelihood*
*I'll come out the same type this time?*

*Yes, but is this type stuff real?*

*How do self-estimates of type compare with*
*Indicator assessments?*

*Do different types really choose different careers?*

*Do different types perform differently on aptitude tests?*

*How does type show up in education...in counseling...*
*in work life?*

# Chapter 7

Using Data From the MBTI Manual to Help Answer Clients' Questions

As TYPE USERS, these are the kinds of questions we get all of the time. People don't usually say, "I have a test-retest reliability question." What they *do* ask is, "How likely is it that I'll come out the same type this time on the MBTI?" Nor do they usually say, "I have a validity question." Rather, they ask, "Does type really relate to the kinds of careers people choose?" Where do you look for the answers to these kinds of questions? The *Manual* is an excellent place to start.

The purpose of this chapter is to orient you to the *Manual* by pointing out resources you can use in responding to clients' questions and needs. In this chapter, we also pull together research from the *Manual* that may be useful to you and informative for your clients when you use the MBTI in particular domains. After reading this chapter, you should feel a lot more comfortable fielding "data" kinds of questions that you or your clients may have about the MBTI and psychological type. If you use the *Manual* along with this chapter, you will also become a more informed reader of research and you will know where to turn to answer even more detailed questions from your clients. It is *not* the intent of this chapter to turn you into a researcher.

In this chapter, we will look at answers to the following questions:

**The reliability questions:**

- Will I come out the same type the next time I take the MBTI?
- Yes, but will I come out the same *type* the next time I take the MBTI?
- Are there certain groups with which I should be careful in using the MBTI?

**The validity questions:**

- Is this type stuff real?
  Are there really four separate preference pairs?
  Are the dichotomies real?
  Are type dynamics and whole types real?
- How does type relate to:
  Counseling, health and stress?
  Education and learning?
  Careers?
  Organizational work?
  Culture?

**WHAT DO I NEED TO KNOW TO READ THE RESEARCH IN THIS CHAPTER?** In this chapter, we will discuss some research where it would be *useful* for you to have a grasp of the concepts of correlations, tests of differences and statistical significance. Don't worry if you don't—you'll still be able to grasp most of what is in this chapter.

If you need a refresher on statistics and measurement, particularly as they relate to the MBTI, we recommend reading *Statistics and Measurement: An Introduction for MBTI Users.* The material in this chapter is not intended to be an introduction to tests and measures. Instead, it is intended to be a summary of useful data from the *MBTI Manual,* and in particular, data relevant to your area of practice.

You *will* find it helpful to have the *MBTI Manual* nearby as you read this chapter. It's not necessary to have a copy to understand what we will review—if you don't have one, you will still get useful information from this chapter. However, you won't learn about pulling further information from the *Manual* when you need it.

## Questions that are really reliability questions

FIRST, WHAT IS RELIABILITY? Reliability is how *consistently* a test measures what it attempts to measure. Why is consistency important? Well, when you measure something with an instrument two times, you want it to come out with the same answer (or close to it) both times. With the MBTI, as with other psychological instruments, you want the person to come out the same type both times they take it (this is *test-retest reliability*, the kind most people care about).

Because personality is "slippery" to measure, psychological instruments cannot have the same consistency you would expect from, say, a ruler. But there are generally accepted standards for psychological instruments. We'll talk more about numbers in a minute, but it should be understood that the MBTI meets and exceeds the standards for psychological instruments in terms of its reliability.

There is also a kind of reliability that addresses the degree to which someone answers questions consistently on any given dichotomy *on the same taking* of the MBTI. This is, not surprisingly, called *internal consistency reliability*. This is of special interest to people who construct instruments because the more consistency there is, the less "noise" there is in the measurement process. It is of interest to us as practitioners because it tells us that there is more "noise" when using the MBTI with some groups of respondents—and this is important to know.

Now to the practical questions.

**Reliability question: Will I come out the same type if I take the MBTI again?** A variation of this question is: I took the MBTI before and it reported a different type that time—what does that mean?

On pages 162–164 of the *Manual,* Third Edition, there are some useful tables describing how consistently people come out the same type on different takings of the MBTI.

Table 8.2 on page 163 shows test-retest correlations for Form M and a brief summary of the same for Form G. In this table it is important to remember that the four dichotomies were treated as *continuous scales*, running from one end to the other. For example, the E–I dichotomy is treated as a single continuum, from low to high, rather than as the bi-polar categories we have been discussing. This was done because the reliability of most other psychological instruments is assessed in this way, and this table allows comparison with the reliabilities of personality instruments in general.

In short, when people take Form M, on a dichotomy-by-dichotomy basis there are test-retest correlations ranging from .83 to .97 across a four-week period. The average of the reliability correlations across that time is .92. The lowest reliabilities are found on the E–I dichotomy with an average of .88. These test-retest reliabilities are quite excellent by general test standards. Remember, a perfect correlation is 1.00—but that doesn't happen with psychological instruments.

Since Form G has been around longer than Form M, there is quite a lot more reliability information for Form G—most of which is reported in the Second Edition of the *Manual.* Reliabilities for Form G tend to be around .81 across a period of several weeks. Test-retest time spans for Form G are often longer, and reliabilities tend to drop off the longer the time span—although even across several months test-retest correlations are in the .70s.

One study of Form G looked at the effect of mood change on reliability of the MBTI. This study is summarized on page 163 of the *Manual,* Third Edition. Results showed that changes in the respondents' moods did not significantly affect test-retest reliabilities (using continuous scores or percentages of agreement by dichotomy).

In sum, Form M reliabilities tend to look better than Form G reliabilities, while Form G reliabilities are still quite good, as they have always been. As researchers continue to use Form M, we will have a better sense of its test-retest stability over longer periods of time.

---

### WILL I COME OUT THE SAME TYPE? WILL THE REAL QUESTION PLEASE STAND UP?

The question about same type is really often a question of "does type change?" rather than a question of "will I come out the same type this time on the MBTI?" It's valuable to know the difference between these two questions. One is really a question about the nature of type itself, while the other is a question about measurement. In reality, there can be some overlap between the questions and answers.

If the question is "does type change?" the answer is, in theory, no. In type theory, especially as it is drawn from Jung's and Myers' perspectives, it is assumed that type is in some way inborn. The *way* type appears in behavior, and the extent to which people develop their type, can vary. Behaviors, and even the scored MBTI type, may change as one focuses on developing different mental processes at different stages of one's life, but the true basic type does not change.

If the question is "will I come out the same type on the MBTI?" the answer is addressed in the section that follows. In addition, remember that even if a person's type never changes, there are all kinds of fluctuations in the *measurement* process that can influence how a person comes out on the MBTI.

---

**Reliability question: Yes, but will I come out the same *type* the next time I take the MBTI?** Now this is *really* the MBTI question because, as you recall, the MBTI is most concerned with which type *category* you fall in.

Table 8.6 on page 163 of the *Manual,* Third Edition, shows test-retest agreement by type category for Form G and Form M. The numbers in this table represent percentages of people who came out the same type category on retest (on a dichotomy-by-dichotomy basis). On Form G, across time periods of less than nine months, people came out the same type category (on each dichotomy) 82–87% of the time. Across periods of greater than nine months, people came out the same type category 75–77% of the time. The test-retest intervals in this latter group ranged from nine months to *six years*.

On Form M, across four-week intervals, two samples of people came out the same type category (on each dichotomy) 84–92% of the time. In one group (the CPP sample), agreement was even higher across the four-week period (92–96%). This group was type-knowledgeable, and thus a realistic percentage of agreement probably lies in the 84–92% range. Time intervals for Form M test-retest data are shorter. In the future, more long-range data will become available.

Table 8.7 on page 164 of the *Manual,* Third Edition, is probably the *most* useful table in answering the test-retest question. This table shows the percentages of people with different numbers of preferences the same on retest. The time of retest was four weeks later. In the three groups, we see that 55–80% of people came out all four letters the same, while an additional 20–38% came out three letters the same. As an aside, people by chance alone would only come out four letters the same 6.25% of the time.

In looking at the table, we can see that across four weeks, 75–100% of people came out three or four letters the same on retest (this comes from adding together those who came out four and those who came out three preferences the same). Again, one group was type knowledgeable and these time spans are relatively short. Thus, a realistic range (including Form G data) is probably to expect people to come out three or four letters the same 75–90% of the time.

**Reliability question: Are there certain groups with which I should be especially careful in using the MBTI?** This is not a trick question! It is a reliability (as well as a validity) question. The assessment "noise" on the MBTI is greater with some groups, and it helps to know with which groups this may happen. Noise in testing can come from the limitations of the items themselves (with specific groups), from testing conditions, and/or from certain characteristics of the people taking the instrument. For example, we might expect that clients who are younger or who have less development would respond less consistently to items on the instrument.

Table 8.3 on page 163 of the *Manual,* Third Edition, shows reliabilities for Form M for various groups. In fact, reliabilities are high (.91–.92) and consistent across all ages. Data from the second edition of the *Manual* (Form G) showed that reliabilities for those younger than age eighteen did tend to be lower. There are not enough data on Form M to know whether or not lower reliabilities in those younger than eighteen will hold true for Form M as well. Ethical practice would suggest that we treat results with greater caution in those younger ages.

Reliabilities across ethnic groups also tend to be quite high, though some dichotomies tend to have more noise (lower internal consistency) for some ethnic groups. Compared to the general national sample, reliabilities tend to be somewhat lower on: T–F for African Americans adults (.84); S–N for African American college students (.80); S–N (.82) and T–F (.83) for Asian or Pacific Islander college students; and S–N for Latino/Latina/Hispanic college students (.84).

This is, again, information for the professional who may wish to consider that results on those dichotomies for those groups be treated with somewhat greater caution. In practice, as we noted in the introduction, we always assume that the type a person comes out on the MBTI is a hypothesis to be verified.

To summarize some of the data from the second edition of the *Manual*, higher reliabilities on the MBTI have been found for groups that are over-achieving, in college preparatory courses or in advanced placement. Relia-bilities are also higher for college and university students than for high school students, and higher in groups with greater average intelligence. In the latter group, reliabilities may be higher due to greater development of perception and judgment and/or due to higher reading level. Underachieving students can show much lower consistency in their MBTI responses. Appropriate and ethical use of the MBTI suggests being extremely cautious in using the instrument with those individuals or groups where reliabilities are demon-strably lower. If you do choose to use the MBTI with those groups, results are best seen as experimental or as a jumping-off point for discussion.

---

**SUMMARY: WHAT CAN YOU CONCLUDE ABOUT THE RELIABILITY OF THE MBTI?**

1) Reliabilities (when scores are treated as continuous scores, as in most other psychological instruments) are as good or better than other personality instruments.

2) On retest, people come out with three to four type preferences the same 75–90% of the time.

3) When people change their type on retest, it is usually on one dichotomy, and in dichotomies where the preference clarity was low.

4) The reliabilities are quite good across age and ethnic groups, although reliabilities on some dichotomies with some groups may be somewhat lower. The T–F dichotomy tends to have the lowest reliability of the four dichotomies.

5) There are some groups for whom reliabilities are especially low, and you need to exercise greater caution as you think about using the MBTI with those groups.

## Questions that are really validity questions

WHAT IS VALIDITY? Validity is the degree to which an instrument measures what it intends to measure, and the degree to which the "thing" that the instrument measures has meaning. Why is this important? If type is real (or rather, if it is an idea that reflects the real world with any accuracy), then we should be able to use type to understand and predict people's behavior to some degree. Type should help us make useful distinctions in the values, attitudes and behaviors of different people. Otherwise, why use type? This section on validity is intended to help you and your clients understand the "realness" of type, and to use research on type constructively.

**Validity question: Is this type stuff real?** This is essentially what validity questions are asking—"Is this type stuff real?" Chapter Nine in the *Manual,* Third Edition, broadly describes the kind of research that is done to demonstrate the validity of the MBTI, and large amounts of data are summarized in that chapter. Three broad categories of data are summarized: 1) evidence for the validity of four separate scales; 2) evidence for the validity of the four preference pairs as dichotomies; and 3) evidence for the validity of whole types or particular combinations of preferences. These three categories of data all speak to the same question, "Is this type stuff real?" In the sections that follow, we will briefly look at the validity research summarized in Chapter Nine to help answer that question.

After answering these three general questions, we will look at the validity research by specific application area. That is, we will ask and begin to answer the question, "How does type relate to counseling (or education, or careers, or organizational work, or culture)?" In this way, you can get useful data related to your area of interest quickly and directly. All research that is not about reliability is really research on validity anyway. Thus, when we look at the research by application area—whether it's in careers, organizations or education—we are still answering the question, "Is type real?"

**Important note!** Remember that virtually all of the research you will read about is based on *group* data. While a particular study may show that, say, Sensing and Intuitive types differ on tests of aptitude, this doesn't mean that any given Sensing type might not score higher than any given Intuitive type on the SAT. Such group data demonstrate there is indeed something to type because the results could be predicted from type theory. That is, type theory and the Indicator have validity in the arena of educational behavior—specifically, behavior on aptitude tests. *However*, it must be clearly understood that group data might not hold true for any given individual.

In many of the tables in Chapter Nine of the *Manual*, you will see relationships (correlations) between type preferences and some other behavior or assessed quality (e.g., sociability, responsibility). These also need to be understood as evidence for the validity of type, but should not be assumed to hold true *for every individual.* While Extraverts on the whole might demonstrate more sociability than Introverts on the whole, any given Introvert might in fact be more sociable than any given Extravert.

Using data to say "you are an Introvert and therefore unsociable" is a misunderstanding and a misuse of data. Always hold data loosely as you use them. Please bear this issue in mind also as you read the "quick and dirty" research summaries in the applications area of this chapter. The results are group data that are statistically significant, and demonstrate the validity of type in that domain of application. The results do *not* allow us to assume they are true of any given individual.

**Validity question: Are there really four separate preference pairs, i.e., four scales?** On pages 172–173 of the *Manual*, the authors summarize the *factor analytic studies* of the four scales. In a way, this is like the internal consistency of the scales we talked about earlier. Factor analytic studies look at all possible correlations between items on an instrument to see which items hang together as groups. In short, most factor analytic studies show clearly that the four scales of the MBTI are solid and largely independent scales. That is, the four scales have validity and make sense as they stand, rather than in some other item configuration. Many other informal type "questionnaires" out on the market don't have this kind of rigorous research behind them.

Even *more* useful for the practitioner are the studies relating the four scales to other measures of behavior or scores on other assessment tools. If type is real, it should relate to other things we can see or measure. Specifically, type should relate to things we expect it to (e.g., Extraversion would correlate with a measure of sociability), and it should not relate to things we would expect it not to relate to (e.g., Sensing would not correlate with a measure of sociability). Chapter Nine in the *Manual* summarizes dozens of studies showing that people's preferences on the four scales relate (correlate significantly) to such other measures in ways that make theoretical sense.

In brief, studies summarized on pages 174–184 of the *Manual* have shown that each of the preference scales does in fact relate to things to which you would expect each to relate. For example, Extraversion has been found to relate to comfort with the environment, a preference for acting on the environment, sociability and relatedness to others, use of social resources in coping, and a preference for social and enterprising interests and public speaking. Likewise, Feeling has been found to relate to concern for others, warmth, adaptability to others, and career interests in social and artistic areas. On a scale-by-scale basis, there is a great deal of evidence that type as measured on the MBTI is "real."

One of the contributions Jung and Myers made to personality theory was their understanding that Introversion is a healthy and normal personality preference. However, many theories and models of personality seem to have an inherent assumption that healthy behavior looks more extraverted. As a result, some personality assessment tools tend to see introverted behaviors in an unhealthy light—that is, reporting introverting kinds of behaviors on those instruments can lead to a lower assessment of "mental healthiness."

As an aside, this is a fine chapter to turn to when a client says, "I took the Strong Interest Inventory (or 16PF, CPI or Jungian Type Survey). How does my type relate to those instruments?" When you read the correlations in the tables in this chapter, be sure to read pages 173–174, which tell you how to read the correlations for each table.

**Validity question: The dichotomies—are they real?** As we have noted throughout this book, type is about qualitatively different *categories* rather than trait-like scales. That is, Extraverts and Introverts have qualitatively different world views. If type theory is true, then we expect to find evidence that the scales on the MBTI reflect dichotomies—two different categories of people. In fact, there is some reasonably good evidence that the MBTI scales are getting at something that looks like dichotomies—though not all studies demonstrate this, and not all personality theorists buy this assumption.

Figure 9.3 on page 188 of the *Manual* gives an example of the kind of data showing that Extraverts and Introverts, regardless of their score on the E–I scale, are seen as categorically different. Faculty rated students on a measure of gregariousness (without knowing their types). The table shows clearly that Extraverts (even those with a preference clarity just over the midpoint towards Extraversion) were seen as clearly more gregarious than Introverts (even those Introverts with a preference clarity just over the midpoint toward Introversion).

This section of the *Manual* summarizes other studies that examined differences in brain activity, behavior, creativity and time-orientation to demonstrate that there do appear to be qualitative differences between the types. In these scale-by-scale studies, it seems that the strongest evidence for differences is often found on the E–I and S–N scales, although dichotomous differences can be seen on the T–F and J–P scales as well.

**Validity question: Type dynamics and whole types—are they real?** Now we are getting at the crux of type. Type theory and the MBTI are based on a model that assumes dynamic interactions among the preferences. If type theory is real, then there should be evidence that the four sets of preferences interact in ways that demonstrate that the whole type is more than the sum of four preferences. The final section of Chapter Nine (pages 196–219) in the *Manual* summarizes studies that relate to the question of the reality of type dynamics.

Studies addressing this issue and which are of special interest to us as practitioners may be broadly grouped as follows:

1) comparisons of the reported MBTI type with other self-estimates of type

2) studies specifically testing type dynamics theory and studies of whole types

**1) Comparisons of the reported MBTI type with other self-estimates of type.** Some critics of the MBTI have suggested that the type descriptions can be read as simple horoscopes. That is, people can find themselves in any of the sixteen descriptions. In fact, the research shows this is *not* the case. People find the type descriptions of their reported type to be like them, while they find descriptions that are to varying degrees opposite of their reported type to be very much *unlike* them.

Table 9.17 on page 197 of the *Manual* is a summary of studies that looked at the agreement between reported type and best-fit type. In brief, respondents find the type descriptions of the type they came out on the MBTI to be more like them than type descriptions that varied from that reported type. Respondents tend to feel the most confidence in the report of their preferred functions (S, N, T or F). Respondents are also likely to "find" themselves in a description that varies from their reported type by the one letter on which their preference score was slight. This really fits with our experience as practitioners. Further, if respondents are given a description that is the opposite of the type they came out on all four preferences, they are very unlikely to say the description fits them.

Many of us conduct type explanation sessions in which we have participants do an informal self-estimate of their type (based on our description of the preferences) before we give back their MBTI results. In another group of studies that are very much like this real-life feedback process, comparisons have been made between the *reported* MBTI type and a *self-estimate* based on either a description of the preferences or on participation in training programs. The first part of Table 9.17 on page 197 summarizes these studies. Most were done with Form G and some with Form M.

In brief, agreement on all four dichotomies between MBTI type and self-estimate is in the 60–80% range. Agreement at the chance level would be 6.25%. When we look at agreement between MBTI type and self-estimate on three or four dichotomies, agreement is typically over 95%. When disagreement occurs, it is typically on a dichotomy on which the preference clarity is slight.

**2) Studies specifically testing type dynamics theory and studies of whole types.** Why are these studies important to us as practitioners? The MBTI is based on a theory that assumes there are dynamic interactions among the preferences. For example, Extraverted Feeling is assumed to be qualitatively different from Introverted Feeling. Or Extraverted Feeling as a dominant function is assumed to be different from Extraverted Feeling as an auxiliary.

If the situation permits it, we practitioners may actually teach our clients about type dynamics and development! Dynamics are core to what we do when we use the MBTI, even if we don't teach clients about dynamics. Thus, this group of studies is important for at least two reasons: 1) as practitioners we might want to know if dynamics and whole types are real; and 2) we might want to be able to answer our clients when they ask, "Yes, but are dynamics real, and why can't you just treat the dichotomies separately?" Certainly, clinical experience is one powerful kind of evidence, but sometimes it's also useful to have evidence for our more data-concerned clients (and our data-concerned selves!).

On pages 203–210 of the *Manual*, you will find a discussion of studies of type dynamics theory. One way of testing the validity of type dynamics is to look at the degree to which observer ratings (observers who do not know a person's type) of people's behavior correspond with what would be expected from type dynamics theory. For example, do those who have dominant Thinking (INTP, ESTJ, ENTJ) behave differently from those who have auxiliary Thinking (ENTP, INTJ, ISTJ)? If type dynamics are real, then there should be little overlap in the descriptors across those two groups. In fact, the research shows there is very little overlap. External observers who do not know a person's type see very little similarity in the behavior of people who have Thinking, Feeling or Intuition as a dominant function versus those who have those functions as an auxiliary. In this research, there were not enough Sensing types to perform an adequate statistical analysis.

As practitioners, this reminds us of the difficulty in presenting descriptions of Thinking vs. Feeling when we present the dichotomies separately. Some descriptions of Thinking fit better for some Thinking types than others, and the same is true for Feeling types. Introverted Thinking differs from Extraverted Thinking, and even Extraverted Thinking can look different in different people depending on whether it's dominant or auxiliary. This difficulty speaks to the importance of using descriptors that are well tested. See page 98 in Chapter Six of this guide for examples of those kinds of descriptors.

Another way of testing type dynamics theory relies heavily on complex statistical analyses and interpretations—do the scales in interaction predict behavior better than any scale alone? This approach often looks to see if types with different forms and attitudes of the four functions differ from each other statistically in ways that cannot be explained by trait theories. For example, do dominant Introverted Thinking types (ISTP, INTP) differ from auxiliary Extraverted Thinking types (ISTJ, INTJ)? If type is just a collection of traits of the four preferences, then statistically these types should differ from each other on some external measure (e.g., values) only on the J–P dichotomy. In fact, the types do differ from each other in ways that make sense in light of type dynamics. For example, the ISTP/INTP group (those who introvert their Thinking) valued friendship more highly than the ISTJ/INTJ group (those who extravert their Thinking). For a more in-depth look at these kinds of analyses, see pages 205–210 of the *Manual*. This kind of study as reported in the *Manual* does hint at the reality of type being something beyond simply adding traits from the four preferences. However, the evidence is not consistent or compelling in every case.

Validity of the types as a whole is usually shown through demonstrating that whole types (four-letter types) behave in ways that cannot be understood in light of separate preferences alone. Studies of differing type distributions in different careers is one well-documented demonstration of how whole types differ. If different types choose different careers in ways predicted by type theory, then we can begin to say that type theory has validity. The Selection Ratio Type Table (SRTT) is a method of comparing different type tables (the statistic used is the chi-square) to determine if certain types are over- or under-represented in a particular group. For example, we might want to compare a type table of family practice physicians to a type table of physicians in general to see if certain types are more or less represented in the specialty of family practice. In fact, some types are more frequent (e.g., ESFJs). The evidence in this domain is compelling—different types do choose different careers, and different specialties within careers. Examples of analyses using SRTTs can be found in Chapters Eleven and Twelve of the *Manual.*

Again, when external raters (who are not familiar with type and don't know the participant's type) observe the different types, there are dramatic differences in behavior not attributable to a dichotomy-by-dichotomy type interpretation. In a study summarized on pages 215–217 of the *Manual,* for example, INTPs and INTJs were described in very different ways by observers, even though they are only one letter different. INTPs were seen as original, imaginative, complicated, hasty, rebellious, individualistic and restless. INTJs were seen as formal, deliberate, logical, serious, aloof and reserved. Raters saw very real behavioral differences between these types not attributable to simple J–P differences. Observers saw equally dramatic differences between other types in the study.

We can feel comfortable telling our clients there is evidence that there is more to type than simply adding together adjectives that describe the four preferences separately. The whole types have a validity beyond a preference-by-preference interpretation based on traits. There is some emerging statistical evidence that type dynamics as described by Myers has some validity—although the picture is not yet complete.

**Can you use the MBTI if you don't believe in type dynamics?**

Yes, absolutely. You can treat the dichotomies separately and interpret, as best you can, someone's preferences on each of the four preference pairs. Many practitioners don't fully understand dynamics, and some practitioners don't believe in type dynamics. Even if you don't believe in type dynamics, ethics and appropriate use ask you to understand dynamics, since the MBTI was constructed based on the dynamic model of type.

If type dynamics are real—and there's good reason to believe that some kind of dynamic interaction is happening—then your use of type and the MBTI will be a great deal more powerful if you understand and use the dynamic model.

**Validity question: How does type relate to counseling (or education, or careers, or organizational work, or culture)?** The question here is, "Does type have validity in the area of…(counseling, education, etc.)?" That is, does type help us understand or predict behavior in these particular application areas? The information in the following sections is intended not only to demonstrate type's validity in these domains, but also to help you make use of clinical experience and research data in specific areas of practice. At the end of each section, you will find further resources for learning about theory and research in that area of practice.

An exceptionally valuable resource for practitioners and researchers alike is the book *MBTI Applications: A Decade of Research on the Myers-Briggs Type Indicator* (Hammer, 1996). In addition, Chapters Ten through Fourteen of the *Manual* provide excellent overviews of theory and research for the different domains of practice. Remember again that research data are typically group data, and that any given individual may differ from the pictures presented in the research summaries. Also, the lists of "quick and dirty" research findings (all of which are statistically significant) for each application area are *not* exhaustive, but rather are a sampling of research demonstrating that type appears to have validity in that domain.

## Specific application areas

### Counseling, health, and stress

PSYCHOLOGICAL TYPE originally arose from Carl Jung's work with his psychotherapy clients. He saw fundamental differences in the way people approached the world—differences that were not attributable to pathology, but differences in the way people attended to the world, took in information, and made decisions. Type is an exceptionally powerful tool in working with counseling clients. Type helps counseling practitioners by giving them a tool for:

- gaining insight into the counselor's own style and approach to counseling
- building rapport with clients
- building client self-esteem and self-valuing
- helping clients see differences in relationships as healthy differences
- providing a framework for understanding individual development
- forming hypotheses about potential strengths and/or blind spots in the client's development
- providing clients with insights into how they manifest stress, and their coping styles

One of the most critical insights counselors can have related to type is that different types of clients have different expectations in counseling and that clients approach the process in different ways. Of course for most counselors, this is a given. However, we must always remember that we "look out" at the world through the lens of our own type, and that how we differ from our clients can and will affect our assessments as well as the process of counseling. Thus, an ENFP counselor needs to understand that an ISTJ client may not be "compulsive," and an ISTJ counselor needs to understand that an ENFP client may not be "histrionic"—in the absence of other data. In addition, the two different clients will have two different "paces" in counseling.

Pages 226–229 of the *Manual* summarize some of the issues to which counselors might want to attend in working with clients of different types. *Remember, your clients may have fundamentally different typological views of the world than you do and it will affect how you perceive and interact with them.* Enough said to the wise practitioner.

Type dynamics and the developmental model provide a valuable framework for assessing client developmental strengths and needs. Good type development requires good development of both the dominant function and the auxiliary function—*in their appropriate attitudes*. Recall our discussion of balance in the chapter on dynamics. Extraverts who extravert both their dominant and auxiliary or Introverts who introvert both their dominant and auxiliary functions will be too one-sided. Individuals need good access to both the outer and inner worlds for mental health. They also need good development of a way of perceiving (Sensing or Intuition) and a way of judging (Thinking or Feeling). Beyond development of the dominant and auxiliary functions, good type development demands some reasonable attention to and comfort with the tertiary and inferior functions—although by no means equal development.

The inferior (least-preferred) function can erupt in such a way that an individual is "in the grip" of that function. In short, the individual begins to behave in an exaggerated, albeit unconscious, way that looks like an immature version of his or her opposite type—that is, the type whose dominant function is the opposite of his or her own. Naomi Quenk's books *Beside Ourselves* and *In the Grip* describe these eruptions of the inferior function; these books are extremely valuable resources for counselors.

Couples work is a fertile domain for the use of psychological type. Type can help couples understand differences in values, communication style, decision-making, and issues of order and lifestyle. For example, Extraverts and Introverts differ in the amount of time they wish to devote to relationships outside the primary relationship. *Intimacy and Type* by Jones and Sherman is a useful guide for professionals and clients alike.

Are type differences also linked to differences in physiology, health, stress-response and coping? The answer appears to be yes. Type can be a useful tool in helping clients understand their typical responses to stress and the behaviors that may lead them to compromise their health. Type can also help clients gain insight into how they may develop wider and different coping skills.

**Quick and dirty research summary for counseling, health, and stress**

- Thinking type counselors tend to prefer the more logical and analytical (cognitive and behavioral) approaches to counseling, while Feeling type counselors tend to prefer the humanistic and affective approaches.

- Intuitive types in general and Intuitive Feeling types in particular are more drawn to counseling as a way to address their personal difficulties.

- Perceiving type counselors appear to be more successful with crisis clients.

- Feeling type counselors appear to be more successful with clients who express emotions openly.

- Clients in general and in midlife in particular seem to report discomfort with out-of-character behavior associated with their inferior function.

- Contrary to popular opinion, research shows that similar types seem to be attracted to, and to marry, one another. This pattern is particularly evident in Intuitive and Feeling types.

- There appear to be differences between Extraverts and Introverts at the level of brain activity, both in degree of arousal in response to stimuli and in areas of the brain that are highly active. Extraverts seem geared to avoid under-arousal, while Introverts seem geared to avoid over-arousal.

- There seem to be type differences in proclivity to some diseases. Heart disease is the most studied and is found significantly more often in Introverts, especially Introverted Sensing types.

- As a response to stress and illness, Introverts tend to have a smaller range of coping resources than Extraverts, particularly Introverts with Thinking (ITs) and Introverted Feeling types (IFPs). Research also shows that using knowledge of type in a stress reduction program can result in a significant reduction in stress.

- Some researchers believe that reporting of type preferences can shift under stress, and that the likelihood of reporting preferences for Introversion, Sensing and Thinking may increase under stress/illness.

### Primary research resources for counseling, health, and stress

Myers, I. B., McCaulley, M. H., Quenk, N. L., & Hammer, A.L. (1998). *MBTI Manual: A guide to the development and use of the Myers-Briggs Type Indicator* (3rd ed.). Palo Alto, CA: Consulting Psychologists Press.—Chapter Ten: Uses of type in counseling and psychotherapy.

Quenk, N. L., & Quenk, A. T. (1996). Counseling and psychotherapy. In A. L. Hammer (Ed.), *MBTI applications: A decade of research on the Myers-Briggs Type Indicator* (pp. 105–122). Palo Alto, CA: Consulting Psychologists Press.

Shelton, J. L. (1996). Health, stress, and coping. In A. L. Hammer (Ed.), *MBTI applications: A decade of research on the Myers-Briggs Type Indicator* (pp. 197–215). Palo Alto, CA: Consulting Psychologists Press.

### Other useful resources for counseling, health, and stress

Corlett, E. S., & Millner, N. B. (1993). *Navigating midlife: Using typology as a guide*. Palo Alto, CA: Consulting Psychologists Press.

Jones, J. H., & Sherman, R. G. (1997). *Intimacy and type: A practical guide for improving relationships for couples and counselors*. Gainesville, FL: Center for Applications of Psychological Type.

Provost, J. A. (1993). *Applications of the Myers-Briggs Type Indicator in counseling: A casebook* (2nd ed.). Gainesville, FL: Center for Applications of Psychological Type.

Quenk, N. L. (1993). *Beside ourselves: Our hidden personality in everyday life*. Palo Alto, CA: Davies-Black Publishing.

Quenk, N. L. (1996). *In the grip: Our hidden personality*. Palo Alto, CA: Consulting Psychologists Press.

**Education and learning**

TYPE HAS GAINED increasing acceptance and use at all levels of education. There is a wide range of research on type and the many facets of education. Some of Myers' earliest research was done with students, and she was very interested in the relationship between type, type development, academic interests, and academic performance. Type has also found increasing application in elementary education. The Murphy-Meisgeier Type Indicator for Children (MMTIC) is the instrument of choice when using type concepts for students in grades three through seven. In all settings, an understanding of type can help:

- teachers learn about their natural strengths and biases in teaching
- students learn about their learning styles, motivations, and needed strategies for success
- students build self-confidence through appreciation of their style of learning
- teachers and students learn about teacher-learner interactions
- counselors working with students who are pursuing higher education, to help students understand the issues their types might face in that pursuit
- academic counselors working with students to maximize their strengths and build skills to address their blind spots

Different types need different kinds of attention and support in the learning environment, and they are "turned off" by differing aspects of the learning environment as well. Clearly, learning needs to build on the strengths of our type, but learning also appropriately asks us to draw on the lesser-preferred sides of ourselves at times. In addition, the research, as well as common sense, tells us that the teaching-learning process is far too complex for such simple solutions as matching a teacher's type to a student's type for the "best" results.

Knowledge of single dichotomy preferences can provide both teachers and learners with valuable insights into the characteristics of different types of learners. Although all the preferences have an impact, the Sensing-Intuition dichotomy seems to play the most dramatic role in how different types approach learning. Sensing types tend to prefer practical and factual approaches to learning, and move from the particular to the general in building their understanding. In contrast, Intuitive types tend to prefer imaginative and theoretical approaches to learning, and move from the general to the particular in building their understanding. The Judging-Perceiving dichotomy seems to play a role in the process or order in which learners want to take in information. Judging types tend to prefer approaches to learning that are sequenced and methodical, while Perceiving types tend to prefer approaches that are more random. In short, the preference for S or N tells us what kind of information learners prefer, while the preference for J or P tells us the way in which they prefer to receive it.

In addition, it is clear that percentages of students with a preference for Intuition increase as grade level increases from elementary and secondary through the levels of higher education. The percentage of Intuitive teachers also increases in the same way.

Although knowledge of one preference alone (particularly the preference for Sensing or Intuition) can provide a great deal of insight into teaching and learning styles, it is clear that "whole type" information provides us with far more profound insights into the values, needs, motivations, strengths, and challenges of different learners. Pages 245–258 of the *Manual* provide a fine summary of education-related research for whole types.

In the domains of academic achievement and aptitude, it is probably not surprising that Judging types tend to have higher GPAs than do Perceiving types. However, it also seems that Introverts and Intuitive types *as a group* tend to perform better than Extraverts and Sensing types on standard tests of academic aptitude (e.g., the Scholastic Aptitude Test and the Graduate Record Exam). As Myers has noted, these results do *not* suggest that INs are more intelligent than ESs, but that scholastic aptitude tests measure the Introverted and Intuitive aspects of intelligence (internal quickness with images and symbols) rather than the applied and practical aspects of intelligence possessed by Extraverts and Sensing types. This information is critically important for students and those who work with them to help students understand how and why ESs may perform as they do on such tests—and not to take such tests as evaluations of their skills, worth or intelligence. These studies and this issue are well addressed on pages 267–270 of the *Manual*. Again, it bears reminding that these are group data only. Any given Perceiving type might have a higher GPA than any given Judging type, and any given Sensing type might have a higher SAT score than any given Intuitive type. In addition, Sensing types tend to perform as well as Intuitives once they are involved in their major field.

In all educationally-related behaviors (homework, extracurricular activities, persistence), type can probably be most helpful to us in developing greater awareness of the differing *motivations* of the types. For example, some types may be more likely to be referred for discipline problems. However, in the mixed group of types that *are* referred, it can be useful to explore the reasons and motives for their actions in light of their differing type dynamics. If type is seen primarily as a tool for development, then looking at education-related behavior in light of individual dynamics is most consistent with the spirit of type.

**Quick and dirty research summary for education and learning**

- Extraverts tend to value active experimentation and collaborative learning.

- Introverts tend to value lectures, reflective observation, and abstract sequential learning.

- Extraverted, Intuitive and Perceiving teachers tend to have more student movement and noisier classrooms.

- Introverted, Sensing and Judging teachers tend to have quieter and more orderly classrooms.

- The effects of teacher-learner type similarities and differences on satisfaction and achievement are not clear—type-matching alone does not lead to success or satisfaction.

- Intuitives seem to perform better than Sensing types in academic tasks requiring manipulation of symbols.

- Sensing types seem to perform better in and prefer academic approaches that involve a reliance on memory, and where the teacher gives a clear sense of direction.

- Research on the relationship between type and learning and behavior disorders has yielded mixed results. There are no types that are clearly more often labeled *learning disabled* or diagnosed with attention deficit disorder.

- The frequency of Intuitive type teachers and administrators increases as the level moves from elementary and secondary through higher education. Percentages of Judging types remain constant for all levels of teachers and administrators. The percentage of Intuitive type students increases with educational level as well.

- Vocational education students and teachers tend to report preferences for Sensing and Thinking more often than general student and teacher populations.

- There are some relationships between type preferences and student life in higher education. For example, Extraverts report they are helped to persist by active involvement in campus life. Sensing types are more likely to participate in athletics and to attend basketball games. Preferences for S, T and P are frequent among male scholarship athletes. Extraversion, Thinking and Perceiving are related to referrals for judicial offenses. Extraversion, Intuition and Perceiving are related to referrals for substance abuse offenses.

- College students reported experiencing their living environment as most supportive when they and their roommates share all four preferences (also when dominant or auxiliary are the same, although less so). Students' GPAs were higher with roommates who had the same dominant but a different auxiliary function.

- Although a number of studies have been done, the relationship between type preferences and persistence in college is not clear. Results differ widely by type of college and program. It does seem that Feeling types are more likely to withdraw from curricula dominated by Thinking types (military academy, engineering), while Thinking types were shown to withdraw more often from the Feeling-dominated discipline of nursing.

**Primary research resources for education and learning**

DiTiberio, J. K. (1996). Education, learning styles, and cognitive styles. In A. L. Hammer (Ed.), *MBTI applications: A decade of research on the Myers-Briggs Type Indicator* (pp. 123–166). Palo Alto, CA: Consulting Psychologists Press.

Myers, I. B., McCaulley, M. H., Quenk, N. L., & Hammer, A.L. (1998). *MBTI Manual: A guide to the development and use of the Myers-Briggs Type Indicator* (3rd ed.). Palo Alto, CA: Consulting Psychologists Press.—Chapter Eleven: Uses of type in education.

**Other useful resources for education and learning**

DiTiberio, J. K., & Hammer, A. L. (1993). *Introduction to type in college.* Palo Alto, CA: Consulting Psychologists Press.

DiTiberio, J. K., & Jensen, G. H. (1995). *Writing and personality: Finding your voice, your style, your way.* Palo Alto, CA: Davics-Black Publishing.

Fairhurst, A. M., & Fairhurst, L. L. (1995). *Effective teaching, effective learning: Making the personality connection in your classroom.* Palo Alto, CA: Davies-Black Publishing.

Lawrence, G. D. (1993). *People types and tiger stripes* (3rd ed.). Gainesville, FL: Center for Applications of Psychological Type.

Lawrence, G. D. (1997). *Looking at type and learning styles.* Gainesville, FL: Center for Applications of Psychological Type.

Loomis, A. B. (1999). *Write from the start: Discover your writing potential through the power of psychological type.* Gainesville, FL: Center for Applications of Psychological Type.

Meisgeier, C., & Murphy, E. (1987). *Murphy-Meisgeier Type Indicator for Children: Manual.* Palo Alto, CA: Consulting Psychologists Press.

Provost, J. A., & Anchors, W. S. (Eds.). (1987). *Applications of the Myers-Briggs Type Indicator in higher education.* Palo Alto, CA: Consulting Psychologists Press.

Provost, J. A. (1992). *Strategies for success: Using type to do better in high school and college.* Gainesville, FL: Center for Applications of Psychological Type.

**Careers**

ONE OF MYERS' REASONS for developing the MBTI was to help people find work that would fit who they were and in which they could be both satisfied and effective. Consequently, some of the earliest research was done on type and careers; today it is an arena in which there is a large and growing body of research. The MBTI is without a doubt one of the most widely used instruments by career counselors.

Before we review some of the applications of type to careers, it is very important to understand that type alone is not enough information to make a career choice. Virtually all types are found in all careers. People making career decisions need to understand not only their personality type, but also their history, values, interests, skills, resources and goals, among other things. In career counseling and career management, type can be a useful tool for:

- empowering clients and building self-esteem
- knowing which types are attracted to which careers
- understanding one's needs in a work environment
- providing a framework for understanding lifelong development, and differing career needs at different stages of life
- giving clues to how one responds to stress or manifests burnout
- understanding one's decision-making style
- helping clients see strengths and/or blind spots in information-gathering
- providing guidance in developing interviewing skills
- helping clients find particular niches or work environments within careers that are consistent with their style
- understanding differences in counselor and client expectations about counseling

In career counseling, as in all types of counseling, type can help clients develop a sense of self-esteem based in the model of "sixteen different ways of being OK." Understanding that one's style and needs are healthy albeit different from those of others is an important insight. Type can also help counselors and clients see how they may have differing expectations about the process of career counseling (e.g., differing needs for closure, for self-exploration).

One of the classic ways in which the MBTI has been used in career counseling is in attempting to "match" an individual to a career or a job that "fits" his or her type. This is often done by looking at lists or type tables that show careers in which that person's type is relatively frequent—the research is quite clear in demonstrating that different types choose different careers. Although matching can be a very useful and eye-opening approach (particularly when data from other career instruments confirm the high frequency careers), it is probably not the most powerful use of type in career counseling. Exceptionally powerful applications lie in understanding the process of career exploration; that is, how one's type influences decision-making, information-gathering, response to stress, lifelong development, and approach to the counseling process.

Hammer (1996) describes three levels of interpretation of type in career work: static, dynamic and developmental. The application just described is a "static" interpretation—type is treated as a stable snapshot of personality that is mapped onto a list of careers. In the spirit of matching person to career, type tables of different careers may be found in the *Atlas of Type Tables* (Macdaid, McCaulley, and Kainz, 1986), and lists of the most and least frequent careers by type may be found in *Looking at Type and Careers* (Martin, 1995). Pages 295–300 of the *Manual* provide context and guidelines for reading and interpreting career type table data. These data show the power of type in career choice, and also show the limitations of using type alone in career decision-making.

The dynamic level of interpretation focuses on type dynamics: which functions the individual extraverts and which he or she introverts, and the order of preference for the functions. Interpretations at this level give extremely valuable information about decision-making style, information-gathering, response to stress, and approach to career work. In brief, the dominant and auxiliary functions may be favored in the process of decision-making, which can potentially involve *all four* functions: Sensing, Intuition, Thinking and Feeling. Intuitive Feeling (NF) clients, for example, might be inclined to favor Intuition and Feeling in making career decisions, while forgetting to look at the pros and cons of what they value or forgetting to attend to some of the facts about a given career. Dynamics can also give us insight into how clients may look while in the stress of a career crisis—they may be "in the grip" of their inferior function.

The developmental level of interpretation addresses the different path of development that each type faces. Lifelong career development and midlife career issues come into relief here. At this level of interpretation, counselors and clients alike can develop hypotheses about which mental functions (and related career activities) might reasonably be expected to hold the most interest for an individual at a given stage of life. For example, a twenty-year-old ESTJ might typically be more interested in developing and drawing on the strengths of Sensing and Thinking in his or her career work. A fifty-five-year-old ESTJ might be more likely to find pursuits associated with Intuition or Feeling more attractive than earlier in life.

The research shows clear trends for different types *as groups* to have career interests (and to a lesser degree career values) that fit what one would expect given their type. However, the statistical relationships are often moderate, thus assessments of values and interests should always be done in addition to an assessment of type.

Also, given that virtually all types can be found in any given career, counseling can usefully focus on how the differing needs and styles of the different types can be met in any given work setting—particularly if a type is less often found in a career field. For example, although ENFPs are less commonly found in the field of accounting than ISTJs, it can be useful for an ENFP who wants to enter that field to consider how his or her workstyle needs can be met in accounting coursework and eventually in a particular job setting. Management advisory services might be a good niche for an ENFP accountant. Knowing one's type can help individuals consider the degree to which they are willing and able to modify their work environments to fit them and/or modify themselves to fit their work environments.

Another way of approaching this issue is to say that one should never point a person to or away from a career on the basis of type alone—that is, on the basis of that person's type being more or less frequent in a given career. However, it can be useful to know that one's type will be less frequent in a particular course of study and in a career. As Myers said, in this way, one avoids being an inadvertent pioneer.

One of the best uses of type in career work is in giving the client an understanding of his or her work style, decision-making style, response to change and/or stress, and approach to job-creating or job-finding. This is especially true as the world of work continues to change in ways that will lead individuals to many different careers or jobs in the course of a lifetime—rather than one clearly matched career or job that lasts for many decades. Individuals can learn to draw on natural strengths and determine where they may need to expand their skills in order to build a lifelong path of career development.

**Quick and dirty research summary for careers**

- Virtually every type can be found in every career.

- Research shows, however, that there are clear differences in career choice for the types and that the function pairs (ST, SF, NF, NT) play the most important part in predicting career choice. Types are clearly attracted to careers that are predicted by type theory.

- The body of research on career choice is vast, and only a quick summary by function pairs can be given here. Bearing in mind always that all types can be found in all careers, patterns that emerge in the data are as follows:

  - STs are often found in occupations where they can focus on tough-minded analysis and pragmatic details: business, military, technical fields, law enforcement, construction.

  - SFs are often found in occupations where they can connect with and help people in pragmatic ways: health care, education (particularly K–12), religious settings.

  - NFs are often found in occupations where they can help develop people and work with symbols: religion, counseling, arts, teaching.

  - NTs are often found in occupations where they can focus on tough-minded theoretical analysis: scientific or technical fields, law, management.

- Research on satisfaction of the types in careers is not clear. It clearly *cannot* be said that the most frequent types in a career are the most satisfied. All types can and do report satisfaction in a given career.

- Research does show that those who are dissatisfied in an occupation, or who report a greater intention to leave that occupation, tend to be those types who are opposite the most frequent type in that occupation.

- While on the whole, type may not predict a given type's overall satisfaction in a given job, there is evidence that type does relate to satisfaction with *specific aspects* of one's job. For example, Thinking types will report higher satisfaction with administrative responsibilities than Feeling types, while Feeling types will report higher satisfaction with relationships with colleagues than Thinking types.

- EJs tend to be the most satisfied in career choices, regardless of careers. IPs tend to be the least satisfied in career choices, regardless of careers.

- Research shows that having one's "work self" in mind when taking the MBTI can influence results, and the results may thus reflect a person's current work behaviors rather than their true preferences or "best-fit" type.

- Judging types show a higher degree of career decisiveness than Perceiving types.

**Primary research resources for careers**

Hammer, A. L. (1996). Career management and counseling. In A. L. Hammer (Ed.), *MBTI applications: A decade of research on the Myers-Briggs Type Indicator* (pp. 123–166). Palo Alto, CA: Consulting Psychologists Press.

Myers, I. B., McCaulley, M. H., Quenk, N. L., & Hammer, A. L. (1998). *MBTI Manual: A guide to the development and use of the Myers-Briggs Type Indicator* (3rd ed.). Palo Alto, CA: Consulting Psychologists Press.—Chapter Twelve: Uses of type in career counseling.

**Other useful resources for careers**

Bridges, W. (1994). *Job shift: How to prosper in a workplace without jobs.* Reading, MA: Addison-Wesley Publishing Co.

Corlett, E. S., & Millner, N. B. (1993). *Navigating midlife: Using typology as a guide.* Palo Alto, CA: Consulting Psychologists Press.

Hammer, A. L. (1993). *Introduction to type and careers.* Palo Alto, CA: Consulting Psychologists Press.

Macdaid, G. P., McCaulley, M. H., & Kainz, R. I. (1986). *Myers-Briggs Type Indicator: Atlas of type tables.* Gainesville, FL: Center for Applications of Psychological Type.

McCaulley, M. H., & Martin, C. R. (1995, Spring). Career assessment and the Myers-Briggs Type Indicator. *Journal of Career Assessment*, 3(2), 219–239.

Martin, C. R. (1995). *Looking at type and careers.* Gainesville, FL: Center for Applications of Psychological Type.

Tieger, P. D., & Barron-Tieger, B. (1992). *Do what you are: Discover the perfect career for you through the secrets of personality type.* Boston: Little, Brown and Company.

## Organizations

TYPE AND THE **MBTI** are being widely used in organizational development. In fact, a substantial portion of this book is devoted to the issues and strategies in introducing type into organizations. In the past few years, many fine articles, books and resources have emerged on applications of type in organizations. This section is intended to give you an overview of how type is being used in organizations, a summary of the research in this area, and its implications for practitioners. Some of the current uses of the MBTI in organizations include:

- leadership development and coaching
- management training
- team development
- managing organizational change
- communication training
- teaching problem-solving
- career development
- conflict management

Since type provides a framework for understanding individual differences, and provides a dynamic model of individual development, it has found wide application in the many functions that compose an organization.

When type is introduced constructively in an organization, it can serve as the basis for:

- self-esteem and empowerment from understanding the validity of one's own preferred style
- appreciation of one's potential strengths and blind spots in organizational work
- discussing individual differences in a language that is not value-laden, is rational and orderly, and has solid research backing
- building better relationships with others on the job
- building individual or organizational programs focused on employee, management and leadership development, which can be informed by the model of type development
- understanding the different ways people take in information and make decisions
- constructive teamwork as employees see sound reasons for individual differences in work style, management style, problem-solving, communication needs, preferred work environment, response to stress, and the many other behaviors which type may impact
- addressing conflict and differences in ways that empower the individuals involved
- examining corporate cultures and organizational assumptions

Many people are concerned that type and the MBTI have been used destructively in organizations. They have been. And they have been used constructively as well. The destructive ways type has been used are not inherent in type itself, but typically in the lack of knowledge or poor use of type by the practitioner, and subsequently the employees. One of the goals of this book is to help ensure that type is used in effective, constructive and ethical ways when it is introduced into organizations.

When type is misused in organizations, it is often because types are treated as stereotypes (see Chapter Nine of this book for how to address issues of stereotyping), or because type is treated as a static description of an individual; that is, type is not understood within the dynamic and developmental model. There are often time limitations when type is initially presented in an organizational setting. However, as practitioners, we can introduce dynamics and development in our very first presentation of type. This doesn't mean our clients have to be able to "figure out" their dynamics. It does mean that we can talk from the beginning about a favorite function and a second favorite function—and the need to develop both. We can also "plant seeds" by talking about the differences between someone who extraverts their Intuition and someone who introverts their Intuition. It is helpful for participants to have handouts or booklets that show the dominant and auxiliary functions and their attitudes for all sixteen types (e.g., *Looking at Type: The Fundamentals, Looking at Type in the Workplace*). Even if we do not teach dynamics in an in-depth way to our clients, dynamics can inform what we do as practitioners as we conceptualize what is happening and what is needed in any given consultation.

One way type is used in a variety of organizational contexts is to improve communication. Clearly, communication is part of the core of effective organizational work. Type can help members of a group to understand how their communication needs differ, and how to communicate with persons of differing types in ways that "make sense" to them.

Conflict resolution is another clear and valuable application of type in organizational settings. Types differ on how they define conflict, what generates conflict, and how they respond to conflict. Some conflicts are type-related (e.g., differences in work and communication styles), but type can also serve to build communication for addressing other conflicts. Chapter Thirteen of the *Manual* has useful information on type and conflict, and *Looking at Type in the Workplace* gives insights into how each type responds to conflict and how to address the differences.

The problem-solving model (see the zig-zag exercise in Chapter Ten of this guide) provides a useful framework for helping individuals and organizations make informed decisions that look at the facts, the possibilities, the logical consequences, and the people consequences—that is, decisions that draw on all four mental functions: S, N, T and F. Feeling analysis is often ignored in business, which can lead to internal personnel difficulties as well as difficulties with customers.

Organizational change is a fact. An understanding of individual differences can help us respect the needs of different types in that process, and can help us to listen to the perspectives and gifts each type brings to the change process. *The Challenge of Change in Organizations* (Barger & Kirby, 1995) provides a guide for helping different types through the many stages of organizational change.

Teams are also a given fact of current organizational life, and this is an arena in which type is used extensively by organizational practitioners. Clearly, type is not an appropriate tool for choosing individuals to be on a team. However, looking at an existing team through the lens of type can help the team ask and answer the question: what are our strengths and how do we use them? Also, if certain types or mental functions are not well represented (e.g., N and F), how do we ensure we cover those "bases" in our work and in the development and delivery of our products and services?

Leadership development and executive coaching is an exploding field of practice and research. The research on type, management and leadership is enormous, and only highlights can be given in the "quick and dirty" research summary that follows. For an in-depth review, see the management and leadership chapter in *MBTI Applications: A Decade of Research*. Ongoing research is also presented at the leadership conference offered by CAPT.

There are multiple applications of type in the arena of leadership and coaching. Perhaps the most powerful application lies in the use of dynamics and the developmental model. Pages 356–357 of the *Manual* give an overview of ways the model of type dynamics and development can be used in leadership development. Dynamics provide insight into the "order" in which the mental functions are consulted in the variety of processes of leadership—visioning, relating, strategizing, problem-solving, motivating, and conflict management, for example. Dynamics can also give leaders and coaches a model for exploring the effectiveness of their balance between perceiving and judging, and the balance between extraverting and introverting—which impact on everything the leader does. The developmental model gives insight into the needs and natural paths of development for individuals with different leadership styles, and provides a framework for exploring life (e.g., midlife) and career changes, and personal and professional growth.

Interestingly, there is little evidence that certain types prefer one leadership *style* over another, but there is clear evidence that type is associated with some particular leadership *behaviors*. Some of this research is noted in the research summary. Leaders and coaches can use type to become aware of their behavioral strengths and work through the potential blind spots associated with their type. For example, it is clear that certain types are over-represented among managers and leaders—the TJ style in particular. The strengths (e.g., emphasis on decisiveness, competence and goal-orientation) and potential blind spots (e.g., not attending to group process, failing to involve others in decision-making) associated with this style can impact everything that leader does in the organization.

In all of the work we do in organizations (as in all work using type), it is important for us to ask: to what end am I using type? What purpose does it serve? Type is a tool that helps us accomplish some end, and that end may be self-awareness, improving communication, leadership development, or team-building. "Doing" the MBTI in an organization in and of itself serves no purpose. Type is only *one tool* in organizational work (whether that work is team-building or leadership development)—there are many other tools and skills that need to be used. As practitioners, we should ask ourselves how using the MBTI in a particular setting at a particular time furthers the purpose of our work with that organization. Chapter Eight of this book addresses issues in introducing type to an organization and can help you answer this very question.

### Quick and dirty research summary for organizations

- There are statistically significant differences in the work environment characteristics preferred by different types. For example, co-worker cohesion is more important to EFs; opportunities for innovation are more important to Intuitives; loyalty, security and managerial control are more important to SJs; and autonomy is more important to IPs. Tables 12.5–12.8 on pages 289–291 (the career chapter) of the *Manual* provide more data on work environment research.

- Those who extravert the same function report more satisfying and effective communication than those who extravert differing functions.

- In communicating, Extraverts want to focus on a wide variety of topics, while Introverts want to focus on one problem. Sensing types want well thought out, detailed plans, while Intuitive types want challenges and possibilities. Judging types want plans with timetables and supervisors who don't surprise them, while Perceiving types want flexible plans and supervisors who are spontaneous.

- In responding to conflict, Extraverted Thinking type (ETJ) males prefer to compete, while Extraverted Thinking females prefer to compromise. Introverted Thinking types (ITPs) prefer to compromise. Extraverted Feeling types (EFJs) prefer to collaborate, and Introverted Feeling types (IFPs) prefer to accommodate.

- Hard research on differences in decision-making and response to change is missing or suffers from lack of appreciation of different type dynamics. Results from large-scale questionnaire data collection suggest that types do have differing needs during organizational change.

- Preferences for Intuition and Perceiving correlate with a preference to change through innovation, while preferences for Sensing and Judging correlate with a preference to change through adaptation.

- In a group of managers, the Extraversion-Introversion dichotomy was the best predictor of stress and coping. Extraverts show higher social hardiness and Introverts show higher levels of social stress. Different types prefer different coping resources. For example, ENTJs prefer physical over emotional resources, while ESFJs prefer emotional over physical resources. Table 13.12 on page 347 of the *Manual* gives a summary of which resources are more used by which types.

- Research shows that teams with similar communication styles perform their tasks more quickly, experience less conflict, and like and listen to each other more. Although the research is mixed, a number of studies show that teams with diverse communication styles are more effective and produce better outcomes, but they may take more time in doing so. In short, type similarity seems to be positively related to process variables (e.g., working together and getting along) and negatively related to outcome variables (e.g., quality of the product).

- Managers and leaders with preferences for E and F are generally rated higher on teamwork variables.

- Managers and leaders with preferences for NTP, particularly for INTP, value self-oriented individualism, a value that research on teams shows interferes with teamwork.

- Leaders different from the team on the Thinking-Feeling dimension were rated by team members as more effective than leaders who were the same as the team on T–F.

- Attempts to find relationships between type and overall leadership *style* have found little.

- Type has been found to relate to particular leadership *behaviors*. Sensing and Feeling are more associated with participative decision-making than Intuition and Thinking. Preferences for E, N and F are more associated with facilitating and interactive leadership behaviors, while preferences for S, T and J are more associated with administrative behaviors. Preferences for N and P are associated with creativity, managing change, and transformational leadership behaviors. In response to conflict, Feeling types are more likely to avoid, accommodate or compromise than Thinking types.

- In one study, all types were able to learn the needed skills for participative leadership, but Feeling types were more able to use a participative style.

- Although there is an increasing selection for Intuition as one moves up in management level (and for Extraversion at the executive level), *type does not appear to predict success in an organization—no one type characterizes the successful CEO.* Training is a better indicator of success.

- Extraverts tend to have a positive sense of well-being that may help them manage the stress of executive positions better than Introverts.

- Type does seem to predict the kind of task on which a leader spends time (e.g., Introverts spend time on paperwork and problem-solving; Extraverts spend time socializing and politicking). These behaviors may indirectly affect performance depending on organizational culture.

- NTs appear more likely to make decisions in unstructured environments and to recognize problems and patterns and request information for problem-solving in open-ended environments. NPs tend to identify creative and integrative solutions to problems—and also appear more unpredictable, rebellious and undependable. As we have noted, there are potential strengths and blind spots associated with every style.

- There is some evidence that managers of all types learn to value the managerial culture of pragmatism and orientation to goals and results—in type terms, STJ.

**Primary research resources for organizations**

Hammer, A. L., & Huszczo, G. E. (1996). Teams. In A. L. Hammer (Ed.), *MBTI applications: A decade of research on the Myers-Briggs Type Indicator* (pp. 81–103). Palo Alto, CA: Consulting Psychologists Press.

Myers, I. B., McCaulley, M. H., Quenk, N. L., & Hammer, A. L. (1998). *MBTI Manual: A guide to the development and use of the Myers-Briggs Type Indicator* (3rd ed.). Palo Alto, CA: Consulting Psychologists Press.—Chapter Thirteen: Using Type in Organizations.

Walck, C. L. (1996). Management and leadership. In A. L. Hammer (Ed.), *MBTI applications: A decade of research on the Myers-Briggs Type Indicator* (pp. 55–79). Palo Alto, CA: Consulting Psychologists Press.

**Other useful resources for organizations**

Barger, N. J., & Kirby, L. K. (1995). *The challenge of change in organizations: Helping employees thrive in the new frontier.* Palo Alto, CA: Davies-Black Publishing.

Demarest, L. (1997). *Looking at type in the workplace.* Gainesville, FL: Center for Applications of Psychological Type.

Fitzgerald, C. R., & Kirby, L. K. (Eds.). (1997). *Developing leaders: Research and applications psychological type and leadership development: Integrating reality and vision, mind and heart.* Palo Alto, CA: Davies-Black Publishing.

Hirsh, S. K., & Kummerow, J. M. (1998). *Introduction to type in organizations* (3rd ed.). Palo Alto, CA: Consulting Psychologists Press.

Hirsh, S. K. (1985). *Using the Myers-Briggs Type Indicator in organizations: A resource book.* Palo Alto, CA: Consulting Psychologists Press.

Pearman, R. R. (1999). *Enhancing leadership effectiveness through psychological type.* Gainesville, FL: Center for Applications of Psychological Type.

## Multicultural uses

IN THIS SECTION, multicultural use of the MBTI is defined as the use of the Indicator with individuals or groups whose culture is different from that of the group with which the Indicator was developed and validated. This introduction is intended to sensitize you to some of the practical issues that can arise in using the instrument multiculturally. Chapter Five in this book (*How to Administer and Score the MBTI*) also highlights some specific issues when administering the MBTI to persons for whom English is a second language. This section also departs somewhat from the format of the other "quick and dirty" sections in that the emphasis here is more on issues and principles of use than on data summaries.

In using type in multicultural settings, we need to:

- recognize that the MBTI was developed and validated with persons who are predominantly English-speaking middle class white Americans
- understand that in spite of this background, type does appear to have meaning and validity in a variety of countries and cultures
- know that there may be some groups with whom we should exercise extreme caution when using the MBTI, and that it may be inappropriate for some cultural groups
- be aware that culture and type can interact such that type differences are expressed differently in different cultures
- ensure we are sensitive to how culture and language can impact administration and interpretation of the MBTI

While the MBTI was developed primarily with English-speaking middle class white Americans, there is substantial evidence that the MBTI has reliability and validity in other predominantly English-speaking cultures, as well as with persons for whom English is a second language. Research has demonstrated validity for various applications of the Indicator in Canada, the United Kingdom, China, South Africa, and students from Spanish-speaking countries. On the whole, studies support the validity of type and the Indicator in a variety of cultures—*assuming they are used sensitively and appropriately.*

When we say that type does appear to have meaning across cultures, we must always remember that both type and culture are powerful influences on people's ways of being and behaving in the world. Using type and the MBTI in multicultural settings asks us to understand the influence of a particular culture on people as well as the influence of type on behavior. Culture influences when and how an individual's psychological type is expressed. The Center for Applications of Psychological Type regularly offers a conference on multicultural uses of type and the MBTI, where these very issues are addressed. Proceedings from those conferences are an excellent source of theory and data on multicultural applications.

Of course, when using the MBTI with people for whom English is not the primary language, the preferred approach is to use a translation of the MBTI in that person's native language. As we noted in the chapter on administration, the issue is one of acculturation rather than simply language comprehension. Which set of cultural values and norms (as well as language) is the best fit for this person?

It is important to recognize that a *larger* question often arises among MBTI users, "Does *type* have universal meaning and application?" Jung and Myers believed that it did. In addition to the more than two dozen research translations in progress, there are currently sixteen commercially available translations of the MBTI, including: Bahasa Malay, Chinese, European French, German, Korean, Spanish (Castellano) and Swedish. There is growing evidence that type has meaning and application in a variety of countries and cultures—that is, the concepts of type make "sense" to those learning about type, and the translations make "sense" to respondents.

There *are* cultural groups for whom the MBTI may not be appropriate. While the Indicator has been successfully used in cultures where group social values are important (e.g., Latin American and Asian countries), it may be less appropriate to use the MBTI in cultures in which group or communal identity is a very central value ("collectivist cultures"), and where those values may also be combined with an experience of oppression. In these groups, reporting of individual preferences may have less meaning than for other groups. As always, the sensitive type practitioner needs to work within his or her area of competence and use the MBTI and type cautiously with any individual or group for whom validity has not been established.

Part of the sensitive use of the MBTI multiculturally, as with any other use, is to ask: "To what end are we using the MBTI? Whose needs are we meeting (ours or the client's)? Are there other methods and tools that can help us meet the needs of this group or this individual—methods developed and embedded in this particular culture?" Type is not always the best tool to develop self-understanding or to enhance effectiveness.

Another important issue is that culture and type can interact such that type is expressed differently in different cultures. For example, while the actual percentages of Extraverts and Introverts are very similar in the U.S. and the U.K., the expressions of those preferences appear to differ. That is, American

Introverts may appear more comfortable with "small talk," self-disclosure and fast-paced conversation than British Introverts. In short, Extraverts and Introverts exist in both the U.S. and the U.K, but they look different in the two countries. In this regard, it is important to recognize that behavioral descriptions of preferences based on U.S. patterns may not fit how those preferences are expressed elsewhere.

As we look at the relationships between type and culture, another question often arises: does a country or a culture have a type? Moody (1995) gathered data on psychological type, ethnicity and culture and found some clear relationships between descriptions of type and descriptions of culture among diverse populations: Japanese, Hawaiians, Chinese and Filipinos. As we consider the possibility that there *may* be national or cultural "characters," we need to understand that all types are substantially represented in all type tables collected by nation or culture. This kind of research suggests again that the expressions of type may differ by culture. Type researchers and practitioners alike have expressed concerns that culture and type both be understood in their own right, as well as in their combined contribution to behavior and individual expression.

A very practical issue in multicultural use of the MBTI is the impact of culture on the administration of the instrument. Chapter Five in this book gives the specific reading, age and language issues to which you need to give attention when administering the MBTI with any client, and addresses cross-cultural concerns as well. The *MBTI Manual* notes that, in general, clients who have English as a second language "find most items easy to answer, and with attention to reading level, age and possible language issues, both practitioner and client can feel confident of the validity of their overall results on the MBTI" (p. 373). In practice, if you have concerns about your client's ability to understand the meaning of MBTI items, it is best to discuss this issue before administering the Indicator.

When administering the MBTI, it is very important to help clients report their true type as much as it is possible for them to do so, and to recognize cultural factors that may hinder this process (e.g., a cultural norm of agreeableness, or coping strategies developed by minorities within a majority culture). When verifying and teaching about type, it is also important to recognize cultural differences in approaches to learning. Relationship to authority, pace, "classroom behavior" and other factors can influence the process of uncovering one's best-fit type. Chapter Fourteen of the *MBTI*

*Manual* provides many useful guidelines for administering, interpreting and verifying type when using the MBTI in multicultural settings.

**Quick and dirty research summary for multicultural uses**

- Type tables *may* differ by country and co-culture within a country, but the evidence is too limited at this time to make generalizations or to accurately answer the question: "Does a country or a culture have a type?" The data are also too complex to easily summarize here. For specific differences between countries and cultures, refer to the type tables in the multicultural chapter of *MBTI Applications*, and be sure to read about the limitations of the various studies reported there.

- In studies that have examined interactions *between* culture and type, there is some evidence that certain behaviors may be more supported in particular cultures. The degree to which a person's preferred behaviors are consistent with a culture's expected behaviors will affect that individual's expression of type.

- Samples seem to show a preponderance of SJ types across the cultural groups studied both inside and outside the U.S., as well as almost universal gender differences in preferences for Thinking (males) and Feeling (females).

- There is not sufficient data to report on reliabilities of the MBTI with groups other than those on which the instrument was developed. However, reliabilities for *translations* of the MBTI (specifically the Spanish, Korean, French and Norwegian) have been reported to be good to excellent.

- Although it is still emerging, multicultural research provides evidence for the validity of the MBTI in many cultures. That is, the Indicator does indicate people's Jungian type preferences in the cultures in which it is being used.

- In the U.K., Canada, Australia and New Zealand, the percentage agreement between reported and best-fit type was essentially the same as for a similar United States study (80% agreed on all four dichotomies).

- Evidence for the validity of type cross-culturally can be found in similarities of type distributions for similar occupations, fields of study and work roles across cultures. That is, different types choose arenas of work and study predicted by type theory, and those patterns are similar across cultures. There *do* also appear to be differences across cultures. Refer to *MBTI Applications* for more specifics of this research.

- Studies of managers and executives across cultures (U.S., Mexico, Canada, U.K.) demonstrate over-representations of ST and TJ relative to the general population.

- Studies of student majors, teachers and educational administrators show type similarity across cultures (U.S., Canada, Australia, China). Thinking types are attracted to sciences, Feeling types are attracted to liberal arts, and administrators are likely to be TJ.

- In Finland, problem-solving behaviors, and in Italy, specific leadership behaviors, have been found to relate to type in ways that are consistent with U.S. studies.

**Primary research resources for multicultural uses**

Kirby, L. K., & Barger, N. J. (1996). Multicultural applications. In A. L. Hammer (Ed.), *MBTI applications: A decade of research on the Myers-Briggs Type Indicator* (pp. 167–196). Palo Alto, CA: Consulting Psychologists Press.

Myers, I. B., McCaulley, M. H., Quenk, N. L., & Hammer, A.L. (1998). *MBTI Manual: A guide to the development and use of the Myers-Briggs Type Indicator* (3rd ed.). Palo Alto, CA: Consulting Psychologists Press.—Chapter Fourteen: Uses of type in multicultural settings.

The *Proceedings of the Multicultural Research Symposia* offered by the Center for Applications of Psychological Type (1993, 1996, 1998) are excellent resources. Specific articles are listed in the section below.

**Other useful resources for multicultural uses**

Casas, E. (1990). The development of the French version of the MBTI in Canada and in France. *Journal of Psychological Type*, 20, 3–15.

Casas, E. (1995). Diversity of patterns of type distribution among cultures: What do the differences mean? In R. A. Moody (Ed.), *Psychological type and culture–east and west: A multicultural research symposium* (pp. 65–76). University of Hawaii, January 1993. Gainesville, FL: Center for Applications of Psychological Type.

Inclan, A. F. (1986). The development of the Spanish version of the Myers-Briggs Type Indicator, Form G. *Journal of Psychological Type*, 11, 35–46.

Moody, R. A. (1995). Psychological type and ethnicity: How do ethnographic and type descriptions compare? In R. A. Moody (Ed.), *Psychological type and culture–east and west: A multicultural research symposium* (pp. 157–192). University of Hawaii, January 1993. Gainesville, FL: Center for Applications of Psychological Type.

Nordvik, H. (1994). Two Norwegian versions of the MBTI, Form G: Scoring and internal consistency. *Journal of Psychological Type*, 29, 24–31.

Ohsawa, T. (1995). Introduction to characteristics of Japanese management style: For better understanding of cultural differences in comparing MBTI data of Japan with other countries. In R. A. Moody (Ed.), *Psychological type and culture–east and west: A multicultural research symposium* (pp. 241–260). University of Hawaii, January 1993. Gainesville, FL: Center for Applications of Psychological Type.

Sim, H. S., & Kim, J. T. (1993). The development and validation of the Korean version of the MBTI. *Journal of Psychological Type*, 26, 18–27.

Uhl, N. P., & Day, D. A. (1993). A cross-cultural comparison of MBTI factor structures. *Journal of Psychological Type*, 27, 3–10.

## Resources

Resources for each application area are listed at the end of each data summary. The books below are good overall sources for research, data, and reviews of the data.

Bayne, R. (1995). *The Myers-Briggs Type Indicator: A critical review and practical guide*. London: Chapman & Hall.

Myers, I. B., McCaulley, M. H., Quenk, N. L., & Hammer, A. L. (1998). *MBTI Manual: A guide to the development and use of the Myers-Briggs Type Indicator* (3rd ed.). Palo Alto, CA: Consulting Psychologists Press.

Hammer, A. L. (Ed.) (1996). *MBTI applications: A decade of research on the Myers-Briggs Type Indicator*. Palo Alto, CA: Consulting Psychologists Press.

Macdaid, G. P., McCaulley, M. H., & Kainz, R. I. (1986). *Myers-Briggs Type Indicator: Atlas of type tables*. Gainesville, FL: Center for Applications of Psychological Type.

Thorne, A., & Gough, H. G. (1991). *Portraits of type: An MBTI research compendium*. Palo Alto, CA: Consulting Psychologists Press.

Zeisset, R. M. (2000). *Statistics and measurement: An introduction for MBTI users*. Gainesville, FL: Center for Applications of Psychological Type.

*A group has asked me to administer the MBTI and help them use the results in their work. What kinds of questions do I need to ask before I get started?*

*I'm working on a team where I believe knowledge of type would help. What do I do?*

*How do I roll out the MBTI in my organization?*

*I am introducing type into an organization, but I believe they have had a bad experience with this kind of program. What steps do I need to take?*

# Chapter 8

**IMPROVING THE FUNCTIONING OF GROUPS.** There will be times when you give the Indicator to a group of people who are not part of an organization. For example, students in a career orientation workshop, residents of a retirement home, or members of a church congregation may or may not play an active part in the organization. Their intention is to consider using type in their personal lives, and they are usually not considering type as a tool for helping the organization or group function better. In effect, they are individuals receiving a type explanation for individual, rather than group reasons. Later in this chapter there are guidelines for giving a type explanation in any group setting. The rest of this chapter is about the challenge of introducing type into an organization, where improving the functioning of groups is a primary reason for teaching its members about type. It is a challenge that takes careful planning.

If we are to be effective in introducing type into an organization, we must always think of it as an organic system about to be altered by what we do. If we do it right, the system incorporates type and benefits from it. Otherwise, the type concepts bounce off or are degraded by the system's resistance to change.

Included in this chapter are suggestions for:

- describing and analyzing the organizational situations you will encounter
- deciding on possible points and means of entry
- using type theory to help you plan
- identifying the factors supporting and resisting the use of type concepts
- making a specific plan with a good chance of success

**WHAT'S THE PROBLEM?** Consider the following situations. What do you need to know and do to get type well established in the organization?

- **Situation:** The manager of a twenty-person department has learned about type, thinks it should help with communication and morale issues, and asks you to plan an MBTI workshop for them. What do you need to know before you say yes and start planning?

This chapter is adapted and used by permission from *People Types and Tiger Stripes*, Third Edition, © 1993 Gordon Lawrence.

- **Situation:** You have conducted a two-hour introduction to type for the top management of your organization. They were pleased with it and see the potential for use of the MBTI throughout the organization. They ask you to develop a staged plan for doing that. How do you start and what might be the stages of the plan?

- **Situation:** After learning about type from you, a member of a team in your organization is very enthusiastic about type being introduced to the other team members. What is the next step, and what data do you need to gather?

The three situations are typical—probably straightforward and not too complex, right? That would almost always be a bad assumption. The situations in most organizations where type might be introduced have complexities and issues that should be uncovered—at the beginning. There may be a pile of issues in each situation that you need to sort through before you start a type workshop.

Many of us who use the Myers-Briggs Type Indicator have introduced type into organizations with the intention of it becoming part of the organizational culture. Sometimes we are successful, but too often we are disappointed in the results: some individuals in the organization benefit, but we see no widespread effect.

We know the value of type in our own lives and expect through our teaching skills and enthusiasm to energize an essential core of fellow enthusiasts in the organization who will also see the value and spread the benefits of type throughout the organization. We expect a kind of chain reaction. We expect type concepts to become part of the language the members use in working with each other, because they recognize the constructive qualities of type theory.

Such expectations are not realistic. Some organizations are ready to be influenced by our teaching skills and enthusiasm, but most situations require more. What does it take to successfully influence an organization—beyond what is needed to effectively teach individuals about type?

This question is at the heart of the career of those who specialize in organizational development. Some of them have added the MBTI and a sound knowledge of type theory to their other skills and are sharing what they know with others through the Association for Psychological Type and various publications.

## Describing and analyzing the situation

In this chapter we answer the question by describing the approach we generally use. The readers we have in mind want to introduce type into their own organizations. We believe readers who want to introduce type as an outside consultant or trainer will also find the chapter helpful—much of it applies to them as well.

THOSE OF US who want to influence other people's use of type encounter widely varying situations with different ingredients that have to become part of each plan. We have helped many people plan ways to introduce type into their organizations, and every situation is different, requiring a plan designed to fit it specifically. What we have written here is *a general strategy for devising situation-specific plans.*

**DESCRIBE THE SITUATION IN DETAIL.** As you start thinking seriously about how to introduce type into your organization, begin by writing a description of your situation. Whether you put it in good prose form or just phrases, it pays to write it in detail. Our suggestion is that you write it in the form of answers to some key questions.

**What goal or ongoing effort of the organization can type be linked with?** This is the first issue to address in your analysis of the situation. Unless the leaders of the organization, or of a unit within the organization such as a work team, are open to and looking for tools to help them deal with problems or pursue particular goals, they are not ready for you to introduce type. The importance of this attitude cannot be stressed too much. Are they seriously committing resources to improving individual effectiveness, teamwork, mission clarity, the quality of products and services, and other such goals that can be enhanced by uses of type?

Even if you know that type knowledge is what the organization needs, your attempts at teaching type will probably not influence organizational behavior to any extent unless the leaders are actively inquiring into means of improvement and see type as a possible means of improving their situation. In most cases, learning about type and using the ideas will not be accepted as a goal of the organization solely on the merits of type theory. The time and hard work it takes to learn and develop the skills of type can be justified in the members' minds only to the extent that they are committed to the goal that type is supposed to help them reach.

If type takes hold in an organization, it will be because its members link it in their minds to the goal they are pursuing. Their energy and momentum for reaching the goal are then available for learning about and using type concepts.

**How can you judge the readiness of the organization to use type?**
Even when you know there are leaders and others committed to improving organizational processes, that fact is no assurance they are ready for type. Do they seriously believe that people's individual differences need to be used more constructively? Are they committed to giving people time, training and resources to work on developing their individual effectiveness? Are they ready to use a tool like type ethically, or is there a real risk that they may use it as a weapon? If it is hard for you to find positive answers to these questions, a direct introduction of type into the organization is not realistic. Perhaps a small-scale introduction is feasible; some means for that are given in the paragraphs that follow.

An important step in introducing type into an organization is to find out the goal that the knowledge of type is intended to serve, the members' clarity about that goal, and their commitment to achieving it. In the absence of these, type knowledge is likely to be simply a curiosity that some will appreciate and others will forget; the organization will not be broadly affected.

**What is my position of influence in the organization?** Who listens to me and regards my ideas as credible enough to be given serious consideration? Who is in my circle of influence, and are they people who have credibility with others outside my circle?

Your answers, carefully thought out, will suggest the pathways for spreading type ideas. The circle is your base for introducing type. In many kinds of organizations, psychological theories, including type, are suspect and negated. Your credibility will have to carry type through the initial stages of introduction until the base group members see for themselves the value of type and are willing to commit to supporting the next step of its extension into the organization.

If you are the top administrator or a high-level resource person who is expected to bring new ideas into the organization, you have a different set of opportunities and constraints than do other employees who may not have those expectations attached to their jobs. All of the questions that follow apply to people lower in the organization; some will apply to the top leaders as well.

**What are my purposes and motives in this situation?** It pays to examine carefully your motives in introducing a change into the organization: Do I have purposes other than the obvious ones of using type to improve the ways we work? Do I have other motives I may not have acknowledged to myself?

Am I hoping that by taking the lead in introducing type I will become more visible as a leader or potential leader? What other agendas do I have that may ride on the coattails of the change I hope to introduce?

The answers to these questions are for your own consideration, to clarify what is energizing you in your plan for introducing type. Being clear about your purposes will help you make better judgments about the plan and the situations that come up as you act on the plan. *If your personal reasons do not mesh with the organization's objectives and active commitments, do not try introducing type.* Once you have tried it and type is not received well, the organization is likely to turn off to other attempts; reintroducing type may be impossible once the door has been closed.

**Do I have a client or am I my own client?** One way of looking at your role in introducing type into your organization is to consider yourself as a change agent. In introducing type you are proposing that people change some aspects of their ways of thinking and relating to each other, and that is what a change agent does. We are using the term change agent in a way that is somewhat different from general usage. We do not mean that you are necessarily someone who orchestrates and directs a change process. With respect to type, you are the bringer of a resource, and in doing that you may be simply a helper to the designated change agent.

Whatever your role in the change process, you have to have a client—a person or group—who, in effect, authorizes you to bring a proposal for change into the organization. Tacitly or explicitly, you negotiate with the client to find out what the client wants. If you introduce type to co-workers without considering whether they have a client relationship with you, you may have no client and no support, so what you are trying to do may seem to them an unwanted intrusion into "the way things are done around here." If you bring in something the client doesn't anticipate, or something the client objects to when you bring it, it will be ignored or rejected. If the client does not see type as helpful, your work with type will not be accepted as help. In other words, you need to be sure a welcome mat is laid out for type ideas by the people who will be responsible for nurturing a change in the organization.

Sometimes the welcome mat doesn't go out until after they have had an initial orientation to type, such as taking the MBTI and getting a face-to-face explanation of the ideas. In any case, your first client needs to be in your circle of influence. From that base, you can build the next base that includes the next client or set of clients.

This caution may feel like a wet blanket, an attempt to stifle your enthusiasm. That's not the intent. We urge careful planning so that your first effort to introduce type is successful, and that success will sustain your enthusiasm.

*If you do not have a client* in the sense described here, then start out as your own client. That is, use type in your own work, and invite others to observe you using type. To those who are interested in what you are doing, explain type concepts and your reasons for using type. Your aim is to interest those who themselves are credible, and are informal status leaders among co-workers. We suggest that your invitations to them be informal, casual opportunities to see how you use type. If you are a teacher or trainer, show them specific ways type helps in your teaching. These people can then become a client group and help you plan the next steps in introducing type to the larger group. If you learned about type from a co-worker, you and that person most likely would be part of each other's client group, part of the base for the next steps.

**Can I find members who share the values implicit in type theory?**
What has attracted many of us to type theory is the way it represents viewing human differences in a new light. By showing the complementary strengths and blind spots of the types, and showing that all types are valuable, Myers provided basic guidelines for the constructive use of their differences. Implied in the theory are values such as the worthiness and dignity of individuals despite their differences; the importance of collaboration for best results; and the necessity of trust, mutual support and openness to allow the collaboration to happen.

People who hold these values and try to practice them are the ones most likely to be ready for learning about and using type. They will see type as a practical tool for advancing their values. As you decide which people make up your base for introducing type into the organization, consider people you know who appear to share these values and try to act on them. If most members of your organization pay lip service to these values but are actually steeped in habits of distrust of differences, the task of selecting the base is more difficult.

**When and how should I involve the organization's leadership?**
Whether you have a client or you are your own client to begin with, your aim will be to involve the top person of the organization as soon as you feel sure he or she will see type as a credible and feasible set of ideas for the organization to use. It is a truism that people are likely to support a change they help

to design. The reverse is true, too: the chances of their resisting a change go up to the extent they were not involved in planning the change. These rules of thumb certainly apply to the top people, who see facilitating or resisting change as a major part of their leadership.

The top person or people also want to know that you are loyal to them, and that introduction of type into the organization will contribute to their success. They know that most innovations fizzle out, so they will be skeptical until they can clearly see the likelihood of success. No leader wants to advocate an idea that gets rejected or ignored by others in the organization.

This may seem a very slow process. If type ideas took you by storm, you may be hoping they will surge through the organization as well. Organizations resist and slow down change for a lot of reasons. The resisting forces won't be bulldozed or bandwagoned away; they exist for reasons that can be understood. But they can be anticipated and, with careful planning, can often be converted into supporting forces.

The process will move more slowly than you want for another reason. There is a natural progression in the absorption of type concepts that takes time. At the beginning people start to see the usefulness of type in terms of the separate dimensions: E–I, S–N, T–F and J–P. While work applications may be their initial motivation, they soon find that their use of type seems superficial until they begin to study the meanings of type differences in their own families and among other people they are close to. Before they can get beyond the surface in applications of type to their work, they need time to explore with family and friends the personal experiencing of their own type preferences—for example, how daily life is experienced differently through the Extravert's and Introvert's viewpoint. People getting more deeply into type have to ask many questions of each other. They try out language about type. For example, they have to learn what language about Introversion and Extraversion fairly represents these two ways of being in the world—with a minimum of stereotyping. Similarly, they must develop their understandings of S–N, T–F and J–P. Understanding the even deeper levels of type takes still more time, of course.

**How does type fit into the organizational culture?** Some organizations are open to new ideas, with leaders who actively look for them. Some leaders are quick to attend to new ideas, but resist using them. They enjoy playing with the idea of an innovation while most members of the organization do not want to make changes in their practices. In other organizations, leaders are slow to consider new ways, but, when convinced of their value, will give solid support for change.

One way of looking at these organizational differences was described in a training handout developed by Earle Page (1985). Page saw that an organization's culture was strongly influenced by the type preferences of its leaders, either the current leaders, the founding leaders, or both. An organization tends to attract and hold members who fit well in that culture. He saw the energy of an organization being distributed into four categories corresponding to the type preference combinations of Extraversion or Introversion, and Sensing or Intuition: IS, IN, EN and ES. An organization needs the perspective of all four tendencies, but usually it is steered by one of them.

- **IS energy**, reflective and always practical, is directed toward conserving what has proven itself to work well enough. Drawing strength from continuity, from protecting and enjoying the proven, it resists novel and unproven ideas, expecting them to be more disruptive than beneficial.

- **IN energy**, reflective and engrossed in possibilities, is directing the organization to question the tried and true, take the long view and imagine new ideas. Focused on anticipating the future, it assumes that a better way can, and must, be found.

- **EN energy**, pushing toward action on fresh ideas, is focused on vitalizing the organization to take risks in trying new ways. Drawing strength from surges of enthusiasm for the new ways, the EN viewpoint assumes organizations are at their best when caught up in pursuing important changes.

- **ES energy**, directed toward action on life's practical realities, steers the organization to get on with its obvious responsibilities. The emphasis is on staying on track, doing what is needed and getting results.

All four perspectives or energies may be active in the organization. If they are recognized and valued for their positive characteristics, and used in appropriate ways, the tension between them will be constructive. Otherwise, the tension will be seen as negative, and adherents of each viewpoint will see the others as having "excessive" influence and squandering the organization's resources.

One of the four is likely to be a major shaper of your organization's culture, with the others playing a lesser role. Whichever of the four dominates the others will have a bearing on your approach to introducing type. The credibility of type will be an issue with all four, but for different reasons.

**If IS dominates**, and the organization is perceived as working well, you will need to show at the beginning that type helps to continue and protect well-accepted values and ways of working. That is quite a challenge, considering that uses of type are usually promoted as *new* ways of communicating and working, meant to replace the familiar. But if the IS organization is experiencing pain in areas where type could be helpful, it may well be open to considering *practical* new tools. In either case, in the IS organization, as you plan out your credibility base, you will need to draw into it some status leaders who are IS stalwarts, and let them help you pace the introduction of type.

If your organization is energized around **IN or EN values**, change and newness are not unwelcome, but the credibility of type is an issue in another way. IN and EN leaders are likely to have given considerable thought to the ideas they see as the guiding principles of the organization. For type to become one of those ideas, the leaders will need to see type as consistent with their vision for the organization.

**If ES values** are paramount in the leadership of the organization, to see type as credible the leaders must believe that it is clearly practical and will help the organization get better results on its accepted objectives.

The best of the values and skills of IS, IN, EN or ES may not be steering the organization. The blind spots associated with each are important to consider. The leaders of most organizations can recite research that shows what makes organizations effective, but they may not be using that knowledge in their own organizations. Earle Page also saw the negative side of the four tendencies. *If not balanced* by other perspectives, the IS influence "may dry up the organization, narrowing leadership and productivity;" the IN influence may weaken the organization by pulling too much energy into "irrelevant ideas and alternatives;" the EN efforts for change may fail to see practical limits and exhaust the organization's resources; and the ES view may keep leaders from seeing the necessity of change, and keep the organization stuck in a rut. If you see some of the negative tendencies in your organization, they may help you size up the situation for introducing type.

It is also useful to consider the organization's culture in terms of the type preferences that seem to be most emphasized in the day-to-day work of the organization. Does the work mostly call upon and reward introverted or extraverted behavior? Does the work attract and hold Introverts more than Extraverts, or vice versa? Similarly, consider S–N, T–F and J–P. Combining the four preferences gives you a hypothesis of the composite type of the organization. Read the type description of that type and you will get some clues about the approach to introducing type that will be most appealing.

**What are my assumptions about the specific influential people in this situation?** At this point in your analysis, you have a fairly clear idea about which people are most influential in the situation, those who most affect the plan you are forming for introducing type. As you begin to see the roles you expect them to play in the plan, it is time to examine your assumptions about the ways they will act and why they will act that way. If you are assuming a key person will act in a certain way and he or she doesn't, your plan may be upset. Try to test your assumptions ahead of time. Often you can ask people directly about how they will act: "For this to work, here is what I will need…" Talk it out whenever you can. Go over your assumptions with someone you trust who can give you a different perspective.

## Deciding on possible points and means of entry

YOUR ANSWERS TO THE NINE QUESTIONS in the previous section should give you a fairly complete description of the situation for introducing type. They may also suggest possible points of entry; that is, where, with whom and how to start introducing type. Your own position in the organization may dictate the point of entry. In any case, except perhaps the latter, you will need to have the leadership endorse and support the entry plan. You may be in a position that allows you only to plant the seeds of type with someone who then takes responsibility for the entry process, perhaps with you as a helper.

## Analyzing the forces for and against uses of type

IN WHATEVER POINT OF ENTRY being considered, the specific situation of the entry needs to be analyzed. The force field technique for analyzing a situation is very useful in cases like this. There are four basic steps in force field analysis:

1) **Make a goal statement.** In any situation where one has a desired goal, there are forces working for and forces working against the reaching of the goal. For a successful analysis of these forces, you need a statement of the goal that is clearly focused. It is all right to begin with a fairly general goal such as, "to introduce type so that it is accepted, used, and disseminated from the point of entry." Then the task is to decide what forces at this possible point of entry are working for and against the reaching of the goal.

2) **List the forces.** Begin the force field analysis with two lists, side by side, of forces for and forces against. When you are a member of the organization and want to assess the rightness of a possible entry point, your questions to yourself will be to estimate what people and what conditions in the situation would be favorable and unfavorable to the use of type.

3) **Consider the strength of the forces.** The next step in force field analysis, after the lists have been made, is to weigh the relative strength of each

force in the equation: Which favorable forces can I strengthen and which unfavorable ones can I weaken, with the resources at hand? What specifically can be done to each? The situation, as it is, is an equilibrium of the forces; to get energy into accomplishing my goal—the acceptance of type through this entry point—I have to change the balance of forces, change the status quo that does not now include uses of type.

Consider the situation of a young high school teacher who was eager to extend uses of type in his school. The school had a record of serving well the academically oriented, college-bound students, but not doing well with the others. As a distributive education teacher, he taught mainly the latter students. The principal put him on a committee of teachers charged with the task of finding out what was needed to better serve the students who were likely to enter the workforce after graduation, if they made it to graduation. The committee members were given time during the school day to do their work. The young teacher saw this committee work as an entry point for introducing type. As part of the force field analysis, his goal statement was "to have the committee support type as a way of looking at learning needs of students and improving their instruction."

He listed these favorable forces:
- the committee appreciates my energy and ideas
- the committee has agreed to consider type
- the principal knows about type and supports its use
- type data about SP types being disadvantaged by the standard academic programs should help us see ways to improve instruction
- some teachers of academic subjects, and all of the administrators, are concerned about the students who aren't college-bound
- nearly all the teachers are interested in improving instruction
- the other committee members are well known and respected by the faculty
- we have funds to give the MBTI to students and faculty

He listed five unfavorable forces:
- the committee members don't know about type, nor do most others on the faculty
- I am one of the younger teachers and not well known
- the teachers usually resist changing the curriculum and their ways of teaching
- the committee has no idea how much support its recommendations will receive

- the teachers mostly ignored some learning styles work (not type) we did on an inservice day two years ago.

He went through his lists to see what favorable forces could be strengthened and what unfavorable ones could be weakened. For our purposes here, we don't need the details of his analysis.

He came to four conclusions:

- The committee is a good point of entry, because the other members are open to ideas and I have credibility with them.
- I will need to go step by step, first introducing type to the committee, and getting their approval to collect some type data on students.
- Although most of the faculty don't know me well, the teachers of ninth graders do, and I probably can get their OK and the principal's approval to administer the MBTI to all freshmen, and have the teachers of ninth graders take it too. I expect to get some data that will show the committee the value of using type in their work and including it in their recommendations to the faculty.
- Because two committee members are department heads, the next step would be for the committee to try out ideas, including type, on all the heads.

These conclusions were the basis for his entry plan. After the committee members took the MBTI and got an orientation to type, they supported taking data on the freshman class. Administering the MBTI to the ninth graders and their teachers did provide some data of importance. Most interesting was the fact that more than one third of the students were reported as SP types, while only three of their teachers (less than 10% of them) were SPs. These entry activities opened the door for a wider introduction of type into the school.

**4) Revise the force field analysis after entry has been made.** Once you start using type—you make your entry—you'll probably need to revise your force field analysis as the forces change. You'll also need to revise your goal statement as you enter the next phase of introducing type into the organization.

## Deciding on strategy: The long view

ALL OF THE ANALYSIS you have done to this point suggests a strategy, a big-picture plan. Strategy is a military term. It is distinguished from tactic, a plan for action within the strategy. A tactic is consistent with the strategy and is one part of carrying out the strategy.

Write out your strategy. It can begin with summary statements from the analysis you have done and with your ideas for entry. When you have it written fully, we suggest you try to boil it down to a few phrases or sentences. As your plan progresses and you bring others into the planning of next steps, the strategy statement in its brief form (perhaps amended by the base group) will serve to keep everyone's eye on the target. The young high school teacher had a beginning strategy—introduce type through the committee and the department heads.

## Deciding on tactics: An action plan

AN ACTION PLAN DEALS WITH DETAILS: who will do what, when and how. The high school teacher in this example needs to decide specifically what he will say and to whom he will say it and exactly *how* he will introduce type to the committee and department heads. This aspect of planning means setting realistic, specific, concrete and achievable goals. It is an aspect many of us know well, at least in theory. The key is to plan the specifics of our introduction, and then to act on that plan. When you move into action, you will have done a thorough job of anticipating many of the issues that may arise. The box on the following page has a checklist to remind you of important issues to address when setting up the conditions for introducing type to an organization. In the next chapter, we will explore the specific kinds of ethical issues that can arise when introducing type to your clients.

When you plan to administer the MBTI and/or explain type to people in an organization, you may wish to use the following questions as a checklist in your planning.

**1) The people taking the MBTI. What do *they* see as...**

- **the purpose for taking it?** Watch for hidden agendas and misunderstandings. Don't rely just on reasons and reported perceptions given to you by an intermediary whose motives you don't know.

- **the potential value of it?** You may need to clarify their understanding.

- **their option of taking it or not?** What do they see as the consequences of not taking it?

- **the uses to be made of the type report itself?**

- **their control over the MBTI results?**

- **the leader's or supervisor's expectations of them that are implied in introducing type to members of the organization?**

**2) The formats and approaches used: How might I fit the administration of the MBTI and the type explanation to the people?**

You will want to anticipate the dynamics of the group and fit the introduction to its members. Design the explanation session around their purpose for taking the MBTI. For example, if work-team dynamics is the theme, then the session should give the team members opportunities to practice using type in team dialogue, and they will need to discuss their types with each other. When type is introduced appropriately into the team-building process, team members report that type concepts provide a concrete, objective way for them to talk about their personality differences in teamwork—their differences in perception, decision style, pace, priorities, etc.—without getting personal; that is, without feeling that the mention of differences constitutes a personal attack.

**3) Administration and scoring of the MBTI: What options fit my situation?**

Whether it is administered in a group session or individually, filled out during work hours, or at home, it is important to follow the guidelines for administration and scoring given in this guide or in the *Manual.*

**4) Resources and follow-up support: How much should I provide?**

What materials will the participants need to have during the type explanation session, to take home as a reference, and to have available in a resource library within your organization? What resources will new people need to help them learn type-related skills and to explore type beyond your knowledge? Their continued and constructive uses of type will depend on such follow-up support. At a minimum, they will need a sheet of words and phrases that characterize the type preferences, a report of their MBTI results, and a set of the full descriptions of the sixteen types. That is the basic set for any explanation session and for their personal, further exploration at home. In addition, they should have handouts related to their purpose for taking the MBTI.

**Resources**

Barger, N. J., & Kirby, L. K. (1995). *The challenge of change in organizations: Helping employees thrive in the new frontier*. Palo Alto, CA: Davies-Black Publishing.

Bridges, W. (1992). *The character of organizations: Using Jungian type in organizational development*. Palo Alto, CA: Consulting Psychologists Press.

Demarest, L. (1997). *Looking at type in the workplace*. Gainesville, FL: Center for Applications of Psychological Type.

Hirsh, S. K., & Kummerow, J. M. (1998). *Introduction to type in organizations* (3rd ed.). Palo Alto, CA: Consulting Psychologists Press.

Lawrence, G. D. (1993). *People types and tiger stripes* (3rd ed.). Gainesville, FL: Center for Applications of Psychological Type.

Page, E. C. (1985). *Organizational tendencies*. Gainesville, FL: Center for Applications of Psychological Type.

Stein, M., & Hollwitz, J. (Eds.). (1992). *Psyche at work: Workplace applications of Jungian analytical psychology*. Wilmette, IL: Chiron Publications.

*Everyone is worrying about being pigeonholed by type. How do I address this issue?*

*How do I handle it when I hear one type saying things that I know are stereotypical about another type?*

*A company president just asked me to help them use the MBTI to hire some Feeling types. She says her organization needs them to improve their customer service. What do I do?*

*How do I respond to a client who says, "I really liked our feedback session. Can I take one of those MBTIs home to give to my wife?"*

# Chapter 9

WE HATE TO LEARN about people who had a bad experience with the MBTI. When we ask them to tell why it was a bad experience, we learn that one way or another the person who was explaining the MBTI did something inept or unethical. The trouble was not in the MBTI or the concepts of psychological type. The skills and ethics of the user were the problem. Any instrument that is used incorrectly is a blunt instrument that can do damage.

When you introduce someone to the MBTI, the credibility of type concepts—as well as your own credibility—is on the line *for that person*. Anyone using this book wants to be skillful and ethical in presenting type to clients. In our view, ethical use and skillful use of the MBTI are the same thing. Any skillful use of the MBTI will be ethical and vice versa. This applies to all the skills we have emphasized in this book. It is unethical to disregard them. However, while we all intend to use them well, there are pitfalls along the way that can interfere with or confuse our intentions. This chapter is about some of the less obvious pitfalls.

In this chapter, we highlight two kinds of ethical issues:

- stereotyping, and how to minimize it
- how to deal with pressures to bend the ethics, pressures that you will encounter especially when using the MBTI in organizations

The chapter starts with a case problem of stereotyping. You have the choice of working on the problem first or skipping to the material on stereotyping that follows the case problem.

## Case problem: Stereotyping of the Thinking and Feeling preferences

Here is a stereotyping problem for you to work through. You are consulting with a work team of nine people. They took the Indicator, and you led them through six hours of orientation to the type concepts. You used several exercises, including the E–I exercise in which Extraverts form a group and identify what they admire about Introverts, and what it is that Introverts do that baffles them. Meanwhile, the Introvert group had the parallel discussion. When the E and I groups came together, they had

*Portions of this chapter are adapted by permission from *People Types and Tiger Stripes*, Third Edition, ©1993 Gordon Lawrence.

a very useful discussion of the two lists they made separately. The discussion helped them see some stereotyping they had been doing. They were pleased with the insights they got, helping them separate type from stereotype. In a later session with the same team, a session about communication issues, you find that the insights they had about E–I stereotyping don't seem to carry over to other aspects of type. You hear the following dialogue between team members.

A Feeling type says to the group, "Learning about the reality of type differences doesn't change the fact that most Thinking types strike me as cold and condescending when we work on a team problem together. When I say what I want to say about the topic we're working on, some T immediately seems to point out what's wrong with my idea, or at least tries to put a different spin on it—as if what I said was flawed and needed the T comment to fix it or put it in its place."

A Thinking type member of the team says, "I think you might be talking about me. Nothing personal, but I hate it when someone takes my comments as an attack. All I'm trying to do is clarify for me what I heard—to get it clearer in my head. And I don't see what's wrong with politely showing the logic or lack of logic in what someone else says."

Another Feeling type comes in: "Yeah, but when Thinking types 'clarify' they seem to do it in such a condescending way, as if we need coaching on how to speak our minds in a better way. They assume their 'logic' is superior, and often dismiss what we say as not serious, not 'logical,' and not worth a response."

And another Thinking type says, "OK, but it seems to me that Feeling types' ideas often come out in a fuzzy and roundabout way that needs some clarifying if the group is going to use the ideas. And they repeat things, sometimes two or three times, seeming to imply that I wasn't alert or smart enough to get it the first time."

"Of course we repeat things, reword them and say them differently, because you give us no clue that you heard them the first time," responds the same Feeling type.

As the consultant, you get the impression that this kind of dialogue will drag on and not turn constructive until you intervene. What will you do and say at this point to help them truly recognize the stereotypes and get past them to common understanding?

Here are four steps to follow.

1) First, identify the stereotypes in this situation, as fully as you can.

2) Next, decide what your specific goal(s) will be when you intervene.

3) Then, write out how you will intervene and the specific language you will use in dialogue with the team.

4) When you have completed these steps, take what you have written to a partner/colleague who is opposite you on the T–F preference.

 • Ask the person to look for any stereotypes you may be unconsciously using in your goal statement(s) or in your intervention scenario.

 • Ask the person also to tell how the Feeling types on the team are likely to react to your intervention, and how the Thinking types might react.

 • See if the two of you can edit the plan to make it more likely to succeed.

Before you start to write on the tasks just described, you may want to read the material that starts below. It will give you ideas about how stereotyping happens and how to help people get past it. You do need to read it, either before or after your writing.

After you have written your response to the case problem, you can compare your approach with the one we have written on page 181.

## Type and stereotype

STEREOTYPING IS A RISK that is always with all of us. We tend to stereotype those who are most different from ourselves because we understand them less—a rule that holds true for differences in type as well as for differences in culture, race, and other characteristics. For example, Extraverts may stereotypically project onto Introverts the awkwardness they themselves would feel when stuck without having something to say or some action to be involved in. The comfort the Introvert feels in reflection and silences may not occur to the Extravert.

The opposite projection, of course, is a risk for Introverts. Seeing the Extravert jump into a conversation with half-formed thoughts might cause the Introvert stereotypically to project onto the Extravert's behavior the rudeness and shallowness they themselves would feel guilty of if they had displayed the same behavior. The energy the Extravert gets from letting thoughts flow aloud with other people, and shaping the thoughts in dialogue, may not occur to the Introvert, whose choice would be to keep a thought inside and polish it until it is ready to be exposed.

MBTI users have a special responsibility to examine their own stereotypes and to teach about type in ways that minimize clients' stereotypical use of type concepts. How can we teach type concepts in an unbiased way if we are not aware of our own stereotypes?

**WHY DO WE STEREOTYPE?** Everyone has to sort life's experiences into categories to make sense of them. We can't deal with each experience as a unique event, so we categorize experiences to get mental order and comfort in our thought processes. Why do we stereotype when all we mean to do is have helpful labels for experience? In our drive for order and mental comfort, we tend to take shortcuts and to form poorly constructed categories that are too simple and biased.

**TYPE AND STEREOTYPE.** We who use type theory certainly want to avoid stereotyping the sixteen psychological types. No doubt most of us who use type were drawn to it because it gives us categories to think with that are vast improvements over the familiar unconstructive categories by which people sort each other. Our common goal is to give people more helpful categories to put in place of less helpful ones. Carl Jung, Katharine Briggs and Isabel Myers worked hard to select terms for psychological type that would avoid bias and minimize stereotyping. We continue that process. It surely is not a finished job.

*But we are all caught with our biases showing. Being an Intuitive type, my dominant Intuition colors and steers my perceptions in such a way that I cannot be sure that my views of the Sensing process or of Sensing types aren't stereotypes, at least in some respects. Time and again my Sensing friends have helped me see the stereotypes I was using. Type theory tells me that Sensing is my least developed mental process, and the most unconscious of my four mental processes. I believe it. Sensing just doesn't get much respect in the flow of my thought processes, so how can I expect it to assert itself and show up my stereotypes for what they are?*

*How wonderful to have some Sensing friends who help me break my stereotypes about Sensing! If I, who have been studying type for more than twenty years, unwittingly use language that stereotypes people when I talk about the types, what happens in the minds of those I teach, who first learn about type from me? Perhaps the stereotypes get embellished and hardened as they are passed on.*

*With Intuition and Thinking as my dominant and auxiliary mental processes, my Sensing and Feeling processes are less mature, less conscious, more worrisome, and less controllable and predictable when they come into my conscious life. So when people and situations call on my Feeling and Sensing processes, my shadowy and immature versions of these processes color my perceptions and give me an unconscious bias that results in stereotypes.*

*I am likely to see immaturity or threatening motives in those who are so different from myself, who remind me of the parts of myself I would rather keep hidden. So I project onto their behavior the dark meanings that come out of my shadowy side, and I have produced a stereotype.*

*Just as I am guilty of unfavorable stereotyping of people with type preferences different from my own, so I am guilty of favorable biases creeping into my language and thoughts about my own type preferences.*

— Gordon Lawrence

**IT HAPPENS TO ALL OF US.** None of us is immune from stereotyping. One person, very knowledgeable about type, and whose name we know well, wrote these descriptive phrases about Thinking types: "Thinking types…are relatively unemotional people and uninterested in people's feelings…[They] tend to relate well only to other Thinking types…[They] may seem hard-hearted…"

We all know *some* Thinking types who are accurately described by these phrases, but do you detect stereotyping here? These are Isabel Myers' words, from the 1962 *MBTI Manual*\* and from the first edition of *Introduction to Type*\*\*. They are part of the section called "Effects of each preference in work situations."

Isabel Myers was a very careful writer, to say the least. It is impossible to overstate the exquisite care she took in finding the right words for describing type—clear words that would not stereotype or have misleading connotations. Her perfectionism in writing is typified in the fact that the manuscript of *Gifts Differing*, her major writing about type, was essentially complete twenty years before publication. She would take it off the shelf every week or so to change a word.

Isabel Myers was a dominant Feeling type, an INFP. If stereotyping were to appear in her descriptions, where would it most likely be? It would be in her description of the mental process opposite her dominant, her least conscious process—Thinking. Several MBTI users with a preference for the Thinking process objected to the phrases and called them to her attention, and she changed them to read, "Thinking types…do not show emotion readily and are often uncomfortable dealing with people's feelings…[They] tend to be

---

\* Myers, I. B. (1962). *Manual: The Myers-Briggs Type Indicator. Princeton, NJ:* Educational Testing Service.
\*\*Myers, I. B. (1962). *Introduction to type* (1st ed.). Swarthmore, PA: Author.

firm-minded… " Later editions of the *Manual* and *Introduction to Type*, edited by others after Myers' death, show other changes in the descriptions of Thinking types.

Are these wording changes nit-picking? Not at all. Our job is to find and use language that reduces the risk of ourselves and our clients distorting type into stereotype.

**WATCHING OUR LANGUAGE.** What are some signs of stereotyping, some red flags, we can watch for in our language? Phrases containing absolutes, like "always" and "never," are suspect.

> "You can always count on Sensing types to…stuff envelopes…
> take minutes of the meeting"—an example of Intuitives relegating
> mundane tasks no one likes to do.

> "Never trust an NF with balancing a checkbook."

In dividing up jobs, some people who know a little about type are quick to assume that the decisions about who gets what jobs can be based on a superficial (stereotypical) look at type preferences, without other considerations such as familiarity, desire, skillfulness, etc.

> "We sure could use an ISTJ for this job…Ralph's an ISTJ,
> let's use him."

> "This committee is going to die if we don't get an Extravert on it."

Another sign of stereotyping is excusing one's behavior on the grounds of type.

> "I'm allowed to be spacey; I'm an Intuitive."

> "That's my J compulsiveness."

Any time stereotypes creep into the terms we use to describe and explain about the types, we are passing them along to those we teach about type— and chances are, the stereotypes will get more flagrant as our clients pass the language on to others.

**WHAT WE CAN DO.** Stereotyping in our conceptions and language about type is natural and inevitable, but we can guard against it and head it off—and we must if we are to grow.

- We can be alert to the spots where we ourselves are most vulnerable to stereotyping, which will differ for each of us as our types differ.
- We can be aware, those of us who use and teach others about type concepts, that we have in common a very big problem. In our enthusiasm, in our desire to convince people of the value of type, we overstate and over-generalize—a sure source of stereotyping.

- We can ask people whose preferences are opposite ours to help us spot our possible biases as we talk about type, and to suggest alternate, unbiased language.
- We can realize that improving our language about type requires an improvement in our understanding of our opposites, a deeper knowledge of type.
- And, finally, we can assume that the quest to drive out our stereotypes about type never ends.

We can help each other. Isabel Myers was known for the effective way she helped people improve their understanding of type by gently offering them a non-stereotyping word to replace a biased one they had used. She'd say, "I believe they'll understand better if you say…" or, "I used to say it that way until my ISTJ husband showed me a better wording…" In the same spirit, we can help each other.

HERE ARE OUR RESPONSES to the case problem. There will no doubt be other sound ways to approach it as well.

**1) IDENTIFY THE STEREOTYPES IN THE SITUATION.** The dialogue was heavy with stereotypes. The stereotyping terms the Feeling types used to characterize Thinking types were:
- cold and condescending
- immediately seems to point out what's wrong…flawed
- [assumed I] needed a T comment to fix it (my idea) or put it in its place
- 'clarify'…as if we need coaching on how to speak…
- assume their 'logic' is superior
- dismiss what we say as not serious
- give us no clue that you heard…

The stereotyping terms used by the Thinking types to characterize Feeling types were:
- takes my comments as an attack
- [Fs took offense at my] politely showing the logic or lack of logic…
- Fs' ideas often come out fuzzy
- imply that I wasn't alert or smart enough to get it the first time.

**2) DECIDE WHAT THE SPECIFIC GOAL(S) WILL BE WHEN YOU INTERVENE.**
- Get team members to start talking about the assets of the Thinking and Feeling ways of mental processing.
- Help them see the stereotypes as defensive reactions that emphasize differences and obscure the common ground.

## Our approach to the case problem: Stereotyping of the Thinking and Feeling preferences

- Help them devise some language, perhaps some code words, which they can use in their work to trigger a *focus on the positive values* in the T–F differences, when the differences show up.

**3) DEVISE AN INTERVENTION PLAN WITH SPECIFIC LANGUAGE.** Here's our suggestion for one way to approach the problem. The consultant is talking. "Let's take a few minutes to talk about the dialogue that just took place. We heard about the irritations we feel in the differences between the styles of mental processing of Thinking types and Feeling types. We certainly spotted irritations. How about the plus side…what would we identify as the *assets* of the Thinking way and the Feeling way of reasoning? Let's do it individually first, as we did in the Extraversion and Introversion activity the last time we met. Remember it? Thinking types, please take five minutes to write down the assets of the Feeling process or what you admire about Feeling types. And Feeling types likewise write down the assets of the Thinking process or what you admire about Thinking types."

"…Now let's hear what you wrote and discuss it a little. Let's start with assets of the Feeling types…" The consultant guides the dialogue, getting agreement on statements of assets and checking with Feeling types to get their perception on what is said about the Feeling process.

Then the consultant says, "Now let's look at the terms used to describe Feeling types when we were talking earlier about what irritates us. I jotted down some of the language…(reads from stereotype list). In light of the assets we just listed for the Feeling process, can we see how the irritations might happen?" The consultant guides the discussion of the Feeling stereotypes and then steers it onto the assets of Thinking types and the T stereotype list.

The consultant's job here is to help team members see that the people of the opposite preference, T or F, aren't intentionally irritating us. The Thinking types, for example, instinctively clarify—not to annoy, but to get things said in a precise way, because they value precision. The Feeling types who don't yet appreciate type differences may get annoyed because the T's aim for precision seems to be criticizing the F's way of saying something.

Similarly, Feeling types explain things in a way that can be less direct than a Thinking type prefers—not to annoy, but because they value getting a complete picture that shows the interconnection of people and events. Thinking types value a linear, impersonal way of reasoning, and when they don't yet appreciate type differences, they may dismiss the more inclusive explanation as "fuzzy-minded" rather than seeing the value that the F speaker added to the dialogue.

This is a good point for the consultant to call attention to two resources the clients received earlier:

1) The word lists in *Looking at Type* (by Earle Page). Look at the pairs of words used to characterize the Thinking and Feeling preferences on page 27 (see also the *Key Words* listed in Chapter Six of this guide).

The consultant points out the pairing of words on the list and helps the team members identify the reasons for the words to be paired as they are. For example, *critique* and *appreciate*. These represent two contrasting ways to help a situation. The T way of making improvements is through impersonal, critical analysis— pointing to something specific that needs to be fixed. The F way of making improvements is to show appreciation for what is right in the situation so that the person whose job it is to make the improvement will feel personally encouraged, understood and supported in doing the needed job. Neither way is wrong. People who appreciate type differences know the benefits of each way. They can avoid being annoyed by the differences. More about that later.

2) The booklet, *Descriptions of the Sixteen Types*. Start with page 2.

The consultant points out three features:

- The bulleted parts of the type descriptions are *values* associated with each of the types.

- Opposite types are across from each other on the same page. This arrangement helps us see the contrasting values between opposite types.

- The contrasts suggest the kinds of stereotypes that can easily happen. For example, within the ENTJ and ISFP descriptions are listed the contrasting values of "Foresight; pursuing a vision" (ENTJ) and "Finding delight in the moment" (ISFP). When someone is deeply absorbed in a future vision, what's being neglected? The present moment. A person who highly values the quality of the present moment and how to improve the moment can easily fall into an attitude of seeing dark motives in someone who regularly neglects the present to give energy to shaping the future, and vice versa. That kind of projection of motives is the root of stereotypes of the psychological types. Those people who neglect the values we care about are the ones we most likely will stereotype as immature or having bad motives.

The consultant asks the team members to:

- find the page with their type description on it
- read the description and the one opposite
- identify five or six stereotypes they could easily attach to their opposite type, if they weren't careful
- share with the other members one of the stereotypes they have to guard against

If you are working through this guide with other people, we suggest you use the activity above as a group.

Finally, in your intervention plan for the case study clients, you may want to include something to help them when they have a negative (stereotyping) reaction to the words or actions of their opposite—in this case, Thinking or Feeling. Here is a mental gimmick to focus them on the *positive* values of the Thinking and Feeling mental processes. When one co-worker says or does something that triggers a negative reaction based on type differences, the other team member can call to mind *The Four As*: Alert, Acknowledge/Appreciate, Accept, and Ask.

**Alert:** Recognize your negative reaction, your irritation, when it happens.

**Acknowledge/Appreciate:** Look for the possible positive meaning of the irritating statement or action, and acknowledge to yourself or aloud the potential value of it.

**Accept:** Accept the statement or action *as if* it were positive and helpful.

**Ask:** Ask the co-worker to say more to help your understanding.

**Exercise:**

**Identifying
stereotypes in
the terms we use**

Stereotypes creep into the terms we use to talk about type. To be effective—especially with people whose type preferences differ from ours—we need to spot the stereotypes and root them out. We never fully succeed, but we need to keep trying. (You may want to use this activity with some of your client groups. If you suppose you may use it sometime, work through it yourself now.)

This is a group activity—first with pairs, then two sets of pairs, and then with the whole group. It can be used with any of the type preference pairs: E–I, S–N, T–F or J–P. Pick one of the pairs. We will illustrate with E–I. There are three tasks.

**DIRECTIONS:**

1) Each participant will team up with another participant whose E–I preference is the same. After they are sitting together, each of the participants individually will bring to mind someone he or she knows well whose E–I preference is opposite his or her preference, and write a few words about that person. Each Extravert participant, for example, will think of an Introvert he or she knows well and write down four or five words or phrases that accurately describe the Introverting characteristics of the person, taking care to use unbiased descriptors. Using the same care, the partners in each Introvert pair will individually use the same process to identify the Extraverting characteristics of their sample Extravert. Allow three or four minutes for this step.

2) Next, the partners will discuss the words they wrote individually and edit them as needed to replace words that might be seen as stereotyping. Schedule five minutes or more for this step. The job for the Etravert pairs is to produce a list of terms that work to give unbiased descriptors for Introverting—one list of terms they agree are unbiased.

3) Finally, each pair of Extraverts will get with a pair of Introverts to present both sets of descriptors, to discuss any stereotyping suggested in the two lists, and to find unbiased replacement words. In your discussion, you will find more stereotyping than you suppose. The foursome's job is to produce one list of E and I terms that all four participants agree are unbiased. If time permits, all the foursomes can report their lists to the others.

After the discussion, we believe you'll agree with us that stereotyping is natural and inevitable. We have to be on our guard to minimize it.

**IDENTIFYING STEREOTYPES IN OUR DESCRIPTIONS OF TYPE PREFERENCES.**

Sometimes when we use the activity you just read, *Identifying stereotypes in the terms we use*, we take the foursomes' lists of E and I words and combine them into one composite list. Some words appear on several lists. On one recent occasion, these were the Extravert and Introvert descriptors on two or more lists:

| Extravert | Introvert |
|-----------|-----------|
| • active | • thoughtful |
| • open | • quiet |
| • talkative | • reserved |
| • sociable | • shy |
| • outgoing | • serious |
| • friendly | • deep |

As a whole group, we examined these words and others on the lists looking for stereotypes or terms that could lead to misunderstanding. We applied **three stereotype-detecting criteria** to each term:

1) Does the term *raise a red flag*, suggesting *bias for or against*? The words listed above did not seem biased to the participants, but others on the composite lists raised red flags very quickly: for example, "superficial" and "entertaining" on the Extravert list, and "loner" and "quiet assurance" on the Introvert list. We all knew people for whom the words were accurate, but we all agreed the terms applied to special cases and not the general categories of Extraversion and Introversion.

2) Could the term be misleading by implying a *negative opposite characteristic* for people of the other preference? We decided this criterion eliminated most of the twelve words listed above. For example, using "active" for Extraverts could imply "passive" or "inactive" as characteristics of Introverts; "open" could imply "closed"; using "thoughtful" for Introverts could imply "thoughtless" or "unthinking" as a characteristic of Extraverts; and "quiet" could imply "loud" or "noisy" for its opposite. Each time we use this activity, participants come to the conclusion that *explicitly stating the opposite you intend* is important to avoid misunderstanding, so it helps to generate the words in pairs. For example, "active" and "reflective" are a good pair, as are "outgoing" and "reserved," and "expressive" and "quiet." By finding good pairs, we returned most of the twelve words to the list.

But good pairs were hard to agree on, and our "good" lists never get very long.

3) Does it *distinguish between the preferences*, or could it be applied also to the opposite or *other preferences*? We decided that "friendly" didn't distinguish between Extravert and Introvert. And some Extraverts regarded themselves as "shy," so those words were eliminated. Also eliminated were "open" and "thoughtful" because they were not distinctive to Extravert or Introvert. Four out of five words on the composite lists are not mentioned above; they were eliminated, mainly because they did not meet this criterion—words such as "lively," "people-oriented," "enthusiastic," "expansive," "careful," "brief," "self-encouraged" and "discreet." They were dropped because they could apply to more than one of the eight preferences that make up the types.

This activity always has the effect of making participants alert to the need for care in choosing descriptors for the type preferences. They uniformly speak of it as a powerful learning experience, and it makes them appreciate the carefully chosen lists of word pairs that are in some of the resources on type. Very good lists are included in *Looking at Type*. Turn to the Extravert/Introvert lists on page 11 and compare them with the ones produced in the example given above. We ourselves use these *Looking at Type* word pairs when explaining type to people and we recommend them to others. Stay with the tried and true terms.

## Avoiding ethical pitfalls

**HOW DO I RECOGNIZE ETHICAL PROBLEMS?** When you use the MBTI with groups and organizations, you will *often* experience pressures to bend the ethics. It helps to be prepared with a clear view of what to do when the pressure comes. In this section are brief descriptions of a dozen situations, all of them real, which raise typical ethical decisions encountered when using the MBTI. Read the situations and ask yourself how you would respond to them.

Following the twelve problems are our responses—compare ours with yours. In many situations, there is more than one ethical alternative. The solution, however it is resolved, should follow ethical guidelines. To help you, we have included here a summary of the ethical guidelines adopted by the Association for Psychological Type (APT), the membership association of MBTI practitioners. One of the main reasons APT was formed was to develop and support principled, ethical uses of the Indicator. You may want to read these guidelines before you take on the problems we have given you.

At the end of this chapter you will also find a list of ethical guidelines developed at CAPT that can be followed when administering and interpreting the Indicator. Those guidelines address some scenarios commonly faced by the MBTI practitioner.

## ETHICAL GUIDELINES FOR USING THE MBTI

The Association for Psychological Type has adopted a statement of ethical principles for using the MBTI. The most basic ones are condensed here.

**VOLUNTARY.** The client has the choice of taking the MBTI or not. Even subtle pressure should be avoided. In situations where the success of using type depends on every member trying out the ideas of type, as in teams or families, offer the MBTI to all members, score it for those who choose to take it, and then provide a group type explanation to all, including anyone who didn't take it. After the explanation and during introductory activities, those who didn't take the instrument are almost always willing to hypothesize a type for themselves and may ask to take the MBTI.

**Confidential.** The practitioner gives the MBTI results directly to the person and not to anyone else. An individual's type does not go to the boss or into a personnel file unless he or she offers to give the information. People are usually comfortable talking about their type, but the MBTI outcome is theirs to reveal or not.

**Enhances, does not restrict.** MBTI results and type concepts are used only to enhance someone's understanding and opportunities, not to restrict their options. The career counselor, for example, does not counsel a client away from a particular occupation because his or her type is rare in that occupation. The counselor instead provides information in the context of discussing opportunities and challenges of that career in relation to the strengths of the client's type.

**Face-to-face explanation.** The MBTI respondent always gets a face-to-face explanation of type from the practitioner. He or she always has an opportunity for dialogue about the results and for exploring the ideas to find a best-fit type. For that reason they never get their results through the mail or secondhand.

**Full type description.** The respondent always gets a full type description to accompany the MBTI scored results. Always give them a type resource booklet that includes not only a full description of their reported type, but also all the other types—which some may want to explore to find a better fit. We use *Looking at Type: The Fundamentals, Introduction to Type,* or *Descriptions of the Sixteen Types.* Respondents need good resource materials in their hands when they are later considering type or explaining it to family or colleagues.

**What's indicated, what's not.** In explaining MBTI results and the type concepts, the practitioner needs to distinguish between what the Indicator indicates and what it does not: type characteristics are tendencies, not imperatives; they are preferences, not abilities or achievement potential; and they represent one view of personality, not a complete picture. And the MBTI indicates types, not stereotypes.

## Exercise:

## What do I do in this situation?

**DIRECTIONS:** Write a brief statement of how you would handle each of the twelve situations. You can check your responses with ours, listed at the end.

1) **The boss's expectations.** Your arrangements are complete for introducing type concepts to the management level personnel of a manufacturing company, including the boss. You have their MBTI results and have arrived to start the workshop. The boss, who knows something about type, asks you for a copy of the managers' MBTI results, saying, "It will help me tune into them better."

➤ You say: "Tuning into each other better is what it's all about. But it is my job to give people's MBTI results directly and only to them. It is their decision to tell others their type, if they want to."

➤ The boss replies: "I understand. But I do know about type, and I *am* paying for this."

➤ You say…

2) **The absent participant.** One of the workshop participants has an emergency and leaves before you hand out the MBTI results. At the end of the session, a colleague of hers offers to take the MBTI printout to her.

➤ You say: "Thanks for your thoughtful offer. But I'm bound by the ethical rule of giving each person her results directly."

➤ The participant replies: "It's really OK. I'm her best friend."

➤ You say…

3) **The sophomore class.** You are working with a high school. More than 90% of the sophomore class has taken the Indicator and received the MBTI results, and you have shown them how study style may be improved by understanding one's type. Their teachers have also learned about their own types, and you showed them how to use type concepts to improve instruction. The assistant principal wants to have each student's type entered into his or her computer record.

➤ He says: "With that in the record, a teacher can look up the file on a student and get some idea of the learning style to take into account with that student."

➤ You say…

**4) Fix this guy.** The leader of a work team has approached you to help the team with its members' communication. Several members get on each other's nerves a lot. They have heard about the MBTI and want you to teach them about type. Later, after working out the arrangements, you learn from the leader that one team member refuses to take the Indicator.

➤ The team leader says: "Could you please explain to him individually that the MBTI gives only positive results? He *is* the main problem in the team, and we do want this workshop mainly for his benefit. There isn't any point in doing the MBTI workshop if he doesn't participate. Would you try persuading him?"

➤ You say…

**5) Filling the vacancy.** You are working with an organization that consists of four teams. While they are learning about type, one person from team B comes to you with a question.

➤ She says: "The five people on our team get along just great and we work so smoothly together. But we do miss deadlines sometimes and have a hard time getting closure. We just figured out that we all have a P preference. No Js on our team. One of our members is leaving next month. What would you think about our asking the boss if we could be in on the hiring so we can get a J on the team?"

➤ You say…

**6) Finding a Feeling type.** The CEO of the organization, conversant with type, wants you to use the MBTI to help find the right person to head the customer relations department.

➤ The CEO says: "I believe we really need to get a Feeling type, an Extravert with Feeling, into this job. Ideally, an ESFJ. Up and down the line, the company has to improve its customer focus—so we need an F orientation in customer relations. Can we set up a candidate search that includes their taking the MBTI?"

➤ You Say…

7) **May I borrow a copy?** You have finished introducing a group to type. A participant comes to you.

➤ He says: "I know my wife will be *very* interested in taking the MBTI. May I take a copy of the self-scorable MBTI home to her? I have all these materials you gave me."

➤ You say…

8) **Over the phone?** A friend and colleague of yours, someone you have known since college days, has learned that you are a qualified MBTI user, and wants to take it. The friend is in another state.

➤ She asks: "Isn't there some way we can do this long distance?"

➤ You say…

9) **Tight budget.** You are arranging to introduce type to employees of a social service agency. Your contact person says they want to start using type for better staff communication.

➤ He says: "But we're on a very tight budget. What's the minimum material we'll need? Can we just use a couple of copies to pass around?"

➤ You say…

10) **Subtle pressure.** The owner-manager of a store wants you to introduce type to her employees. She had a type explanation earlier. She volunteers to hand out the Indicator booklets and answer sheets herself, to save you a trip. You tell her about the importance of your being there to set the right conditions for taking the MBTI: voluntary participation, no right or wrong answers, etc.

➤ She says: "Oh, I understand about the voluntary part, and the other conditions. But I'm sure all of my employees will want to take it when I explain its usefulness."

➤ You say…

11) **Face-to-face?** The dean of a college wants to use the MBTI with incoming freshmen, for two purposes: institutional research on such things as retention and choice of majors; and to introduce students to learning style differences. She wants all incoming freshmen to take the MBTI and two other instruments after they have been admitted to the college.

➤ She says: "I'd like your advice. I want to use all the freshman class type results in the research and keep them in the data bank until after the class graduates. What's the ethical and legal way of doing that? And I want the students to get their own results and get suggestions about type and learning style. Do they need a face-to-face explanation, or can we do something useful through the mail?"

➤ You say…

12) **Before and after.** A friend of yours is planning a training program for human services professionals. The program is called Empathic Facilitation. Your friend believes that Feeling and Extraversion, as identified by the MBTI, would be predictive of skillfulness in empathic facilitation. He wants you to administer the MBTI to participants before and after the training to see if the E and F scores are raised. He would take such a change as a measure of the participants' growth in the target skills.

➤ You say…

Exercise:

Our solutions to
the 12 ethics
problems

1) **The boss's expectations.** You say: "I think you want to have the managers' *true sense* of the type that fits them best. The MBTI may or may not report the best-fit type. Some people have to read or talk about the types before they can decide if the MBTI reported type is the one. My experience tells me they will be enthusiastic about the type concepts and will readily let their type be known in the workshop activities. If you had a boss in the workshop, wouldn't you rather have your boss learn about your type in that way?"

   **Ethical principles: confidentiality; respondent decides best-fit type.**

2) **The absent participant.** You say: "We give the MBTI results directly to people so they have a chance to ask any questions to clarify their understanding of what it reports. I'd appreciate your telling her I'll arrange to have a conversation with her individually. Would you do that?"

   **Ethical principle: the opportunity for dialogue.**

3) **The sophomore class.** You say: "That really might help some teachers who take type seriously. But you need to have a written permission statement from a student before you enter his or her type in the record."

   **Ethical principle: confidentiality.**

4) **Fix this guy.** You say: "Chances are, he suspects you regard him as the problem member of the team. So, he is not likely to change his mind just because I ask him. Even if we did 'persuade' him to take the Indicator, what's the likelihood he'll respond to the MBTI questions in a straightforward way? People taking the Indicator have to want to give answers that truly represent themselves. But there is a simple solution to this. We'll have the workshop, with everyone attending. Because it is on company time, he'll be there. You should not announce to the others that anyone chose not to take the MBTI. At the workshop, I will first explain the type concepts, have people guess how their type will come out, and then return their MBTI results. Then we will form type-alike groups to examine how type affects our communication processes. People will join a group according to their best estimate of their type. He can do that too. Almost invariably, at break or lunch time, the people who chose not to take the Indicator come up to me and ask if I brought any MBTI materials along so they can take it."

   **Ethical principle: voluntary response to the MBTI.**

5) **Filling the vacancy.** You say: "Trying to get a new member whose instincts are for having closure and meeting deadlines sounds like a great idea. Finding the right candidate by using the MBTI is not a good idea, because it shouldn't be used to screen candidates. You remember taking the Indicator; if you wanted to, say in a hiring situation, you could fake your answers in the direction you thought would get you hired. How about this. Your team can help write the job description and the interview questions to emphasize deadline and closure skills, be part of the interview process, and see if you can attract the right person that way. After all, you are looking for skills and not just a personality preference." (Note: Their new hire turned out to be a J.)

**Ethical principle: the MBTI is not used to screen or limit people, but to enhance their functioning.**

6) **Finding a Feeling type.** You say: "The MBTI was not designed as a screening tool. Respondents can fake their answers to the items to give themselves a profile in the direction they think the employer wants. There's one sound and ethical way to use the MBTI for screening. You get the services of a consulting psychologist who administers to applicants a battery of instruments, including the MBTI. The psychologist folds the MBTI results into a composite profile. You get the profiles, without specific MBTI results, and you can use them in the selection process. Tell the psychologist the kinds of skills and traits you are looking for; don't tell the MBTI type you are looking for."

**Ethical principles: don't use the MBTI to screen; it does not report skills.**

7) **May I borrow a copy?** You say: "I hope she is interested. Being able to talk about type differences and similarities is a real plus. There are two reasons why I can't loan you a copy to take home. The MBTI is what's called a 'controlled' instrument, and I have to hang on to them. Also, each time I administer the MBTI to a person, I have to be there to explain the concepts and be available to answer questions the person may have. Maybe your group would want to sponsor an MBTI session for spouses."

**Ethical principles: confidentiality; face-to-face administration; control restricted materials.**

**Exercise:**

**Our solutions to the 12 ethics problems**

8) **Over the phone?** You say: "The ethics of using the MBTI include having a person-to-person session with anyone who takes the Indicator. Because we know each other well, I think the spirit of the ethics would be met if we substituted a phone conversation. I'll send you the MBTI booklet and answer sheet. Send them both back when you're done and I'll score your answers. I'll send you some materials to read, and when you have read them we'll talk." (The person-to-person guideline should be followed, with no exceptions—a face-to-face session is preferable. Sending the MBTI booklet and answer sheet through the mail does not compromise the scoring codes because, unlike the self-scorable version, they contain no scoring key.)
**Ethical principle: person-to-person administration, with dialogue.**

9) **Tight budget.** You say: "At a minimum, everyone needs to have a full description of all the sixteen types. Here are the options (describe them). Using *Descriptions of the Sixteen Types* is the least expensive way to go. You should have a reference copy of other resources that people can check out. I'll bring them and explain them to the group, and you can tell them how to borrow them."
**Ethical principle: everyone should get a full description of the sixteen types, to use in finding or confirming the best-fit type.**

10) **Subtle pressure.** You say: "Thanks for offering to do that. In most cases, it is not a good idea for the boss to hand out the MBTI materials and explain the purpose of taking the Indicator. Some people are wary of any psychological instrument, and others may assume the boss has a hidden motive. In any such cases, the employee may consciously or unconsciously be defensive and not give straight answers to the Indicator questions. It is really best that the MBTI practitioner do it. They also need to know that I will be giving their MBTI results only to them, and they have the choice of telling others their results, or not."
**Ethical principle: voluntary responding.**

11) **Face-to-face?** You say: "The MBTI has been very successfully used in such ways, and I certainly support you in this. It is OK to send the MBTI question booklets and answer sheets to them in the mail, so long as a good explanatory letter goes with them. You also must have the student's written permission to use his or her MBTI results in the research and to put the reported type in the student's records, so I'll include a form for that."

"Students should not get MBTI results through the mail. You will need to set up face-to-face meetings for that. What other colleges have done successfully is to notify students about scheduled times in the new term when they can come to an MBTI explanation session and get their results. If they can't get to one of the sessions, they have the option of an individual session with a college counselor who is qualified in using the MBTI. In the case of students who don't come, you can still use their MBTI results in the research if you have their written permission."

**Ethical principle: when you give MBTI results, you give a face-to-face explanation.**

12) **Before and after.** Your friend has an inaccurate view of the MBTI. You say: "The MBTI does not measure the strength of skills. It identifies mental preferences. A preference for Extraversion, for example, is not an indication of *skillfulness* in extraverting. For a before-and-after measurement, you need a skill-based instrument, not the MBTI."

**Ethical principle: use the Indicator only for what it was designed to do.**

## Exercise:

### How would you handle these client questions?

Now you've had some experience with some of the different kinds of ethical issues that can arise in using the MBTI. You learn to respond to ethical issues by being in the middle of them, and by applying your knowledge and the ethical principles. We'd like to close this chapter with an exercise. Use the questions to test your grasp of a few more of the stereotyping and ethical issues you are likely to encounter. Our responses follow.

**DIRECTIONS:** Here are seven questions typical of those you may be asked by your clients. The questions have stereotypes or misconceptions in them. What will you say to the client in each instance to help the person form a better conception of type? After you jot down your answers, you can compare them with our answers that follow.

1) I live with my sister. She's P off the wall! Do you have any suggestions for living with a super-P?

2) How effective is it to use the MBTI in selecting among applicants for a job? Under what conditions would you recommend using it in the screening process?

3) Why do Feeling types say things over and over when one time is enough?

4) I have a co-worker who acts like a real ESTJ. Can you give me clues about how to get along with her?

5) Why do Extraverts always seem to monopolize conversations?

6) My wife took the MBTI once before and wants to take it again. She won't be here for our meeting. Can I take an extra answer sheet home for her, have you score it, and take the results to her?

7) When I took the MBTI before, my counselor said I probably shouldn't go into engineering because I'm an ESFP. Does that sound right to you?

**Exercise:**

**Our answers to the seven questions**

1) "Super-P" sister.

➤ You say: "What is it she does that leads you to say she's a super-P?"

➤ Likely reply: "She'll put a job aside before finishing and start some thing else that catches her interest. She doesn't live by a schedule."

➤ You say: "She'll leave one interest to move to another, and doesn't seem to follow a plan, and you prefer to have a plan in place and stick to it, right?"

➤ Reply: "Right."

➤ You say: "If she came out P on the MBTI, it means her way of mental processing is to have her perceiving process run her outer life, not her judging process. She gets energized for life's business by the surges of curiosity that come to her; that's her perceiving process in action. You get energized by having a plan and completing things in your plan, right?"

➤ Reply: "Yes."

➤ You say: "The MBTI indicates preferred ways of processing experiences, not good or bad habits, or skills. When two people have differences in their MBTI types, such as J and P, they may annoy each other. The ideas behind the MBTI can help them see that annoyances that come up are probably not intentional and they can use the differences constructively, drawing on each other's strengths. I expect that you and your sister can use the type descriptions to help negotiate ways to manage your living together. Let me show you a couple of things in this booklet..."

2) **Using the MBTI to screen applicants.** We suggest a response similar to the one given to ethics problem six in the previous activity, under the heading, *Our solutions to the twelve ethics problems.*

**3) Why do Feeling types...?** The question is probably one a person with a Thinking preference would ask.

➤ You say: "Here, look with me at the Thinking and Feeling word lists in this booklet, *Looking at Type* (page 27). You see that *precise* and *persuasive* are paired. The terms relate to your question of why Feeling types 'say things over and over when one time is enough.' Thinking types try to report their judgments in terms of impersonal analysis (see those words also on the list), and *precise* statements are something they value. Feeling types, on the other hand, aim to state their judgments in terms that show the caring, personal reasoning they have been doing (see word list), and *persuasive* statements are important to them. A Feeling type is likely to answer your question about 'saying something over and over' with this sort of response: 'When I am telling you about my judgments and you don't show any personal signs of agreement or understanding, I assume you don't get what I'm saying, and I need to rephrase or repeat it with more emotion—use more *persuasive* language—to connect with you. Show me we are on the same wave length and I'll only need to say a thing once.'"

**4) "Acts like a real ESTJ."**

➤ You say: "How does your co-worker act?"

➤ Likely reply: "She is so different from me. Anything I say or do she takes differently from what I intended. She seems very abrupt, and doesn't take much time to process things."

➤ You say: "Chances are, her MBTI type probably is very different from yours. Do you know her MBTI results?"

➤ Reply: "No."

➤ You say: "When someone's type is very different from one's own, it is harder to read the person's motives and meanings. And we run the risk of stereotyping the person, sometimes seeing negative motives when none are there. A good rule is to try to figure out the motivation and values of the person by looking at the type description you suppose fits the person. For instance, let's look at the ESTJ description in *Descriptions of the Sixteen Type*s. These descriptions highlight the values and motivations of the types. Do you recognize her in the description? Try a couple more descriptions too. Now read the description for your own type. Can you spot some contrasts? Can you find some ideas to answer your question of 'how to get along with her…?'"

**5) Extraverts monopolize…?**

➤ You say: "You experience some people as talking too much and not waiting for others to contribute to the conversation?"

➤ Likely reply: "Yes."

➤ You say: "Some Extraverts monopolize conversations, and some are very good listeners. The fact that they are Extraverts says nothing about how good they are at talking with people. When you say, 'Why do Extraverts always…,' it comes across as a stereotype, and that's not helpful. We also should not assume that all monopolizers are Extraverts."

"When long pauses start to happen in a conversation, Extraverts do tend to get uncomfortable and feel they must fill the 'void.' They assume that because they get uncomfortable with silences, everyone else does, too. Without knowing about the differences between Introversion and Extraversion, they aren't aware that Introverts appreciate the pauses as time to polish their thoughts before having to express them."

**6) Take it home to my wife?** You'll want to give an answer similar to that in ethics problem seven in the previous activity.

➤ You say: "The MBTI is a controlled instrument and I have to keep hold of the materials. I also have to give a face-to-face explanation of the MBTI results to respond to any questions the person may have. Even people who have taken it before will have issues to discuss, especially if their MBTI report shows a different type."

7) **I probably shouldn't go into engineering?** What the counselor actually said, we don't know. It is wrong to tell someone they shouldn't do something because of their type.

➤ You say: "It is a very good idea to take your type into account when making career decisions, such as deciding on a college major. Here is a book, *Looking at Type and Careers,* that tells about career choices and type. Among other things, it lists, by type, the careers that are most chosen and least chosen by people of that type. Have you read the materials about ESFP, and are you fairly sure that ESFP is the type that fits you best?"

➤ Likely reply: "Yes, it really describes me."

➤ You say: "OK, as you can see in the book, ESFPs choose a lot of careers ahead of engineering. That does not mean engineering would be a bad choice for you. Your job is to look at the kinds of courses you'll be taking in an engineering major, see if those are subjects that will energize you, and consider what makes engineering attractive to you. If you do decide to pursue engineering, you can anticipate that the large majority of your fellow engineers will not be your type, and you may be doing engineering from a different angle or in a new niche because of your type. By the way, you are more likely to find students with a Feeling preference in environmental engineering than in other engineering specialties."

## Conclusion

As you clearly recognize by now, there is no one right answer to any given scenario you may face. A dilemma wouldn't be a dilemma if it were easy to solve! If you recall the issues raised in this chapter, and if you keep the ethical guidelines in mind as you approach your work with the MBTI, you will be well on your way to the ethical and appropriate use of the Indicator.

## CAPT Code of Ethics

The following ethical guidelines have been compiled by the Center for Applications of Psychological Type to be followed when using the Myers-Briggs Type Indicator.

### Confidentiality in Administering and Providing Results

1) Results should be given directly into the hands of the respondent, whether as an individual or part of a group. A general explanation of the preferences and theory should be given in a face-to-face setting. Results should not be given in impersonal ways such as through the mail. Results should be available only to the respondent unless specific permission has been given to provide the information to a third person. Each person will decide for himself/herself whether or not to reveal his/her type preferences to others.

2) The respondent should be informed in advance of the purpose of taking the instrument and how the results will be used. Taking the instrument is always voluntary. The information is not to be used to label, evaluate, or limit any individual in any way.

3) The respondent should be given an opportunity to clarify their indicated type with the administrator. Each respondent should be provided a written description of their indicated type and preferably a written description of all sixteen types.

4) In using the instrument for research purposes only, it is not necessary to provide individual results to the respondents. However, providing feedback as an option for those requesting it is encouraged.

5) Providing feedback to the individual and/or group is intended to enhance rather than to limit or restrict the functioning of the individual or group.

6) The Indicator should be used according to the instructions on the booklet and in the *Manual*.

7) Specific questions should not be taken from the Indicator to get a "quick reading" on a particular type preference.

8) The Indicator should be used with appropriate populations and results used as suggested in the *Manual*.

### Interpreting MBTI Results

1) The administrator must use terms and descriptors that are non-judgmental and describe type attributes as tendencies, preferences, or inclinations rather than as absolutes. Biased terms may slant interpretation or send messages that a particular preference is "good" or "not desirable."

2) The administrator should be careful not to overgeneralize or oversimplify results and imply that all people or a certain type behave the same way.

3) One should not state or imply that type explains everything. Type does not reflect an individual's ability, intelligence, likelihood of success, emotions, or normalcy. Type is one important component of the complex human personality.

4) The administrator should not impose the results on the respondent nor become defensive if the respondent disagrees with the reported results or does not believe they are accurate. One should explore the perceived differences and help the respondent to be comfortable with themselves.

5) Administrators need to be aware of, and sensitive to, their own type biases and exert every effort to present feedback in an objective way.

6) It is unethical and in many cases illegal to require job applicants to take the Indicator if the results will be used to screen out applicants. The administrator should not counsel a person to, or away from, a particular career, personal relationship or activity based solely upon type information.

7) Administrators should accurately represent their competence and experience to clients.

8) Administrators should continually upgrade their knowledge of the Indicator and advances in the understanding and application of type through education (workshops, seminars, conferences), reading, or other means.

9) Administrators should provide the respondent with materials that describe all sixteen types.

Developed at CAPT and used with permission

**Resources**

Lawrence, G.D. (1993). *People types and tiger stripes* (3rd ed.). Gainesville, FL: Center for Applications of Psychological Type—Chapter 5 ("Type is a four-letter word") covers uses and abuses of MBTI.

Martin, C. R. (1998, April). Unethical MBTI use: What do I do? *TypeWorks,* Issue 22, 5.

Myers, I. B. with Myers, P. B. (1995). *Gifts differing: Understanding personality type*. Palo Alto, CA: Davies-Black Publishing.

Myers, I. B., McCaulley, M. H., Quenk, N. L., & Hammer, A. L. (1998). *MBTI Manual: A guide to the development and use of the Myers-Briggs Type Indicator* (3rd ed.). Palo Alto, CA: Consulting Psychologists Press.

Page, E. C. (1998). *Looking at type* (4th ed.). Gainesville, FL: Center for Applications of Psychological Type.

The Association for Psychological Type's (APT) ethical principles are reproduced in the Winter 1995 volume of the *Bulletin of Psychological Type*. That volume also has several articles on ethical issues in type use.

*That exercise we did on problem solving was really useful. How does it go?*

*What do I do and say when I am facilitating an exercise?*

*What are some good exercises that type trainers have found useful?*

*Where do I go to find more exercises?*

# Chapter 10

**ASSUMPTIONS UNDERLYING THIS CHAPTER.** We all know that adult learners appreciate good exercises that call on them to reflect on prior experiences in light of new experiences introduced in the exercise. As trainers or teachers, we all know that *some* learning objectives are best reached through exercises. We also suppose that psychological type is one of those topics that can best be grasped through experiencing it in interactions with people of differing types, in situations such as small group exercises. The material in this final chapter can play a critical part in our goals of developing people and building effective training programs.

This chapter includes four sets of resources:

- examples of three exercises, with in-depth commentary on how to get solid understanding about type from each exercise
- hints for facilitating group exercises
- sample type exercises that have a wide variety of applications
- further resources for well-tested exercises used by type trainers

## KINDS OF EXERCISES TO USE IN TEACHING ABOUT TYPE.

**Why exercises?** The reality, scope and power of psychological type theory do not register with people until they look at life through the lens of type and re-examine their experiences from this fresh perspective. More bluntly, most people are not really open to the concepts of type until they recognize the reality of type in their own, personal experience. That's why exercises are so important when you are introducing people to type. Well-chosen exercises get people to look through the new lens.

**Objectives.** To match exercises to the teaching of type, MBTI users must first be clear about the instructional objectives the exercises are to serve. We suggest five major objectives to keep in focus and use as quality criteria as you select or develop exercises.

1) *Clarify the nature* of the type preferences, and *show contrasts* between the preferences.

2) *Establish the credibility* of type; establish in people the conviction that the different types and preferences are real and pervasive, not trivial or superficial.

3) Help people experience the *value and necessity* of the contrasting type differences.

4) Help people recognize and learn to manage the *strengths and blind spots* of their type and other people's types.

5) Show people how type can be used to dramatically improve the effectiveness of a range of human endeavors:

- problem solving—gathering data and making sound judgments
- communication processes
- developing relationships
- teamwork
- management and leadership development
- teaching and learning
- self-understanding and personal development
- career decisions

**The first two objectives**—clarifying the nature of and showing contrasts between the type preferences, and *establishing type's credibility*—should be distinctly present in any exercise you consider. Of course, they are essential in any introductory exercise. But once people understand the basic type concepts and accept the reality of type, aren't these two objectives redundant? No. As the basic type concepts are revisited, they become more clear and rich, and people's investment in type deepens. People who have attended the MBTI qualifying training or advanced training programs are amazed that successive exercises have the power to teach them new things about "the basics." The challenge to the trainer is to select exercises that can prompt this deeper kind of learning. It is equally important that the trainer skillfully conducts the activity and leads post-exercise discussions that will stimulate the experienced and novice participants at the same time.

**The third objective**, the *value* and *necessity* objective, should be part of any exercise on *applying* type in some setting, such as teamwork or problem solving. The practical value of type in teamwork, for example, and the need for type diversity, should become crystal clear as the exercise unfolds.

**The fourth objective,** teaching people to manage *type strengths and blind spots,* is different from simply making people aware of the strengths and blind spots. Some exercises focus directly on the skill *training* of using type strengths well and appropriately, such as when to use Thinking criteria and when to use Feeling criteria in making decisions.

**The fifth objective,** teaching people about applications of type in life situations, likewise has two levels. The first is making them *aware* of the role that type can play when people use type concepts. The deeper level is reached by exercises that coach the participants in actual or simulated situations in which they *hone their skills* of using type.

**LEARNING ABOUT TYPE TAKES A PARTICULAR KIND OF EXERCISE.** In the pages that follow, we discuss several exercises and highlight the ways they focus on the five objectives. You will see that the exercises have an essential feature in common: the participants are divided into type-alike smaller groups for the first part of the exercise, and then shifted into type-contrast groups or reconvened as a whole group for the type-contrast stage of processing.

Before the exercise is used, the participants have acquired some basic understanding about type. The exercise is designed to convert their understanding *about* type to an understanding *of* type. In their pre-exercise reading about type, or in listening to you explain the basic concepts, they obtained an abstract, surface knowledge. Their work in the exercise gives them an experiential grasp of the type preferences. It gives them an awareness of how people actually behave or report their experience of being in their type.

This exercise design is based on an essential reality of type. One's type is a framework for mental processing of life experiences. It is not possible to stand outside one's framework, as, for example, a Sensing type cannot take on—even temporarily—an Intuitive framework, and vice versa. The best way available for an S to understand Intuition is to attend carefully to how Ns describe their framework and to how they behave in their typical functioning, and vice versa. The type exercises are structured to do just that—teach participants to attend carefully to the reports and behaviors of those who have the opposite type preference(s).

Most type-alike exercises are designed to show contrasting behaviors and values of the preference pairs—E–I, S–N, T–F or J–P—or for four type groupings, such as: ST, SF, NF, NT (the columns of the type table); IS, IN, ES, EN (the quadrants of the type table); SJ, SP, NJ, NP; or EJ, IJ, EP, IP (the rows of the type table). The rationale for these groupings can be seen in sample exercises published in *Shape Up Your Program* and *Out of the Box: Exercises for Mastering the Power of Type to Build Effective Teams*, referenced at the end of the chapter. In another kind of exercise, participants—individually or with partners of their same type—complete a task or react to something, and then report their type and their response to the whole group. In this way, participants can see how responses differ type by type.

Most exercises on type are designed in two stages.

**1)** Type-alike participants talk and come to agreement on what behavior or viewpoint is typical for them, and record their results on chart paper.

2) Then the type-alike groups report to the whole group, and the trainer guides a dialogue, highlighting the contrasts between the language, viewpoints and behaviors presented by the type-alike groups.

**Exercise on Extraversion/ Introversion**

Let's analyze a well-tested E–I exercise as an illustration of the design described above, and also look at it in relation to the five objectives.

**DIRECTIONS:**

1) Participants divide into groups of about six per group, with about equal numbers of Es and Is in each group.

2) Each Extraverted participant individually writes three things about Introverts (and each Introvert writes three things about Extraverts):

- What is one thing you *admire* about your opposite (E or I)?
- What is one thing that *baffles* you about your opposite?
- What *question* would you like to ask your opposite to clarify your understanding of his or her (E or I) way of doing things? (About five minutes)

3) The Es in the group then share with the other Es in the same group of six their answers to the three questions, and the Is do likewise with the other Is. They combine the admired characteristics into one list, the baffling traits into another list, and ask each other for clarification as needed. (About ten minutes)

4) Each group of six then convenes. They read and discuss their lists. Participants then ask their questions and get answers and comments, alternating E and I questions. (About twenty-five minutes)

5) The whole group is then reconvened, and each group of six has the opportunity to report one insight or new understanding that came out of their group discussion. (About twenty-five minutes)

These instructions are lengthy, so the trainer should probably put them on a handout and/or newsprint and read them aloud as well.

Referring back to the five major objectives for type exercises, the first three are obviously represented in the exercise. Objectives four and five are here to a lesser extent. Let's examine some sample responses to the exercise instructions.

**Participant responses.** An Introvert says, "One thing I admire about Extraverts is their ease in social situations. What baffles me about them is why they seem to need to fill any silence with talk. One question I'd like the Extraverts to answer is: How can you process your thoughts while you're talking all the time?"

An Extravert says, "One thing I admire about Introverts is the quiet reserve I see in many of them that seems to keep them calm and steady. What baffles me about Introverts is why they keep quiet in a group when I know they have something worth saying. A question I'd like them to answer: Isn't it lonely when you do so much processing just by yourself?"

The power of this kind of exercise can be seen here in the language used and in the reactions evoked in the group dialogue. Extraverts hearing the Introvert statements may say (to themselves or aloud), "I don't always *feel* at ease in social situations, even if Introverts see me that way. Some situations take a lot of effort. About filling silences with talk, I guess I feel some responsibility to fill silences. Somehow, silence in a conversation is an embarrassment, making me feel that I dropped the ball. About processing my thoughts, I do that out loud—get my thoughts clear as I speak them. But I don't like to be seen as 'talking all the time,' if that means monopolizing the conversation."

Introverts hearing the Extravert's statements may say (to themselves or aloud), "I may be quiet, but that doesn't mean I am always feeling calm and steady inside. I may be very busy processing my thoughts inside, and the inside action may not show outside. Why do I sometimes keep quiet in a group when I may have something to say? I often feel that the air space is already taken up with other people's talk, and it is hard to get a word in. If I wait a bit, someone else may express my thought well enough, and I won't have to work up the words needed to extravert it. Also, I'm inclined to believe that if the people in the group valued my ideas, they would ask for them. Am I lonely when I am alone with my thoughts? There's a big difference between having quiet time for my thoughts and being lonely. It is not lonely, and it is very comfortable."

**A second layer of responses.** As the group members hear each other's statements, questions and answers, there is a second layer of reactions, a deeper level of understanding about one's opposite. One excellent feature of this exercise design is that participants get these understandings directly from each other—without the trainer having to call people's attention to the key concepts.

**The trainer's role.** The main role of the trainer is to monitor the process closely, identify language that may sustain stereotypes or lead to misconceptions, and supply language that better represents the type concepts. For example, an Introvert may ask a question of Extraverts that shows a bias, such as, "How can you put up with chit-chat when nothing of value is being said?" If the Extraverts respond to the question in ways that don't challenge the stereotype, the trainer needs to take it up: "Are there times when a 'superficial' conversation serves a valuable purpose? …When, and what kind of purpose?"

In most cases, when the trainer sets a positive tone for the dialogue, the participants will spot stereotypes and talk about them until they have been worked out of the language—without the trainer intervening. An important job for the trainer is to capture especially good language and highlight it in periodic summaries during the exercise. The summaries help participants carry away a list of unbiased terms and phrases they can use when talking about type.

As with all exercises, the trainer has to pace exercises about type, keeping them moving. But with exercises that teach about type, the risk is allowing too little time for debriefing. In this E–I example, after the groups of six have processed members' questions and have reconvened into the large group, the discussion of the insights and new understandings gleaned from the group work should not be rushed.

**Exercise on influencing and persuading**

Here is an exercise that divides the sixteen types into four type-alike groups, instead of contrasting pairs, as in the E–I exercise. In this case, the groups are ST, NF, NT, and SF, the four combinations of the mental functions. Type theory tells us these are distinctly different frames of mind, with different values and priorities associated with each. For example, ST represents a preference for Sensing data and Thinking criteria for making decisions. Successfully persuading an ST person about the value of something will take an approach tailored to ST mental priorities and values.

**INSTRUCTIONS** for this exercise are simple:

➤ Without announcing the rationale for the exercise, have participants sort themselves into the four groups. The instructions for all groups are: In your group, please answer the question, and capture your responses on chart paper: *What does it take to persuade/convince us about the merits of some thing or action?*

The contrasts of the groups' responses are usually most dramatic when the order of reporting is ST, NF, NT, SF. The ST group will generally report responses such as, "Is it practical and efficient?" or "What is the objective evidence that the action is sensible?" The NF group will report responses such as, "We can be convinced if the action improves things for people generally and is not just good for a few." The NT group will report responses such as, "Is it conceptually sound?" and "Give me the reasoning and let me evaluate it for myself." The SF group will report responses such as, "Who supports it and how well do they like it?"

During the discussion of the four reports, the trainer should keep in mind the five objectives we listed at the beginning of the chapter, and help participants carry away from the exercise three kinds of personal outcomes:

- some specific language and type concepts they can use
- a recognition of some blind spots inherent in their own type
- an idea of some skills they can work on

The trainer may also want to use a handout such as the following to help participants see the type distinctions more clearly. This one emphasizes the ST, NF, NT and SF high priority values that people try to put into action, especially in group situations such as the workplace.

## ST, NF, NT AND SF PRIORITIES

While each of the sixteen types has a distinctive pattern of priorities and values associated with it, the four STs have some priorities in common, as do the SFs, NFs, and NTs.

### ST Priorities

- conserving valued resources and protecting practices that work
- finding situations where they can use and enjoy their technical skills
- minimizing or eliminating ambiguity and uncertainty
- getting roles defined in specific, objective ways
- knowing exactly what output is expected of them
- having or making objective rules
- dealing with concrete, objective problems that are uncluttered with emotional issues

### NF Priorities

- finding situations where they can pursue their deep concern for broad, human value issues
- finding situations that allow them freedom for creative expression
- exploring the possibilities in relationships
- finding situations that value their insights into complex interpersonal problems
- making institutions responsive to people
- promoting the ideals of harmonious relationships

### NT Priorities

- finding situations that need their objective curiosity and lead to possibilities
- working at the abstract level of broad concepts and general ideas
- analyzing complex, objective situations
- working on problems that respond to their own new techniques and solutions
- pursuing their own idealistic images of how things should be
- having opportunities to independently produce innovative, ingenious solutions

### SF Priorities

- working in harmonious, familiar, predictable situations
- maintaining practical contacts that keep relationships warm and free from conflicts
- enjoying the present moment, making the best of life's conditions
- attending to the tangible needs of individuals
- making a distinctly personal physical environment in which to live and work
- being in situations where their keen attention to the here and now is useful and appreciated

From *People Types and Tiger Stripes*, by Gordon Lawrence. Copyright 1993. Used by permission.

**Exercise on using type deliberately in decision making**

This last exercise is an example of consciously putting type to work in a practical application. It appears in *Shape Up Your Program* and was developed by Candice Johnson. It is used here by permission. It works best when used by an intact group such as a work team, but is also effective when participants have no working relationship to each other. The emphasis in this exercise is on objectives four and five, listed at the beginning of the chapter, both concerned with skill development in the uses of type.

The exercise makes use of the model for problem solving referred to as the zig-zag, which should be explained at the outset. The following excerpt from *People Types and Tiger Stripes* (page 161), used here by permission, gives the rationale for the zig-zag.

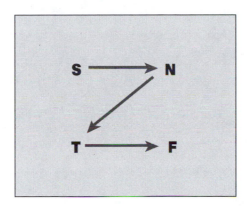

Zig-zag refers to a sequence in using the four processes—S, N, T and F—in solving a problem. When the two kinds of perception are placed at the poles of one line, and the two kinds of judgment are placed on a second line, with arrows connecting all four, the problem solving sequence looks like a "Z" or zig-zag.

Isabel Myers believed that good problem solving could be viewed as a sequential use of the four processes—from S to N to T to F. When faced with a problem, we start constructively with Sensing to identify the facts, the given realities of the situation, that make up the platform from which any changes must be launched. But the raw data by themselves do not settle the problem. The meaning of the data, their relationships to prior experience, are given by Intuition—so the arrow goes from S to N. Intuition also asks: What are new ways to look at the problem and new possibilities in these data for finding a solution?

The arrow moves from N to T when we engage Thinking judgment to analyze and decide the logical consequences of acting upon each of the possibilities. And finally, the possibilities are also weighed by Feeling judgment to assess how deeply we care about the effects of each option; we test the human consequences, the harmony with basic personal values, or the values of others we care about and trust.

A mature settling of the problem will involve the four processes in a balanced way. But, of course, each type plays favorites with the four processes, so balance is difficult to achieve.

The object of the exercise is to have participants experience the problem-solving process using the zig-zag, with each station of the zig-zag well represented. Participants need to be assigned to groups so that the S, N, T and F elements of problem solving are well covered in each group. Ideally, S, N, T and F would be represented by a participant who has that function as the *dominant* function. Each group will work on a problem, ideally a problem of concern to all the participants, as might be the case when the group is an intact work team. Instructions to the groups should be tailored to their situation.

## Steps for the decision making exercise

**INSTRUCTIONS:**

1) In your group, decide on a problem that needs attention, preferably a problem that concerns you all. After you choose a problem, you have twenty-four minutes to work on it. If your problem is a complex one, needing a lot of time, redefine the problem as "how to get started on…(our complex problem)." You may want to work on a problem facing just one of your group members, such as, "Is now a good time for Gary to start his furniture refinishing business?"

2) In the process of dealing with the problem, the objective is to give equal time to each phase of the zig-zag—S, N, T and F—with six minutes for each. Identify your types to each other and try to have each phase led by a member whose dominant matches that phase.

3) When we start working on the problem, engage only in S data gathering for six minutes. (No N, T or F content is allowed during this time!) Then switch to N work for the next six minutes, etc. Have one member keep notes on the content of the *task* progress, and another member keep notes on the *processes* of the group as it works on the task.

4) We will then reconvene as a whole group and discuss the small group work. Sticking to the six minute time frame is, of course, artificial. The objective is to see the essential features of each of the four phases, and to recognize how our individual type differences give us strengths and blind spots in the phases of problem solving. We will discuss these.

After the groups have completed their twenty-four-minute sequence, the trainer reconvenes the whole group to discuss the experience, drawing particularly on the notes of the process observers. This is a good point for participants to talk about applications of the zig-zag to actual situations in their lives. The trainer may want to offer an example of problem solving in his/her experience that produced poor results because some aspects of the S–N–T–F process were neglected, and an example of success using the zig-zag.

## Hints for facilitating group exercises

IN THE DESCRIPTION OF THESE EXERCISES, you have been given some good examples of the kinds of things to say when facilitating the group. The deeper your understanding of type, the more you can bring to processing the exercises, and the more you can highlight behaviors or language that reflect type differences when needed. Nothing is as powerful as having someone say, "But of course you have to start with what has worked in the past when making decisions!" when you can point out that Sensing is this person's preferred function. And then subsequently you can ask a dominant Intuitive type what is the most important thing and get the answer, "To focus on what is the possible outcome." This kind of real-time expression and observation of type leads to powerful learning.

Remember, as the group facilitator *you are the model* of how to use and how not to use type. If you stereotype, you give participants permission to stereotype. If you look for the constructive ways Thinking and Feeling differences can be used in making business decisions, your business clients will look for them as well. When you demonstrate in your language and behavior that you really believe all types are equally valuable, participants are going to be more likely to want to share their types. Participants who are initially skeptical of sharing their type will often choose to do so when the workshop facilitator models a safe discussion of type.

Get training on training. It's a skill. Good reflective listening skills are important for any trainer. Go to training. Watch trainers you like and respect, and remember what they did as you do your own group facilitation.

You will have your own style as well—an ESTJ trainer will look different from an INFP trainer! As we tell our clients, build on the strengths of your type, and tune up your blind spots. If you are an NFP trainer, be sensitive to the needs of STJs in the group who may need structure, agendas and *facts*. If you are an STJ trainer, be aware that the NFPs in the group want more than information—they want a warm and safe learning environment that affirms their individuality. To this end, you will want to know your client before you stand up to train—which you will, if you are following the recommendations in this book. It will also be helpful to review the type table of participants before you begin the program.

Knowing your own style is the first step in building your presentation to meet the needs of different types. Use type to teach type. Preferences for Sensing and Intuition probably have the most dramatic impact on preferences for learning. If nothing else, then, be sure you meet the needs of Sensing types for facts, specifics, and how type will apply in their real-world setting, and the needs of Intuitives for overview, theory, and exploration of possibilities. Beyond that, build the presentation to meet the needs of both Es and Is, Ts and Fs, and Js and Ps.

➤ **A note on time:** When you do an exercise in which participants break into groups, tell them when you want them back. Telling them how long they have for the exercise is good—telling them when you want them back is better. Remember, processing exercises always takes longer than you believe it will.

For further hints on creating a good learning environment while doing exercises, see the section *Processing Exercises: Things to Do and Questions to Ask.*

**PROCESSING EXERCISES: THINGS TO DO AND QUESTIONS TO ASK**

1) When you ask a question (e.g., "Did anyone have any insights from this exercise?"), be sure to wait several seconds before answering it yourself. This gives people in the group time to reflect on the question. Bite your tongue and live with your own anxiety for a few seconds if no one answers right away! Usually, you'll be glad you did.

2) Summarize what a participant said, or what several participants have said ("So it seems that the Introverts in the group are saying they really are involved—maybe even the *most* involved—when they are not saying anything in a conversation.").

3) Ask participants what they noticed in the exercise before you give them too much information. For example, after groups report on an exercise, ask "Does anyone notice any differences between the ST and the NF answers?" Ask also, "How do you believe that relates to type?"

4) Ask open-ended questions (e.g., "How did the Extraverts feel when they couldn't talk?") rather than closed-ended questions (e.g., "Did Extraverts feel tense when they couldn't talk?"). Open-ended questions invite more discussion and spontaneous happenings, while closed-ended questions invite shorter or *yes* or *no* responses.

5) Be genuine. If you don't understand what someone said, don't just gloss it over. Say "I didn't quite get what you meant." If you are running out of time, don't rush the exercise. Rather, say, "We're about out of time; let's hear from one more person."

6) Don't insist that everyone say something. Look and listen for cues that a person is telling you they don't want to participate—and honor that wish.

7) At the same time, be sure everyone has a chance to speak if they want to. Make the group a place where people who might not be heard get a chance to say something. If it seems that someone in the group got *run over* by another group member in the exciting rush of ideas, then come back to that person (e.g., "It seems like there was something else you wanted to say.").

8) Make the group as safe as possible. Let members know that we are trying to understand how different types approach the world. If you hear any *type bashing*, be sure to re-frame the statement in a way that honors that type, and *also honors* what the speaker was attempting to say. For example, "It sure does feel like Extraverts are not respecting you when they jump into the middle of your response. At the same time, we are hearing from Extraverts that rapid exchanges of ideas—what seem like interruptions—are the way they think. They think *out loud* with others."

9) Trust that most people have good intentions, but remember also that the group is looking to you to set the tone. Is it safe? Can I say what I think? Can I disagree without being attacked?

10) Look at the process—not just the product—in the group exercises. For example, you might note not only that the ESTJ group answer differs from the INFP group answer, but also that the ESTJ group came to consensus, and started and finished writing quickly.

11) Remember, type doesn't explain everything. Don't try to force-fit a group process or individual behavior into a type explanation when there might be better explanations.

12) If the exercise goes differently from your expectations (type-related or otherwise), be sure to note it and talk to the group about why it might have gone the way it did.

## Sample Exercises

THE EXERCISES ALREADY DESCRIBED in this chapter can be adapted to a variety of domains. For example, the exercise on the zig-zag approach to problem solving can easily be adapted for team-building programs, career workshops, curriculum development applications, and leadership development. The final section of this chapter is devoted to describing some exercises that can have broad application in a variety of domains.

Exercises become effective as they are tried and fine-tuned through successive use. Keep a log of what went right and wrong, along with ideas for improvement. Also remember how important it is to build your exercises so they meet the needs of different types of people. The zig-zag analysis can be exceptionally useful in looking at how you do exercises and can support you in your efforts to make them even more effective.

## S—N Exercise: Perceiving a leaf

This S–N exercise has been used a lot by type trainers, always with valuable results. Its intent is to demonstrate the differences in the kind of information to which Sensing and Intuitive types attend. Variations on the exercise are given at the end.

➤ Allow fifteen to twenty-five minutes for this exercise.

➤ You'll need easel pad paper, markers, and two spaces that are as separate as possible so the groups won't overhear each other.

1) Have the Sensing types gather in one group and the Intuitive types in the other.

2) Before the two groups go their separate ways, write on a sheet of newsprint and read the following instruction. Ask that there not be any discussion before the groups meet separately. The instruction is this:

➤ *Write a few words or phrases about a leaf.*

Be careful not to use the word "describe" as you give this exercise.

3) Let the groups meet and work separately for five to ten minutes before bringing the two groups back together. Cover the groups' responses so they can be viewed one group at a time.

4) Ask the Sensing types to report first on their list. Responses will tend to be physical descriptions of a leaf, or different kinds of leaves (e.g., green, veins, stem, crinkly, colorful), or specific things that are done with or to a leaf (e.g., raking, burning, piling). Answers are often concrete characteristics, real memories, or concrete associations (e.g., Halloween, fall).

5) Ask the Intuitive types to report on their list. Responses may begin with physical characteristics and things that can be done with a leaf, but will move quickly to (free) associations, moving further and further from the actual description of "a leaf." Associations such as a table leaf, tea leaf, leaf in a book, Leif Ericsson, and a symbol of life and death are not uncommon.

6) Ask the group if they notice any differences between the two lists. Do they see differences that might be related to type? Note that although they had the same instruction, the two groups immediately had different takes on what was relevant information in the process. Remind them that Sensing and Intuition are *irrational*

functions—we do not give order to perceiving information, but rather, that information presents itself in our minds and we go with that information.

7) Note that there is often overlap in the two lists. The Sensing group will often have free associations on their list, while Intuitive types will have physical descriptors on theirs. This is a reminder that everyone uses Sensing and everyone uses Intuition—but different types give more weight and attention to one kind of information than to the other.

8) Because styrofoam cups are so often available in the training setting, another variation is this:

   ➤ *Write a few words or phrases about a styrofoam cup.*

   Sometimes it's valuable to actually place a cup in front of the group. The stimulus of the actual cup can be an even more powerful drive for Sensing types to "describe" the cup, even though the word "describe" is not used.

9) Other variations:

   Ask the groups to write a few words or phrases about a poster, picture or painting. Any object that can provide concrete images as well as metaphorical or symbolic elements is good.

   Without telling them the nature of the exercise or dividing them into groups, you can give the group as a whole the exercise. Have them individually write their ideas on a piece of paper. As you process the exercise, have some Sensing types read their ideas first, then have some Intuitive types read their lists. STs and NFs will tend to have clear contrasts.

**T–F Exercise: Appreciation**

This exercise demonstrates some of the qualities that Thinking and Feeling types value in themselves, and also shows how we might miss the boat when expressing appreciation and giving feedback to others. Variations on the exercise are given at the end.

> ➤ Allow thirty to forty minutes for this exercise.

> ➤ You'll need easel pad paper, markers, and two spaces that are as separate as possible so the groups won't overhear each other. As the trainer, it will be important for you to recognize that other preferences will spill over into the Thinking and Feeling responses. For example, some Thinking responses will be colored by Judging, while others will be colored by Perceiving.

1) Have the Thinking types gather in one group and the Feeling types in the other.

2) Before the two groups go their separate ways, read the following instruction and write it on a sheet of newsprint. Ask that there not be any discussion before the groups meet separately. The instruction is this:

> ➤ *For what do you like to be appreciated?*

3) Have the groups work separately for about ten minutes and then bring them back together. Cover and view the groups' responses one at a time.

4) Ask the Thinking types to go over their list first. Typical responses include: my intelligence, ability to solve problems, insights, ability to get things done or make them happen, objectivity, impartial sounding board for friends' and colleagues' problems. Items listed are often related to tasks, getting the job done, specific skills, and mental attributes.

5) Now ask the Feeling types to review their list. Typical responses include: empathy, tact, supporting others, helping friends and colleagues through tough times, sensitivity to climate, showing concern, caring about people's development and their personal lives. Items listed are often related to attention to relationships, sensitivity to "quality" of the environment or communication.

6) Ask both groups to comment on any differences between the lists. Do the differences make sense in light of type? If they aren't

distinct, can anyone explain the similarities? If the same word appears on both lists (e.g., supportive), there is value in having the groups describe what they mean by that word and how it is demonstrated (e.g., how Ts show support vs. how Fs show support).

7) Point out that there are at least two insights to be taken away from this exercise. First is that the lists can be read as lists of what the different types consider to be valuable and important qualities in themselves. Second is that we often miss opportunities to recognize and appreciate what other types "bring to the table" in our personal and work lives—because what we value may differ from what they value. People may express appreciation for something we do, but it doesn't have much impact on us because it doesn't strike us as something important to us!

8) You can also add to this exercise by further breaking the group down into ETs, EFs, ITs, and IFs, and then asking the additional question:

   ➤ *How do you like appreciation shown?*

   Extraversion and Introversion will often impact how people like to be recognized and appreciated (e.g., how public or private the appreciation is, notes vs. awards).

9) Another variation on this TF exercise is to ask the two groups:

   ➤ *What do you look for in an ideal partner (in your personal life)?*

   This exercise is interesting because it may elicit qualities that describe the respondents' own types—that is, the qualities they look for in others are qualities they value in themselves. Sometimes people consciously list qualities that are very much unlike them. When they do this, they often comment that they are looking for someone who complements their own style.

**J–P Exercise:
Work and Play**

This is a J–P exercise that has also been used extensively by type trainers in many variations. Its intent is to demonstrate the differences Js and Ps have in how they perceive work and play, and to what degree they distinguish between the two.

Depending on how "safe" the setting feels, you may need to vary the content so that a split is not set up between Js and Ps with regard to workplace behavior. Although the exercise is presented here as a "work-play" exercise, variations are given at the end.

➤ Allow twenty to thirty minutes for this exercise.

➤ You'll need two large sheets of paper and enough room for everyone in the group to spread out in a line.

1) Post two sheets of paper, one each on opposite ends of a wall or room.

   ➤ One says—*I must finish my work before I can play.*

   ➤ The other says—*I can play anytime.*

2) Tell people to imagine a continuum running from one sign to the other, and to stand on the line at the point that fits them best. That is, they stand closer to the sign that fits them better.

3) When everyone has settled on some point along the line, and before you ask their types, you can begin with some questions:

   ➤ *To the people at the "finish my work" end: what does this mean to you?*

   ➤ *To the people at the "play anytime" end: what does this mean to you?*

   ➤ *After hearing this discussion, would anyone move?*

   You will probably find that the "finish work" group tends to make distinctions between work and play, and play is often a reward for work. The "play anytime" group will often say that work and play flow in and out of one another and that they are working in their minds when they may not look as though they are working on the outside. There will be variations in between along the line.

4) Now tell participants—"if you had to choose, please turn to the sign that fits you the better." You are asking them to group themselves.

5) Have people identify their types (if known), by raising their hands:

➤ *Would the Js raise their hands?*

➤ *Would the Ps raise their hands?*

As a rule of thumb, Judging types, and SJs in particular, will be closest to the "finish my work" end. Perceiving types, and NPs in particular, will be closest to the "play anytime" end.

6) Note that this is essentially how MBTI items work. People are asked to choose one side or the other of an item, and the item is kept on the Indicator if it correctly sorts known types into the category that is right for them. If this were a J–P item, would we want to keep it in the Indicator?

7) Note how Js and Ps often have what appear to be different work ethics, but how it is really often a difference in perception of what constitutes work and play. Often, too, people will say they wished they had more of the qualities of folks at the opposite end of the line!

If this exercise as presented would be too "hot" a topic in a particular work setting, there are variations that can be useful.

• *When approaching a new project: plan my approach vs. jump in*

• *On a nonworking weekend: plan my weekend vs. see what happens*

• *On visiting a theme park: look at the park map vs. just go and explore*

**Function Pair
(ST, SF, NF, NT) Exercise:
Communication**

This exercise, or some variation of it, can be used for just about anything, depending on the needs of the group. The function pair groupings are very powerful, and exercises that use this grouping highlight the different beliefs, assumptions and world views of people who prefer those mental functions. Remember, the mental functions tell us what kind of information we prefer and how we like to make decisions—they are the *core* of our type.

The function pair exercise is presented here as a "communication" exercise in an organizational context, but can be varied to address many issues: intimate relationships, leadership style, parenting style, teaching/learning style and so on. You've seen one variation already in this chapter in the exercise on influencing and persuading. Other variations are given at the end of this exercise.

> ➤ Allow forty-five to sixty minutes for this exercise, depending on the size of the group.
> ➤ You'll need at least four sheets of newsprint, markers, and enough room for four groups to meet relatively separately.

1) Break the larger group into four groups: ST, SF, NF, and NT.

2) Give the entire group the same assignment (write the following on a large sheet of newsprint):

   > ➤ *What is good communication?*

3) Send the four groups to different areas and have them come up, as a group, with answers to the question. They have ten to fifteen minutes. Give them a sheet of newsprint and a marker to record their answers. This exercise is most valuable if you can post the results, and compare/contrast the answers of the different groups.

4) Come back together as a large group, and have each group hold up their newsprint and report on their group's results. We usually have them report out in the following order for maximum contrast: ST, NF, SF, NT. However, any order is fine.

5) Sample responses that often come up:

   > ➤ ST—paraphrasing, you repeat what I say and I repeat what you say to be sure we understand each other, we focus on the facts and don't let emotions get in the way, we agree to disagree, people are direct about the important content and don't beat around the bush, the communication is specific

➤ SF—we respect each other, we listen to each others' position, we work toward a harmonious outcome, we look for areas of agreement, we don't yell or hurt each other, we treat each other like people and take the time to connect

➤ NF—we work toward a common vision, we respect each other, we show concern for understanding the other person, we are honest, we look for agreement and an inclusive solution, there is attention to what you say and also how you say it, even when there is disagreement there is still a caring context

➤ NT—the transfer of accurate content with as little noise as possible, there is high signal and low noise, there is a fair exchange of information, content/process/verbals/nonverbals are taken into account, directness is important, "just tell me" without drama, we respect each other

6) As groups report out, note similarities or differences. Typical patterns are noted below. Remember, the patterns noted are all relative, though differences between ST, SF, NF and NT within the group as a whole are always apparent. Career and training of participants will influence results, with counselor answers looking different from engineer answers. Patterns are still typically apparent.

➤ ST patterns—behavioral descriptions of what constitutes good communication, focus on content/facts rather than "atmosphere" or relationship, more impersonal/direct

➤ SF patterns—focus on listening, seeking of harmony, no hurt feelings, respecting/caring for each other from a "real people" perspective, very personal and relationship-oriented

➤ NF patterns—a more abstract sense of our "getting along" with each other, ideals about how people "in general" should treat each other, a description of vague relationship qualities or atmosphere (vague to other types, not to NFs), concern for harmony and respect

➤ NT patterns—a more abstract, impersonal (often systemic) description with few precise behaviors described, a "model" of good communication that incorporates "multiple levels" of communication (verbal, nonverbal, content, process, outcome), a matrix model in which ideas from all group members have been incorporated

7) Note to the group that there are some fundamental differences in the ways they define communication. If we don't define it in the same way, is it any surprise that we have trouble making it happen? Ask the group how they can integrate elements from these different definitions to improve "communication" in their group.

8) In addition to the above question, you can also add:

> ➤ *How do you bring about good communication (on a team, at work)?*

Further questions can always be asked of the group for deeper insight. In the following variations on the exercise, you can see the variety of applications:

- *What is your leadership style? What are your strengths and blind spots?*
- *Describe an ideal relationship. What do you look for in a partner?*
- *For what do you like to be appreciated? How do you like it shown?*
- *Describe an ideal teacher.*
- *How do you like to be managed? What encourages you and turns you off?*
- *What is good feedback?*
- *Define conflict. How do you respond to conflict?*
- *Describe an ideal organization.*

**Resources**

Epstein, C. C., Emmerich, R., Jeffers, K., & Patzlaff, S. (1994). *Finding solutions to workplace problems: A team's guide to using Myers-Briggs.* Wausau, WI: Link Publications.

Fields, M. U., & Reid, J. B. (1999). *Shape up your program: Tips, teasers, and thoughts for type trainers.* Gainesville, FL: Center for Applications of Psychological Type.

Hirsh, S. K. (1985). *Using the Myers-Briggs Type Indicator in organizations: A resource book.* Palo Alto, CA: Consulting Psychologists Press.

Hirsh, S. K. (1992). *MBTI team building program: Leader's resource guide.* Palo Alto, CA: Consulting Psychologists Press.

Martin, C. R., & Golatz, T. J. *Out of the box: Exercises for mastering the power of type to build effective teams.* Gainesville, FL: Center for Applications of Psychological Type.

CAPT also offers a wide variety of individual handouts and exercises that come with leader's guides.

# APPENDIX

## Type Descriptions From:

## *Looking at Type: The Fundamentals*

by Charles R. Martin, Ph.D.

### CENTER FOR APPLICATIONS OF PSYCHOLOGICAL TYPE, INC. GAINESVILLE, FLORIDA

## The Sixteen Type Descriptions

These full-length type descriptions are reproduced with permission from *Looking at Type: The Fundamentals* by Charles Martin. Copyright 1997, Center for Applications of Psychological Type.

Now that you know more about the dynamic interactions of the functions for the types, you will be able to see how the type descriptions in the next section are organized by dynamics. In fact, the title of each type description tells you what the dominant and auxiliary functions are for that type (e.g., ESTJ—Extraverted Thinking with Introverted Sensing). As you read about the types, you may notice that the description starts out with an emphasis on the dominant function and how it is the essence of someone's type. The description then moves on to how the auxiliary adds to that type's behavioral style and how the preferences all combine to influence the needs, interests, and relationships of someone with that type. Finally, the description addresses what may happen if the auxiliary is not developed, and how the least-preferred function may show up in that type's life.

# Descriptions of the Sixteen Types

## ISTJ
## Introverted Sensing with Extraverted Thinking

For ISTJs the dominant quality in their lives is an abiding sense of responsibility for doing what needs to be done in the here-and-now. Their realism, organizing abilities, and command of the facts lead to their completing tasks thoroughly and with great attention to detail. Logical pragmatists at heart, ISTJs make decisions based on their experience and with an eye to efficiency in all things. ISTJs are intensely committed to people and to the organizations of which they are a part; they take their work seriously and believe others should do so as well.

ISTJs are quiet, serious, and realistic observers of their environment, who naturally attend to and remember concrete facts. They give great weight to hands-on life experiences; they use their sensing to internally process and file away data for later use. ISTJs usually have a massive amount of information stored inside and an impressive command of the facts. In recalling a past event, they often have a good memory for what was literally said or done. Their orientation to detail can also show as a concern for precision in action and in speech. It was an ISTJ who originally said, "Say what you mean."

ISTJs bring a detached pragmatism to all that they do, and they have a great deal of common sense; ISTJs are typically down-to-earth folk. They learn by doing, and want to know how an idea can be used or applied. As a result, they are often quite skeptical people. "Seeing is believing." They respect the facts and their experience, and they expect things to be logical. Period.

Thinking gives order and structure to ISTJs' experiences and puts their pragmatism in a logical context.

ISTJs tend to be analytical and tough-minded, and they make decisions with an eye to impersonal consequences; they really want their decisions to be objective and fair. Thinking in conjunction with sensing also gives them an eye to the efficient manipulation of real-world phenomena. That is, they like to bring logical order to facts and things in their environment. ISTJs are usually more oriented to the tasks on which they are working than to the people with whom they work, and they may sometimes unrealistically expect all people to behave "logically."

ISTJs do like a structured and organized outer world, and find comfort in developing and adhering to a routine in their work. They like to know what their job is, and generally do not appreciate settings where the rules constantly change; in this sense, ISTJs are conservative. They guard what works, and they want to see evidence that a new way will work before they adopt it. "If it works, why change it?" This attitude gives them an atmosphere of patience and stability, and others often feel settled and calm in their presence.

Above all else, ISTJs are responsible. They do things just because they need to be done, and they have a powerful work ethic. "Work hard, *then* play." ISTJs like getting things done, and they are thorough as they carry a task through to completion. Once an ISTJ commits to complete a task, he or she will do so; they are exceptionally dependable. In fact, they can be difficult to distract once they have begun to systematically work on a project. "Plan your work, and work your plan." ISTJs honor their commitments, and they expect others to do the same; they hold themselves and others accountable for getting things done.

Tradition, stability, and preparedness are usually valued by ISTJs. They respect the fine-tuned performance that characterizes established organizations, and they are often found working in such settings. Through their conscientiousness as well as by quietly building community, ISTJs form much of the backbone of society. They also provide stability through their often clear sense of what constitutes appropriate and inappropriate behavior, and through the keeping of traditions. Ceremonies and anniversaries, such as weddings, birthdays, and holidays, are valued and celebrated.

With their memory for facts and with their attention to getting things done, ISTJs often have great academic success, particularly in subjects that have applications and where results can be seen. Though they tend to have less interest in highly theoretical subjects, they can certainly succeed there as well.

ISTJs are often found in business, production, banking, law, auditing, engineering, and other areas where a mastery of factual data and a tough-minded concern for organization is needed. In their domain, ISTJs work toward efficiency and conservation of resources; they are naturals for quality control. They are often found in management or supervisory positions, overseeing the practical realization of institutional goals. Though they often like to work alone, ISTJs are willing and able to delegate work to ensure the business of the day gets done.

In relationships ISTJs look for fair play and dependability. They themselves tend to be quiet and serious; they are people of few words. They are inclined to be straightforward in their communications and controlled in the outward expression of their emotions. ISTJs do often have a hidden but quirky sense of humor that arises from their highly individual reactions to events. In the extreme, ISTJs may be insensitive and miss the "people part of the equation." At times, they may appear intolerant, and at worst, they may run over others who do not communicate their assertions in a logical and succinct manner.

Development of their extraverted thinking will help ISTJs become more action-oriented and effective in the outer world. Otherwise, they may end up immersed and trapped in their inner world of impressions and memories. Development of thinking will help bring order to their lives by helping them decide which are the most appropriate actions for them to take, and development of flexibility will help them avoid becoming too focused on details. ISTJs may need to work especially hard to understand others' needs for appreciation and emotional support; after all, they are inclined to overlook even their own contributions. Development of feeling will ultimately help them attend more to the people impact of their words and actions. Further, development of intuition will give them a greater respect for the big picture consequences of some of their actions and a greater appreciation for theory.

Under stress ISTJs may withdraw, focus only on their work, and burn out through pushing themselves to get too many things done. They may also become rigid about following rules and become excessively critical of others. Under extreme stress, they can become intensely pessimistic, seeing only negative possibilities in the future, for themselves, for others, and for the world at large.

---

**Key words**

detail ■ precision ■ duty

conscientious ■ analytical ■ critique ■ cool ■ responsibility

# ISFJ
# Introverted Sensing with Extraverted Feeling

For ISFJs the dominant quality in their lives is an abiding respect and sense of personal responsibility for doing what needs to be done in the here-and-now. Actions that are of practical help to others are of particular importance to ISFJs. Their realism, organizing abilities, and command of the facts lead to their thorough attention in completing tasks. ISFJs bring an aura of quiet warmth, caring, and dependability to all that they do; they take their work seriously and believe others should do so as well.

ISFJs are quiet and realistic observers of their environment. They naturally attend to, and have a good memory for, concrete details. ISFJs trust their experience. As they gain hands-on life experiences, they use their sensing to process and file away data for later use. ISFJs usually have a massive amount of data stored inside and an impressive command of the facts. In recalling a past conversation or event, they often have a good memory for what was literally said or done. They like people to be precise in their communications, just as they themselves are.

ISFJs tend to be concrete and pragmatic people. They learn by doing, and they feel that "seeing is believing." They have less interest in abstractions and are more interested in what can be used or applied. ISFJs are down-to-earth in their approach to life, and they tend to have a lot of common sense.

Feeling gives order and structure to ISFJs' experience and puts their pragmatism in a people context. They make decisions based on people values and with attention to human consequences, while sensing ensures that they base their decisions on personal experience. Harmony in relationships is a core value for ISFJs. Feeling also gives them a clear sense of right and wrong and a deep concern for the common welfare. They want their actions to be of benefit to others, and they often quietly radiate compassion. ISFJs at the very least prefer that their actions cause no harm. Though they can be uncomfortable confronting others, they will do so if they believe someone they care about may be harmed.

Above all else, ISFJs take responsibility very seriously and very personally; they have a powerful work ethic. "Work hard, *then* play." ISFJs work persistently and thoroughly, and they hold themselves accountable to get things done. When they promise someone they will do something, they will do it. Because they are so conscientious, ISFJs can be difficult to distract from a task to which they have committed themselves.

Organizational structure, continuity, and security are usually valued by the ISFJs. They want to know the expectations associated with their job and with the jobs of others. If ISFJs can find a cause for which to work, so much the better, because their loyalty will make them tireless supporters of the mission. Through quietly building community, they form much of the backbone of society. In their concern for stability, ISFJs may find themselves acting as guardians of history and tradition. Holidays, anniversaries, and ceremonies are observed, and memories, particularly those of people and relationships, are held in fond regard. Needless to say, family relationships are deep and enduring connections for ISFJs.

ISFJs like to preserve what works. "If it works, why change it?" This attitude gives ISFJs an atmosphere of stability, and others will often feel settled and calm in their presence. Since they often enjoy developing and adhering to a routine in their work, settings where the rules constantly change can be frustrating to them. Though they tend to be conservative, ISFJs are willing to change if there is good evidence of the need. However, they are always concerned that the results be practical and workable.

ISFJs can be frustrated by too much theory and abstraction, and by too much logical analysis; the hard theoretical sciences are often a turnoff. They do, however, learn well in classrooms that give weight to orderly, planful study, and which demonstrate applications of what is learned. ISFJs can master an amazing number of facts.

ISFJs typically like opportunities to interact with people, and they are often found in careers where they can nurture others or attend to their pragmatic physical, emotional, and spiritual needs. They are usually good listeners, and they may have a special affinity with children. ISFJs are often found in health care, religious careers, and teaching (particularly K–12). They are found in business as well, where their pragmatism, organization, and attention to the needs of the customer can lead to great success. Their willingness to take on responsibility can lead to their being placed in management roles, in which positions they are very attentive to the needs of people. They may, however, struggle to learn to delegate tasks.

In their relationships, ISFJs are sympathetic and considerate, and they like to feel a sense of belonging. They tend to be people of few words—quiet but warm. Do not be misled, however, because intimate relationships are of extreme importance to ISFJs. They are deeply loyal to the people about whom they care. They usually make good team members and need to be appreciated for their contributions, though they tend to be modest about their own accomplishments. ISFJs may also have a hidden but quirky sense of humor that arises from their highly individual reactions to events. They may be very sensitive to criticism or lack of appreciation and are in danger of bottling up their emotions and resentments.

Development of their extraverted feeling will help ISFJs become more action-oriented and effective in the outer world. Otherwise, they may end up immersed in their inner world of impressions and trapped in negative reactions. Development of feeling will help bring order to their lives by helping them decide what is most important for them to pursue. In their desire for harmony, ISFJs' own needs may not get expressed or met, and they may respond too much to what others feel or believe. They could benefit from taking the initiative and from being more assertive. Development of intuition and thinking will help them not only to properly estimate their contributions but also to see more of the long-range consequences of their actions, and to be open to new ways of doing things.

Under stress, ISFJs can become rigid, blindly following rules and regulations. If they are not appreciated they may withdraw and/or complain in nonconstructive ways. Under great stress, they may feel deep fatigue and internalize all of their tensions. In the extreme, ISFJs can become exceptionally pessimistic, and see only negative possibilities as they look forward to a fearful future.

---

### Key words
quiet warmth ■ responsible ■ dependable
conscientious ■ systematic ■ realistic ■ pragmatic helper

# INFJ
# Introverted Intuition with Extraverted Feeling

For INFJs the dominant quality in their lives is their attention to the inner world of possibilities, ideas, and symbols. Knowing by way of insight is paramount for them, and they often manifest a deep concern for people and relationships as well. INFJs often have deep interests in creative expression as well as issues of spirituality and human development. While their energy and attention are naturally drawn to the inner world of ideas and insights, what people often first encounter with INFJs is their drive for closure and for the application of their ideas to people's concerns.

Ideas and symbols are real for INFJs. They live for insight and imagination, and they move freely in the inner world of ideas. Their reasoning is abstract, conceptual, complex, and metaphorical. INFJs naturally take multiple or creative perspectives on people, situations, and problems. At times there may also be a philosophical, romantic, or even mystical quality to the way their minds work. Introverted intuition gives a certainty to their insights, and with development of extraverted feeling they may work in a determined way to make their visions a reality.

Feeling provides INFJs with a way of giving structure to and critiquing their vision, and thus their visions are often about possibilities for people or for humanity as a whole. Though feeling is important and necessary, intuition is primary for INFJs, and it pulls them to look to patterns and to possibilities. Feeling puts their future-orientation in a people context, and thus issues of self-realization and human development are often of great import to INFJs. They are usually concerned in an ongoing way not only with their own growth but with the growth of others as well.

INFJs are deeply concerned with fellowship and harmony, and with development of feeling, they are caring and compassionate. They are concerned with what is good for people, and they often see people's hidden beauty. INFJs can be exquisitely empathic, and their sensitivity may almost border on the psychic; at times they may even feel a need to shut out their perceptions of what others are experiencing. With developed empathic skills, INFJs can become powerful and dramatically insightful helpers of others, and indeed they are often found in the fields of psychology, spirituality, education, or in the helping professions.

INFJs usually have a love of learning and they are typically academically inclined. No matter what their field, their great powers of concentration can make them excellent researchers. INFJs need to find a place in the world where their unique gifts can be expressed and used, and they may feel like outsiders in a society that does not have a clear place for those with their unique blend of gifts. They need work that provides opportunities to make use of their creativity, insight, and ability to organize. In their work, INFJs are willing to take on responsibility, and they complete tasks through their quiet perseverance. They may be a behind-the-scenes person who drives and gets things done, or with good development of extraverted feeling, they may be found in positions of leadership. INFJs win followers through magnetism and harmony, through quiet firmness and through a deep-felt belief in their insights. Their certainty of the truth of their intuitions also leads to their developing a strong sense of independence.

INFJs are often quiet observers of people and the human condition. They have an ability to capture the essence of an interaction, a people situation, and to be aware of the timeless qualities of the human condition. With artistic or creative interests (which they often have), they may express these insights in art or writing. INFJs often have facility with the written or spoken word, and with foreign languages, and reading is usually a source of great joy for them.

In relationships, INFJs can be quiet and insightful

friends. Idealists at heart, they greatly value trust and authenticity in relationships. At times, however, others may experience them as certain of—or even stubborn about—their own correctness. Though they typically are concerned with maintaining harmonious relationships and with pleasing others, INFJs may be surprised to hear that others view them as pushy or controlling. Others may also experience them as hard to know or easily hurt, and confrontations and conflict can indeed be terribly painful for INFJs. They are private individuals who may share only a small portion of their inner world with others, not only because they may have difficulty verbalizing their inner experiences, but because they believe others may not understand their insights.

INFJs need development of extraverted feeling to tell them which of their visions or dreams are the most important to pursue. Without that development, they may have difficulty hearing feedback or alternative views from others, and they may neglect to attend to outside realities that contradict their inner vision. Development of feeling and a willingness to move into action will help INFJs avoid becoming trapped in their inner visions of the possibilities, with no way of bringing them into fruition in the pragmatic world. In other words, their dreams and plans will stay just those: dreams and plans. With maturity; INFJs are also able to take in new information and change their stance if they see the need for doing so. Development of thinking and sensing will help them take a hard-nosed look at how they can translate their inner images into outer realities.

Under stress, INFJs may compulsively attempt to organize their outer world but achieve no real embodiment of their visions and ideals. They may also be or appear to be surprisingly critical, perfectionistic, or moralistic. Under stress INFJs may also become self-absorbed in their inner world, have difficulty articulating their needs, and become exceptionally self-critical. Under extreme stress they may become overinvolved in physical experiences (too much exercise), or neglect their physical experience (eat too little), or they may possibly drive themselves to exhaustion.

---

**Key words**

vision ■ insight ■ creativity ■ harmony
sensitivity ■ growth ■ language ■ metaphor ■ symbols ■ quiet intensity

# INTJ
## Introverted Intuition with Extraverted Thinking

For INTJs the dominant force in their lives is their attention to the inner world of possibilities, symbols, abstractions, images, and thoughts. Insight in conjunction with logical analysis is the essence of their approach to the world; they think systemically. Ideas are the substance of life for INTJs and they have a driving need to understand, to know, and to demonstrate competence in their areas of interest. INTJs inherently trust their insights, and with their task-orientation will work intensely to make their visions into realities.

Knowing by way of insight is paramount for INTJs. They want to make sense of the world. To learn, to absorb, and to press the limits of their knowledge are the goals of the INTJ. They are not afraid to think any thought, knowing that all ideas need not be applied or acted upon. They naturally find relationships among disparate theories and systems of knowledge. They want, indeed *must,* see the big picture.

INTJs value logic, but are primarily driven by insight/intuition. Ideas, images, thoughts, and insights emerge spontaneously into their awareness, and only then do they try to make some sense of them using thinking. Their bias in problem solving is to allow the mind to roam freely. Their insights can give them a sense of certainty, and they may appear stubborn. With self-awareness, INTJs are open to new information, though the certainty with which they speak may bar others from trying to argue with them or to provide them with new information. INTJs are willing and able to learn from any source, regardless of status; they are also willing to question ideas, regardless of their source.

Thinking provides the logical analysis to give form and order to the substances generated by the INTJ's inner insight. Thinking helps them critique their visions, but thinking is always secondary to the drive to attend to their intuitive perception. Thinking in conjunction with intuition gives their thinking a systemic quality and they enjoy solving complex problems. They naturally see the world in multiple perspectives, all of which may be seen as true. INTJs mentally play out possible scenarios to determine the consequences of various courses of action; they are the ultimate strategists. They love theory, and they also want to get things done. Ideas are to be implemented, and because they believe in the truth of their insights, INTJs will work tirelessly to turn what is possible into what is real.

INTJs want and need challenge, and they often have a high need for achievement. They have a driving need to be competent, and they often set high standards for themselves. They cannot *not* critique their own behavior and performance; they are always analyzing their own actions with an eye to improvement, whether they are at work or at play. With such high expectations of themselves, they can be quite self-critical. They can also be very impatient with error, inefficiency, and lack of competence, in themselves, in systems, and in others. Whether the focus of their attention is an idea, a person, a product, or a system, INTJs are constantly thinking of improvement.

Looking into the future, seeing trends, and engaging in long-range planning are often areas of interest and skill for INTJs. They tend to keep thoughts and insights to themselves, unless sharing is needed to bring a vision to fruition. It is more important to INTJs to understand other people than to direct them, though they can and will direct others if it is needed. Willpower is of great importance to them, and they believe they can achieve their goals through its application.

INTJs often have interests in scientific and theoretical pursuits, but may have interests in any field where wide-ranging thought is required. With academic interests, they may be excellent teachers and researchers. With business interests, and with their eye to systems and improvement, they are often found in management and planning. Intuition often gives their thinking a philosophical or artistic quality, and INTJs may in fact have interests in philosophy or art. They are driven to be creative whatever their field of interest, and once they have developed and implemented a system, the routine becomes boring and they must either change the system or move on to something new.

INTJs have an exceptionally strong need for independence. They want a problem to solve or a project to complete, and they don't want too many instructions. Authority and hierarchy are understood, and seen as necessary at times, but INTJs are skeptical and willing to question the actions of anyone in that hierarchy. Respect is given to others only on the basis of their competence and understanding, not on the basis of their position. When INTJs are certain of their insights, they will ignore the system and rules.

In relationships, INTJs tend to be quiet and reserved, and they often manifest a cool self-confidence. In general their exterior expression is controlled and little leaks through; as a result they may appear interpersonally distant. Because they also tend to be analytical and by nature to question things, INTJs can appear challenging and insensitive. They may indeed neglect to attend to feeling and relationship issues, and forget to express appreciation or empathy when these are needed.

However, INTJs are usually much more approachable and open than they appear on the outside.

Development of extraverted thinking will provide INTJs with a tool for critiquing their insights and ideas. Otherwise they may end up trapped in their visions of the possibilities, with no way for determining which are the best options or ideas to pursue. INTJs are in danger of becoming over-involved in reflection and/or hair-splitting, and thus they may fail to move into action. Development of thinking as well as sensing will help them avoid this pitfall and also help them find ways to implement their ideas. They could also benefit from learning to express appreciation to others, and from attending to what they themselves and others feel or care about.

Under stress, INTJs may become overstructured and lose the ability to respond flexibly to the outer world. They may also become paralyzed by their ability to take multiple viewpoints and become bogged down in planning stages, seeking perfection before action is ever taken; as a result, their plans may never materialize. Under extreme stress, INTJs can become obsessed with mundane and irrelevant details; they may also become overinvolved in physical experiences (too much exercise), or neglect their physical experience (eat too little).

---

**Key words**

vision ■ insight ■ understanding

learning ■ systemic ■ global ■ improvement ■ achievement ■ competence

# ISTP

## Introverted Thinking with Extraverted Sensing

For ISTPs the driving force in their lives is to understand how things and phenomena in the real world work so they can make the best and most effective use of them. They are logical and realistic people, and they are natural troubleshooters. When not actively solving a problem, ISTPs are quiet and analytical observers of their environment, and they naturally look for the underlying sense to any facts they have gathered. ISTPs often pursue variety and even excitement in their hands-on experiences. Although they do have a spontaneous, even playful side, what people often first encounter with them is their detached pragmatism.

ISTPs are logical and analytical people who believe things in the world should make sense. As quiet and realistic observers of the world, they are intensely curious. ISTPs seek experience in the outer world, and they boil that experience down so they can understand the underlying principles of how things work. ISTPs strive for an objective understanding of things not solely for the sake of understanding, but because they want to use things effectively. They love solving hands-on problems.

ISTPs are naturally critical and come to logical conclusions easily, but since their thinking is brought to bear primarily on their inner world of ideas, others may not see the results of these analyses unless the ISTP chooses to share them. What others typically first encounter with them is their active involvement in the outer world of the senses and their tolerant and easygoing approach to life. Their attitude toward life is playful at times, and when they move into action, ISTPs are spontaneous and flexible, even impulsive. When their principles or independent lifestyle are trod upon, however, they can surprise others by becoming quite firm and possibly stubborn.

Sensing provides ISTPs with a way to stay open to new information, but the gathering of information is always secondary to their need to make sense of things. Their preference for sensing data means that their analysis is brought to bear on the objects, events, and people of the real world, and their thinking tends to be concrete and pragmatic. Thinking in conjunction with sensing also tends to make ISTPs utilitarian; if something cannot be used, than it tends to be of less interest to them. Too much abstraction or theory can frustrate them. In contrast, they do appreciate and have a good memory for factual information. ISTPs tend also to be task-oriented rather than people-oriented and are usually more interested in organizing data or objects than either people or circumstances.

Stimulation of the senses, and sensual experience in general, is of great importance to ISTPs. They often value their material possessions and may also love the outdoors. Having a low tolerance for boredom, ISTPs will pursue excitement and often create action if none is to be found. They enjoy physical activity just for the sheer joy of living in their bodies in the here-and-now. ISTPs may be highly skilled athletes and it is not unusual for them to like adventurous or risky sports. They enjoy honing their ability to respond to the needs of the moment. They are good in crises, and they may also be excellent troubleshooters. ISTPs can be naturals for work in emergency services.

ISTPs often have not only an acute bodily intelligence but a magnificent ability with physical tools and instruments, whether the tool is a computer, a car, or a football. Precision in action and skilled operation of the environment are things to be admired, particularly technical skill, and ISTPs are often mechanically minded. They use their analysis and natural understanding of the world to achieve maximum effect from their efforts; they seek efficiency. In their work, they like to see some kind of tangible result, and thus they are often found in engineering or construction. Since ISTPs often have a very hands-on learning style, traditional classrooms may hold little interest for them. If they can see the practical application of an idea and can learn in a more active way, they will continue in school.

ISTPs are quite independent, and do not have a great deal of appreciation for rules and regulations. What they do respect are skill, logic, and the ability to respond effectively to problems. Competition is certainly not foreign to ISTPs, and they enjoy responding in more "effective" ways than their competitors. They are commonly found in police work, business, and other areas where this need can be met. They are also found in law, computer programming, and accounting, or any career where they can bring logical order to a mass of facts. Whatever their career, ISTPs need variety and opportunities to learn and to apply their skills. Since they often enjoy solitary activities and hobbies, they also need a career where some in-depth interest can be used.

In relating to others, ISTPs often have a reserved and detached style. ISTPs can be tough-minded and a bit cool; they tend to control their emotions, and little leaks out. They may even be shy, but once they know you, they can be quite playful. Much of their expression is nonverbal, because to ISTPs, actions speak louder than words, and when they do express themselves verbally, they tend to be matter-of-fact. They prefer relationships that are collegial, and since they respect skill in others, they often build relationships around shared activities (e.g., scuba diving). ISTPs may frustrate others with their strong needs for independence and freedom.

They resist feeling controlled, which may at times manifest as a lack of commitment, or lack of follow-through.

Development of extraverted sensing will help ISTPs stay open to new information that can be processed using their logical thinking. Without that development, they may get tangled in the world of logic, become certain of the truth of their conclusions, and be unwilling to check out whether or not their "truths" apply to what is really happening in the world outside of their own minds. ISTPs can benefit from learning to establish long-term goals and from adhering to the commitments they make. With maturity, they will also be less inclined to put off decisions. Since ISTPs may sometimes be insensitive to others' needs for feedback and appreciation, they can be seen as unapproachable. Development of feeling will help them attend more to personal and interpersonal issues, including their impact on others, as well as to what others and they themselves care about.

Under stress, ISTPs can feel suddenly trapped or bound by rules or expectations, at which point they may impulsively move out of the constricting situation. In addition, they may become cynical and see only negative possibilities for the future, and as a result put off decisions. Under stress, ISTPs can feel cut off from others, and misinterpret comments made by others as intentionally hurtful. In surprising contrast to their reserved and cool style, under great stress they may even have out-of-proportion explosions of emotion.

**Key words**
logical ■ analytical ■ adaptable ■ pragmatic
problem-solver ■ troubleshooter ■ adventurous ■ cool ■ independent

# ISFP
# Introverted Feeling with
# Extraverted Sensing

For ISFPs the dominant quality in their lives is a deep-felt caring for living things, combined with a quietly playful and some times adventurous approach to life and all its experiences. ISFPs typically show their caring in very practical ways, since they often prefer action to words. Their warmth and concern are generally not expressed openly, and what people often first encounter with ISFPs is their quiet adaptability, realism, and "free spirit" spontaneity.

ISFPs deeply value people, relationships, and all of life. Given the ISFP's reflective nature, other people may not see this intense caring until they know the ISFP well. They are compassionate people who are typically sensitive to the emotional states and suffering of others. ISFPs are perhaps the gentlest and kindest of the types; they tend to be acutely aware of nonverbal messages, and their kindness is often expressed in nonverbal ways. Thus they often have a strong affinity with children and animals. They may also have a love of natural things: plants and bodies of water.

ISFPs are idealistic and would like their work to contribute to people in some way: to their comfort, their freedom, their safety. ISFPs also take a very personal approach to life, and it is important for them to find work about which they can care deeply. When they find people about whom they care, they are intensely and fiercely loyal.

ISFPs are deeply concerned with harmony; they like for their relationships and environment to feel comfortable and free from strife. Since disharmony can be very painful to them, they may act as peacemakers in relationships or groups. If disharmony can not be resolved, they may choose to go their own way. ISFPs are cooperative by nature because they deeply understand that connection and caring are essential to the natural order of the world.

Sensing provides ISFPs with a good grasp of realities and provides them with a way to stay open to new information, though their dominant drive is still a deep process of valuing. ISFPs are usually down-to-earth people who enjoy living in the here and now. They are immersed in the ongoing richness of sensory and sensual experience, and they tend to have a playfully optimistic approach to every day life. As pragmatists, ISFPs prefer the concrete over the abstract, and they often have a good memory for factual detail. Theory tends to hold little interest for them, and they are more interested in how to make something work than in why it works. Sensing also ensures that their caring is practical; they want to help people in hands-on ways.

ISFPs need freedom and variety in their lives, and they may have a low tolerance for boredom or constrictions. Excitement and adventure often call them, and they want to pursue things at their own pace, and in their own way. They *will* fulfill their commitments to people and institutions, but they do not have a great appreciation for organizational structures in and of themselves. In their spontaneity, ISFPs are often good at responding to the needs of the moment. This is particularly true where a pragmatic response is required: helping a person by making them comfortable, by negotiating a dispute, or by keeping their own head in an emergency. In general, ISFPs are flexible and tolerant; however, when a deep value is violated, they can become quite stubborn, much to the surprise of others.

ISFPs are often excited by action for the sake of action. This often shows as a love of sports, crafts, or other hands-on activities. In fact, ISFPs often have athletic interests, and surprisingly, can be quite competitive in this arena, though it may not be obvious. With their immersion in hands-on activity, they may also develop craftsmanlike skill in their manipulation of athletic equipment, tools, or other instruments.

The ISFP's acute sensitivity to color, sound, and atmosphere may manifest itself as a sense of style and aesthetics. These qualities in conjunction with their discerning attention to sensory data can result in ISFPs being excellent craftworkers, artists, or designers; it is not unusual for ISFPs to have interests in art, music, or dance.

The traditional classroom may have little of interest to ISFPs, particularly as the emphasis on theory increases and opportunities for applications or hands-on learning decrease. When they do enjoy school, it is often because they have found teachers with whom they feel a connection. ISFPs often like to work alone and may despair of finding their place in the world. Without planning, they may indeed drift from one career to another. They *can* find a place, however, and are commonly found in hands-on caring and helping careers, such as health care. ISFPs are also found in business and in technical, trade, or crafts careers, where their pragmatic adaptability can be readily applied.

ISFPs are caring and trusting people, if somewhat reserved. Their warmth becomes apparent once a relationship is established, and they deeply value their friendships. They prefer expression through action and artistry rather than through words, and thus their speech may be short and terse. Since they tend not to blow their own horns, ISFPs can also appear modest. In the extreme, this may become shyness or nonassertiveness, and ISFPs can be in danger of underselling themselves, even though they have so much to offer. They do want to be appreciated for their contributions, as they appreciate others for theirs. If they do not get that acknowledgment, they are in danger of withdrawing.

ISFPs need development of extraverted sensing to ensure that they move into action on their ideals, otherwise they may end up feeling trapped in painful disillusionment. This situation worsens if their idealism becomes extreme perfectionism; nothing meets the ideal. Feeling can give ISFPs a sense of certainty about their evaluation of a situation, and development of sensing will help them stay open to facts from the outer world. Development of sensing will also provide them with information on how to move into action on their ideals. At times, ISFPs may also have difficulty in making decisions, meeting deadlines, or following through. As they learn to use thinking and intuition to look to the future, they will see the long-term consequences of some of these actions. They will also increasingly find their place in the world and find work that contributes in the way they would like.

Under stress ISFPs may lose their self-confidence, become passive, and withdraw. They may also take their resistance to rules and regulations to the extreme and neglect their responsibilities, even ones they care about. Under stress, ISFPs can also become overly sensitive to the remarks of others and become very self-critical; under extreme stress they may even become surprisingly and outwardly critical of others.

**Key words**

gentle ■ caring ■ compassionate

modest ■ aesthetic ■ artistic ■ idealistic ■ joyful action

# INFP

## Introverted Feeling with Extraverted Intuition

For INFPs the dominant quality in their lives is a deep-felt caring and idealism about people. They experience this intense caring most often in their relationships with others, but they may also experience it around ideas, projects, or any involvement they see as important. INFPs are often skilled communicators, and they are naturally drawn to ideas that embody a concern for human potential. INFPs live in the inner world of values and ideals, but what people often first encounter with them in the outer world is their adaptability and concern for possibilities.

For INFPs, the world and events are viewed from a very personal and often idealistic perspective. INFPs pursue their ideals, and their desire to find their place in the world and express who they are can take on an almost quest-like quality. INFPs look for meaning; they look for it in their lives, in their work, and in their relationships with others. They may feel a strong need to contribute something of importance to the world or to have an impact on the lives of those about whom they care, though they can also be quiet observers of people and humanity at large.

People and relationships are what the world is about, and harmony in relationships is of great importance to the INFP. They are very concerned with the impact of their decisions on individuals, not only on those about whom they care but on themselves and on their own values as well. Their deep need and desire for harmony can sometimes show as a concern with keeping peace, and with maturity, they are open-minded and egalitarian. INFPs have a desire for harmony which may at times get in the way of their getting their own needs met. Their caring, warmth, and deep valuing of relationships are also difficult to communicate to others and may not be immediately apparent to people in their

lives. INFPs may even appear a bit cool or aloof from the outside, though they would be surprised that others experience them in this way, given the warmth and loyalty they feel inside.

Intuition gives their feeling a future focus and orients INFPs to the abstract and symbolic. Intuition, however, is always secondary to the deep-felt valuing and caring that characterizes their feeling. Their orientation to the future sometimes finds expression in their desire to help others manifest their potential. Their intuition may also find embodiment in creative activity or show itself as an interest in communication. INFPs often have a gift for the written or spoken word, and they typically have a sense of nuance of meaning. INFPs want the freedom to live their ideals, and they do like variety in their lives.

If interested, INFPs may find an outlet for their gifts in the fields of writing, journalism, or foreign languages. Their ideas and their writing are conceptual and metaphorical, with a concern for universals and values, but their writing also tends to have a warm personal tone. Many INFPs also have a deep love and enjoyment of reading. On a subject about which they care, and on which they have had time to reflect, they can be exceptionally verbal and persuasive.

Since creativity is often of importance to INFPs, they may have artistic interests or a concern for aesthetics. They attend to style as well as content in their creative expression, and their creativity is often a vehicle for communicating their values and ideals. INFPs may be strongly attracted to, and enjoy experiencing, the human condition in all its joys and sadnesses, as represented in the works of artists, musicians, writers, and filmmakers through history.

INFPs are excited by new ideas and new possibilities, particularly as they may find expression in people's lives. As a result INFPs are often drawn to areas like counseling, where they can use their caring and grasp of the possible. With interests in academics they may be found in the fields of literature, psychology, and the arts and sciences. Spirituality can also play a large role in their lives, as they look for a personal connection to something larger than themselves. Though INFPs care about people, they are often drawn to fields where they can work independently. Their behavior in the outer world is usually characterized by flexibility and they may be frustrated by routine, structure, and rules.

In their relationships, INFPs are often adaptable people who quietly manifest compassion and sensitivity. Their sensitivity may be seen in their intense empathic responses to the joys and suffering of others, and to those in need. Commitment, loyalty, and love are often of great importance to them, as are family and children. Interestingly, they may be in love with the idea of love, and without maturity, they may become passive and fail to move into compassionate and caring action. Though INFPs often have a strong sense of what is right and wrong, outwardly they are very tolerant; they will, however, let you know if you have trod on their values. Without development, an INFP may fail to express his or her needs clearly, and thus others may be confused or frustrated by not knowing they have violated something of importance to the INFP.

Development of extraverted intuition is necessary for INFPs to help them stay open to new ideas, new information, and new experiences. Otherwise they may feel deeply, but never move into action, or they may fail to check whether their beliefs about people are true. As a result, their strong sense of right and wrong can lead to their being perceived as moralistic by others. Development of intuition will also give INFPs possible ways to pursue their ideals. Without this development, INFPs' energies may become trapped inside, squandered on worrying about meaningless issues, or brought to bear on issues that are so big that they do not know where to start or how to have an impact. Development of sensing and thinking will also help them take a hard real-world look at their plans, and give them the firmness needed to manifest their ideals.

Because INFPs are often attracted to new possibilities, and because they may have difficulty saying no, they may bite off more than they can chew. They can have too many projects going to successfully complete any of them. Under stress, they may also become rigid and perfectionistic, feel inadequate, and become critical of themselves. Under extreme stress, and in surprising contrast to their tolerant and caring style, they may even become outwardly critical of others, feeling that others are failing to meet the ideals the INFP has set for them.

---

**Key words**

deep-felt valuing ■ quiet caring ■ relationships
harmony ■ meaning ■ ideals ■ artistic ■ symbols ■ metaphors ■ writing

# INTP

## Introverted Thinking with Extraverted Intuition

For INTPs the driving force in their lives is to understand whatever phenomenon is the focus of their attention. They want to make sense of the world—as a concept—and they often enjoy opportunities to be creative. INTPs are logical, analytical, and detached in their approach to the world; they naturally question and critique ideas and events as they strive for understanding. INTPs usually have little need to control the outer world, or to bring order to it, and they often appear very flexible and adaptable in their lifestyle.

Logic and analysis are paramount for INTPs. They have a drive to analyze, to understand, and to make sense of ideas and events; things simply must make sense, and they *should*. In fact, their internal juggling of ideas almost has a life of its own. INTPs think naturally in terms of cause and effect and logical consequences. They look for the underlying principles that explain the nature of the world or for the principles that capture the essence of their area of interest; INTPs enjoy solving complex problems.

INTPs are naturally skeptical and critical. They question, question, and question some more. As a result, they may appear to others to be challenging, though they do not intend to criticize others. Because they value precision, INTPs are simply looking for logical inconsistencies in writing, speech, thought, and ideas. Exactness in definitions is of great importance to them, and without restraint they may engage in unnecessary hairsplitting. INTPs may also have dramatic powers of concentration, and in using these they may develop an amazingly deep and complex understanding of some area(s) of interest. In fact, they may become so involved in the inner world and in their subject of interest that they may forget about the passage of time.

Intuition orients the INTP's thinking to the future, and to the abstract and symbolic, but intuition is always subordinate to the need to analyze and understand ideas and events. New ideas and new ways of doing things fascinate INTPs. In fact, they are infinitely curious: about ideas, books, systems of thought, computers, or any other current area of interest. They may use their logic and intuition to develop new and highly intricate systems of thought, and thus they can be brilliant and innovative thinkers. INTPs are organizers in the world of abstract ideas; they view things systemically and creatively. They want the freedom to pursue their ideas in their own way, and thus they seek variety and independence in their lives.

INTPs may have scientific, theoretical, or artistic interests, and can be found in computer, physical, or social sciences. They may be teachers, researchers, or thinkers in any field in which abstract and complex thought is required, as in philosophy. For INTPs, experience provides data, and the data is then analyzed for its fit into the complex mental models that they have been developing, possibly over a lifetime. The model is often more important than the experience itself, and INTPs are usually more interested in understanding and solving abstract problems than in the actual application of their ideas. They need to find a career where a deep and intensive understanding of some subject is important.

INTPs are often nontraditional. Their questioning attitude and need for autonomy may even lead to their being or appearing iconoclastic. They do, however, value intelligence and prize competence. INTPs give respect to others based on others' perceived competence and depth of understanding rather than on the basis of position or external trappings of power. This is a natural extension of their strong valuing of autonomy. They are usually tolerant and adaptable and give other people wide leeway of behavior, feeling little need to control others. However, when the INTP's principles (which may not be immediately apparent) are violated, he or she can be seen as very firm, even stubborn.

INTPs are usually more interested in ideas and concepts than in people, though people may certainly be the subject of their acute thinking and analysis. A consequence of this detached and analytical orientation is that INTPs may miss interpersonal nuances, not appreciate the need for social niceties, and end up in hot water as a result. They can appear reserved and impersonal, though they do usually enjoy discussions with other people who share their own keen interest in ideas. Additionally, INTPs may be insensitive to the emotional needs of others and others may see them as aloof or unapproachable. At worst they may be or appear to be arrogant and critical.

Without development of their extraverted intuition, INTPs may remain aloof and incomprehensible, unable to work out or apply their ideas in the outside world. Development of their intuition will also help them take in information that can be processed using their logical thinking. Without that development, INTPs may become entangled in the inner world of logical thoughts and systems, and become too distant from the outer world of people and action. As a result, they may become certain of the truth of their logic, but be unwilling to check whether their "truths" apply to what is really happening in the world outside of their own minds. By attending only to what is logical, INTPs may also forget to attend to what is important to *them* as people. They may at times be weak on follow-through and self-direction, and they may even forget to attend to the details of everyday life. Appropriate development of sensing and feeling will help them avoid these traps as well as help them give greater attention to interpersonal issues.

Under stress, INTPs may feel overwhelmed and misunderstood. However, because they are so adaptable they may remain in a situation rather than leave it or negotiate a change. They may also feel confused when people in general or significant others don't behave "logically." INTPs need to understand that relationships have a logic of their own that the INTP may neglect to register as valid or important. Under great stress, and in contrast to their usual calm cool style, they may erupt with out-of-proportion expressions of emotion, particularly in response to relationship stresses.

---

**Key words**

logical ■ conceptual ■ analytical

objective ■ critical ■ ingenious ■ complex ■ creative ■ curious ■ ideas

## ESTP

## Extraverted Sensing with Introverted Thinking

For ESTPs the dominant quality in their lives is their enthusiastic attention to the outer world of hands-on and real-life experiences. ESTPs are excited by continuous involvement in new activities and in the pursuit of new challenges. They tend to be logical and analytical in their approach to life, and they have an acute sense of how objects, events, and people in the world work. ESTPs are typically energetic and adaptable realists, who prefer to experience and accept life rather than to judge or organize it.

ESTPs are spontaneous and fun-loving realists. They move into action easily, even impulsively. ESTPs live for excitement, pursuing new involvements, new relationships, and new locales. They live in the here and now and are most effective and happy when they can act on the needs of the moment. Flexibility is their hallmark. ESTPs do not have a lot of "shoulds" in their lives. As a result they tend to be tolerant and open to a variety of experiences and people.

ESTPs playfully seek out physical experience in all of its forms, in new food or travel, for example. In fact, things physical are usually of great interest to ESTPs, and they often have the latest electronics, vehicles, tools, and clothes. They may also have a taste for aesthetics. As keen observers of the outer world, ESTPs may have an excellent memory for facts, details, and what is literally happening in their environment. Conversely, abstractions tend to be of little interest to them, and they may not entirely trust theory. In fact, they often learn best by optimistically diving into the middle of things and getting their hands on whatever it is that needs to be learned.

ESTPs are often excited by the sheer joy of activity. For example, they may enjoy participating in a sport for its own sake, their expertise arising from immersion in the action rather than from a focus on achievement. Incidentally, participation in sports or other forms of exercise often provides them with great pleasure and they may be gifted athletes. With their needs for variety and freedom, ESTPs can become frustrated by too much structure and may at times go around regulations they find too constricting.

Thinking gives ESTPs a way to critique and give meaning to their experiences, and to order their perceptions of reality but thinking is always secondary to the drive to gain new experiences. Thinking puts their pragmatism in a logical context; they look for the principles that underlie the working of things in the real world. As realists, ESTPs accept facts as they are, but because they are adaptable, they also know that there are many ways to solve a problem. With their unbending faith in their ability to respond to the needs of the moment, ESTPs are often skilled at managing crises or at solving real-life problems; they can make excellent negotiators and trouble shooters. They can also be tough-minded and a bit cool by nature, in spite of their outgoing personality.

ESTPs are pragmatists at heart. They want to concretely address the *actual* issue or problem at hand. As a result, the traditional classroom tends to hold little of interest to ESTPs, and the more the focus is on theory, the more quickly will their interest be lost. They may literally have trouble sitting still in class. They want to learn how to do something, and they want to learn by doing it, rather than by reading or talking about it; actions speak louder than words. For ESTPs to maintain their interest in school, they need to find active ways to learn and applications for the ideas they are studying.

ESTPs can have magnificent hands-on skills in using the tool of their choice, whether it be a computer, a golf club, a motorcycle, or anything else. As skilled operators of their environment, ESTPs know what resources are available and how to make the best use of them to achieve an end. This skillful operation may also show as an orientation to the arts or crafts, and they can be quite mechanically minded. Whatever the domain, ESTPs prefer working with things that can be seen, and thus are often found in the engineering, construction, technical, and health care or fitness professions.

Adventure, risk, and competition are not foreign to ESTPs, and they enjoy the thrill of responding in more "effective" ways than an opponent. As a result, ESTPs are commonly found in police work, business, and other areas where this need can be met, and where they can demonstrate the skillfulness and even-headedness they so value. They also like to have an impact on others, and since they may also enjoy being "on stage," they can be found working as entertainers, promoters, marketers, and salespeople.

ESTPs are usually seen as friendly, casual, and experienced in life. When they choose to be, they *can* be very perceptive of other people's attitudes and beliefs. However, their preference for matter-of-factness in communications may at times be experienced as tactlessness. Whatever their area of interest, they usually have an enthusiasm that can energize those around them. They are naturals at parties, and can be excellent at group work. Though typically good-natured, ESTPs can engage in one-upmanship. In the extreme, this playful quality can wear on acquaintances, and at worst they may be perceived as manipulative. Since ESTPs also value their sense of freedom, others may at times experience them as lacking commitment in relationships.

Development of introverted thinking will help ESTPs focus, define, and adhere to goals, and help them determine which of their interests are the most important to pursue. In general, ESTPs can benefit from a greater appreciation of the need for structure and follow-through. Setting standards for themselves will also help them avoid the trap of indiscriminately pursuing experiences simply for the sake of excitement. If they find that too many of their decisions are based on the needs of the moment, they may benefit from making longer range plans. They may also benefit from attending to the impact of their behavior on others and remembering that there is more to relationships than people's ability to have a good time together.

Under stress ESTPs may become excessively impulsive, stubbornly ignoring structures, commitments, and deadlines. They may also pursue exciting new experiences at the cost of career and relationships. Under great stress, ESTPs may blow details out of proportion, imagining that they have the worst possible meaning, and see only the negatives in the future. In contrast to their usually confident and adaptable style, they may feel confused, latch onto one *possible* interpretation of their problems and be *certain* it is correct, and ignore all data to the contrary.

---

### Keywords

excitement ■ risk ■ pragmatic ■ realistic ■ adaptable
troubleshooter ■ spontaneous ■ active ■ impulsive ■ enthusiastic

## ESFP

## Extraverted Sensing with Introverted Feeling

For ESFPs the dominant quality in their lives is their enthusiastic attention to the outer world of hands-on and real-life experiences. ESFPs are excited by continuous involvement in new activities and new relationships. They also have a deep concern for people, and they show their caring in warm and pragmatic gestures of helping. ESFPs are typically energetic and adaptable realists, who prefer to experience and accept life rather than to judge or organize it.

ESFPs are energetic, fun-loving realists. They seek fun and excitement and will create them if they are nowhere to be found. ESFPs love life and take obvious joy in drinking it to the full; they continually seek new experiences, new involvements, new friends. Since ESFPs rely heavily on their experience in their understanding and decision making, the more experiences they have, the better! They are more interested in gathering new experiences than in critiquing or evaluating them. Since they seek to know rather than to judge, they tend also to be open to and tolerant of a wide variety of people and activities.

ESFPs are spontaneous, flexible, and playful, and they love activity in and of itself. For example, they can enjoy participating in a sport for its own sake. It is the action itself that is fun, rather than any drive to improve their performance. Incidentally, participation in sports or other forms of exercise often provides ESFPs with great pleasure and they may be gifted athletes.

ESFPs move into action because that is what life is all about, and they easily respond to the needs of the here and now. Above all else, they are adaptable. In fact, they like a bit of adventure in their lives, and in their work too if possible. ESFPs are often good at handling crises, and thus they can make very effective trouble-shooters. They tend to be casual, and may be frustrated by too many rules and regulations. If rules disturb them too much, they will often find ways around them.

ESFPs swim in a sea of sensory experience and thus they often are masters off actual data, noticing and remembering details and specifics. With their immersion in what is real, and in their pursuit of new experience, ESFPs often want to try out the newest fashions, the newest electronics, the newest anything. They appreciate and enjoy their material possessions.

They are also pragmatists at heart. ESFPs are more interested in if and how something can be used, rather than in "why" it works. They are more interested in application than in theory, and in facts than in abstractions. ESFPs tend to have less interest in book learning just for the sake of gathering knowledge, and they usually have a keen common sense.

Feeling provides ESFPs with a way of bringing order to their lives and experiences, but feeling is always secondary to the drive to have new experiences and the rush to be involved in new hands-on activities. Feeling places their pragmatism in a people context; ESFPs like to help and support others in very practical ways. They care about people, and relationships mean much to them. There is a very warm and personal touch in all that they do. When ESFPs make decisions, they are concerned with the impact of those decisions on people, as well as on their own sense of self. They want harmony and tend to be non-competitive people. They may even be skilled at negotiating a common ground between those in conflict.

Since the traditional classroom does not provide as many opportunities as ESFPs would prefer for hands-on learning, they may not enjoy it very much. As they move to higher and higher levels of education, they tend to lose interest with the increasing focus on theory and abstractions. Thus they must find a practical reason and application for what they are learning to get them to continue. ESFPs want to learn by doing, and by being with others who are doing what the ESFP wants to learn.

In general, ESFPs demonstrate their caring for others in very practical ways; they *show* their concern and help others out in direct fashion. For example, they are more likely to give a cold person a blanket than to give them directions to a warmer state.

ESFPs can also be quite empathic, and they often have a special concern for children, animals, and all things natural. As a result, they are often found in helping, teaching, and service careers, and within these careers they tend to work in the hands-on areas. For example, in the helping careers ESFPs are often found in nursing or family medicine, and in the teaching careers they are often found teaching K–12.

With their outgoing nature, ESFPs are also found in business, sales, and entertainment. Whatever their interests, they want and need careers where they have a lot of opportunities to meet and be with others. They are naturals for working in groups, and are usually skilled and comfortable communicators who may be quite persuasive.

ESFPs are people people. They seek company and others seek them out. ESFPs are friendly and enthusiastic, even sparkling. They are often the life of the party, and others can get caught up in their excitement and optimism. Their spontaneity can sometimes manifest as impulsiveness, and though they are caring and generous,

ESFPs may frustrate others by what appears to be a lack of interest in adhering to commitments. As social beings, they want and need feedback and appreciation, and they like to give the same to others. They may be hurt by a lack of positive strokes.

Development of introverted feeling will help ESFPs develop consistency and direction in their lives, and help them determine which of their interests are the most important to pursue. Development of feeling will also help them work on planning and follow-through and in bringing things in their lives to closure. In general ESFPs can benefit from developing a greater appreciation of the need for structures and adherence to obligations. They may also have too much of a concern for here-and-now experience at times. Development of thinking and intuition will help them to look at the longer term consequences of some of their quick actions and to see the need for planning.

Under stress, ESFPs may become excessively impulsive and overcommit without following through. They may also interpret actions and statements made by others too personally and read negative intent between the lines. In contrast to their usual style of pragmatically jumping into action, they may feel trapped in confusion. Under great stress, ESFPs may look to the future with pessimism, and see only negative possibilities, or latch on to one possible negative interpretation of events in their lives.

## Keywords

hands-on ■ realistic ■ excitement ■ people ■ social
expressive ■ enthusiasm ■ spontaneous ■ impulsive ■ new ■ adaptable

## ENFP

## Extraverted Intuition with Introverted Feeling

For ENFPs the dominant quality in their lives is their attention to the outer world of possibilities; they are excited by continuous involvement in anything new, whether it be new ideas, new people, or new activities. Though ENFPs thrive on what is possible and what is new, they also experience a deep concern for people as well. Thus, they are especially interested in possibilities for people. ENFPs are typically energetic, enthusiastic people who lead spontaneous and adaptable lives.

Intuition constantly draws ENFPs to the new. They like, want, even *must* do new things or at least do old things in new ways. This drive arises out of their experience that whatever is over the horizon is always more interesting than what is here and present. ENFPs trust the truth of their intuition and they charge off with excitement and inspiration in whatever direction it points them. With their orientation to the new, they are natural brainstormers, and look to the future with optimism. They are creative, active, and imaginative. ENFPs enjoy starting and becoming involved in the initial stages of a project but usually have less interest in follow-through. They tend to be very spontaneous, flexible, and adaptable people. What may look like difficulty in committing is a manifestation of their desire to miss nothing. After all, deciding prematurely means they might close off many interesting options down the road.

Feeling provides ENFPs with a way to focus and critique their vision, but feeling is always secondary to the driving energy of their intuition. Feeling does often mold their visions into possibilities for people. They are concerned with personal growth, identity, and authenticity, both for themselves and for others. ENFPs want to be free to be themselves, to express themselves, and they want others to feel free to do the same. ENFPs may also be skilled in perceiving what is important to others, and what others are thinking: a valuable skill in any people-oriented profession. They are idealists, believing their vision of the higher possibilities for people are true now or can be made true in short order.

ENFPs want and need involvement with people, and they value harmony in those relationships. They derive great pleasure from meeting and talking with others, and they enjoy opportunities to think out loud. ENFPs are expressive and often have intense emotional responses to happenings and to people in their lives; vital emotional experience is of great importance to them. They like others to be as excited as they are by new ideas and new involvements, and they naturally focus on commonalities in relationships. This focus, in conjunction with their concern for others and their ability to take a global perspective, often leads to skills in negotiation or mediation.

With their combination of intuition and feeling, ENFPs tend to think globally and metaphorically. They are often verbally gifted, particularly in conversation. ENFPs look for the meaning behind statements and events. As a result, they can be skilled integrators of information and ideas, and they are often good at reading between the lines in conversations. They love learning new things, and love looking for new perspectives on facts, events, and people. ENFPs typically learn more by focusing on broad issues and are less concerned with the working out of their ideas.

ENFPs are people people; they are usually gregarious by nature, and they are often performers. They usually have a wide network of friends, acquaintances, and business contacts, and they are naturals for work that requires meeting, persuading, or motivating others. ENFPs are catalysts for change and generators of enthusiasm, and they are often found in counseling, psychology teaching, the helping professions, or personnel work. ENFPs may also have interests in the humanities and the arts, particularly the dramatic arts. Their adaptability and imagination help them to develop skills in almost any area of interest.

ENFPs are typically intolerant of routine, and they need variety in their work. Their perception of time is open-ended, and they like work that allows them to have a variety of projects going on at once. They need to find a place where they can use their abilities to generate new ideas and to look at things in creative ways. Though they are concerned with people, ENFPs are typically quite independent and tend not to be great upholders of tradition. In fact, it is natural for them to push boundaries and to redefine rules.

ENFPs are usually seen as warm, charming, and friendly. At times, however, others may feel overwhelmed by their energy and excitement. In relationships, they are typically supportive, express appreciation freely, and they like to receive feedback as well. They may, however, be overconcerned with harmony at times. As a result, they may be seen as having difficulty standing their ground or confronting others.

ENFPs need development of introverted feeling to help them choose which exciting possibilities they will focus upon and to help them follow through on their visions. Developing a hierarchy of values will help them clarify a direction in life and help them develop self-

discipline. Once a project has started, ENFPs may have difficulty attending to the details: for development they need to realize that implementing an idea is not always as easy as imagining it. ENFPs can also become so excited by a new idea that they may miss cues that others are not as excited by their new interest as they are. Development of feeling will help them avoid this situation. Development of thinking will help them avoid any overconcern with harmony. Development of thinking and sensing will help them attend to the pragmatics of making their visions become realities.

Under stress, ENFPs may have difficulty saying no. Consequently, they may take on too many projects without any practical way of completing them. They can also become rigidly nonconforming if they feel too much structure is being imposed on them. Under extreme stress, ENFPs may also find it difficult to pull themselves away from a project to attend to practical or physical needs. For example, they may forget to eat or sleep, may drive themselves to exhaustion, or may even have inexplicable accidents. In surprising contrast to their usual global style, they can even become compulsively attentive to irrelevant details.

---

### Keywords
enthusiastic ■ visionary ■ energetic ■ possibilities ■ new
many ■ people ■ action ■ excitement ■ creative ■ caring ■ warmth

# ENTP

## Extraverted Intuition with Introverted Thinking

For ENTPs the dominant quality in their lives is their attention to the outer world of possibilities; they are excited by continuous involvement in anything new, whether it be new ideas, new people, or new activities. They look for patterns and meaning in the world, and they often have a deep need to analyze, to understand, and to know the nature of things. ENTPs are typically energetic, enthusiastic people who lead spontaneous and adaptable lives.

ENTPs are continually pulled to new activities, new ways of doing things, and new ways of thinking about things. What is over the horizon is almost always more interesting than what is going on in the here and now. ENTPs can be dynamic visionaries, and they trust the truth of their insights. They believe that if they can imagine something, then materializing it is just one step away. ENTPs work toward their vision or toward solutions in bursts of energy and enthusiasm. They are eternal optimists.

ENTPs are pursuers of change. They are innovators, inventors, planners, and designers. Driven by inspiration, they tend to have a low tolerance for boredom and to become frustrated when things appear to be moving too slowly. They want action and variety in their lives and they typically have many irons in the fire. With their bias toward active learning, ENTPs want to see their visions materialized in the world, though not following through on their visions may at times be their downfall.

Thinking provides ENTPs with a way to focus and critique their visions, but thinking is always secondary to the driving energy of their intuition. Thinking does make them logical and analytical, and thus they value rationality as well as inspiration. Things *should* make sense, and if they don't now, the ENTP believes they *will* eventually after further analytical probing. ENTPs

love to solve complex problems and approach them as challenges.

ENTPs continually look for the meaning behind statements, in events, in data, and in actions. They are often skilled at noticing trends and forecasting the future. Natural conceptualizers, they continually build and rebuild mental models to explain the world, and their thinking tends to be complex, abstract, and original. Because ENTPs are also critical in their thinking, they may be skilled in being able to see several different points of view. They imagine the possibilities of a situation and then strategically analyze those different possibilities to determine which course of action would be the most effective to pursue. ENTPs can be ingenious, and they also trust their abilities to improvise and respond to the needs of the moment.

ENTPs tend to value knowledge and competence, and they are often achievement-oriented. As a result, they tend to value others on the basis of perceived intelligence and ability, rather than on the basis of status. ENTPs, however, are often aware of power and status issues. They can play the game if need be to achieve the realization of their visions.

ENTPs enjoy careers that call upon their ability to look at things creatively and analytically. They may also become bored if they do not feel challenged with a continuous stream of new projects. ENTPs are often drawn to the sciences and technology. They may also be entrepreneurs, marketers, or professors, or anything else that engages their interests.

ENTPs tend to be gregarious, sociable people, and they can be quite exciting company. They enjoy being involved with others, and their enthusiasm is contagious. It may also be overwhelming to others at times. Typically easy-going and casual, they usually look self-confident in their interactions with others. ENTPs do tend to view their lives and people in an objective and analytical manner, and as a result they can be or appear to be insensitive to emotional issues or relationship concerns. Paradoxically, they can be skilled at discerning what others think or believe, when they choose to attend to others in that way.

ENTPs are often verbally skilled and can be energetic conversationalists. They may at times argue for the sake of argument, simply because they enjoy the interplay of ideas with another person. Others, however, may be turned off by their penchant for debate and intellectual sparring. ENTPs also tend to have a high need for autonomy. This need, in conjunction with their belief in their own insights, often leads to their being dyed-in-the-wool individualists. They are not strong believers in rules, and they will often ignore or go around structures that make no sense to them.

ENTPs need development of introverted thinking to help them critique their many ideas and inspirations, otherwise they may waste their energy by being involved in too many projects or in an endless succession of new interests. ENTPs need to make use of their ability to analyze to help them clarify a direction in life and to help them develop self-discipline. They need to realize that implementing an idea is not always as easy as imag-

ining it. Often once a project is begun, ENTPs can have difficulty attending to or following through on details. Development of thinking will help them see the consequences of continual pursuit of the new with no follow-through. Through development of feeling, they can become more aware of their impact on others and of the sometimes negative consequences of continual intellectual challenge and debate. Development of sensing will help them attend to the pragmatics of making their visions a reality.

Under stress, ENTPs may take on too many projects without any practical way of completing them. They may even become rigidly nonconforming if they feel too much structure is being imposed on them. Under great stress, ENTPs may find it difficult to pull themselves away from a project to attend to practical or physical needs. For example, they may forget to eat or sleep, may drive themselves to exhaustion, or may even have inexplicable accidents. In surprising contrast to their usual abstract and global style, under stress they can even become compulsively focused on irrelevant details.

---

**Keywords**

energy ■ enthusiasm ■ new ■ many

abstract ■ theoretical ■ logical ■ complex ■ global ■ entrepreneur

## ESTJ

## Extraverted Thinking with Introverted Sensing

For ESTJs the driving force in their lives is their need to analyze and bring into logical order the outer world of events, people, and things. ESTJs like to organize anything that comes into their domain, and they will work energetically to complete tasks so they can quickly move from one to the next. Sensing orients their thinking to current facts and realities, and thus gives their thinking a pragmatic quality. ESTJs take their responsibilities seriously and believe others should do so as well.

For the ESTJ, logic and analysis are paramount. They believe the outer world should and will make sense, and they strive to bring that world into logical order. ESTJs believe behavior should be logical, and they work to govern their own behavior by strict principles. They have a strong need to organize the facts, projects, events, or people in their area of influence. Since they love *action,* their organizing has a dynamic quality. ESTJs live for decisions; it feels good to settle things. They would rather be certain and be wrong than be uncertain.

ESTJs readily apply their clear standards of what is correct and right to what goes on around them. With their extraverted thinking, they will openly critique anyone or anything that does not meet the standard, but they do so only with the purpose of bringing people and procedures back into a rational and natural order. ESTJs apply standards and measures to themselves and to others only to increase the efficiency and effectiveness they so deeply value. They willingly supervise others to ensure goals are met, whether the goals are those of the community, organization, business, family, or group.

ESTJs naturally gravitate toward management and other administrative or leadership positions. With the sense of certainty their extraverted thinking bestows upon them, they are more than willing to run things

and will decidedly get things done; they are results-oriented. Above all else, ESTJs are responsible. Not only are they *ready* to take on responsibility, they *must* take on responsibility. Accountability is of great import to them, both their own and that of others. As they move to complete projects, they tend to be more task-focused than people-focused.

Sensing orients ESTJs to the present and to the facts, and thus their thinking is both logical and pragmatic. Their preference for sensing gives them a more hands-on approach to life, and they look to the utility of ideas and things. Sensing provides support to the dominant thinking by keeping ESTJs open to new facts, but the dominant force for them is still their drive to analyze and to make logical sense of things.

If ESTJs had a motto, it might be "just do it, and do it right." They have a great respect for the bottom line. And get to the bottom line, they will. ESTJs tend to be industrious people who have a strong work ethic. They value the fulfilling of duty, and if they have taken on a job, it will be completed. Realistic and precise, they attend to detail in bringing projects to fruition. The facts and figures will tell whether the project is done to satisfaction.

ESTJs form much of the backbone of society, and they feel that societal structures are the glue that maintains civilization. Thus, they give weight to institutional and community goals and expectations, and they strive to fulfill their obligations to those groups. They are pillars of the community and respect law and order; ESTJs are conscientious. Needless to say, they tend to be keepers of tradition. Holidays and birthdays, for example, are rigorously adhered to and celebrated. ESTJs appreciate the need for continuity and consistency in life, and thus they tend to value stability and security. If something has worked before, then it doesn't need to be changed—so notes their pragmatism.

ESTJs tend to be acutely aware of hierarchy, power, and authority. Position is earned through application and responsible action, and a person who has fulfilled these obligations competently is to be respected. Competence, in themselves and in others, is a thing to be prized. ESTJs often rise to positions of responsibility whatever their area, and so frequently are managers and executives. They are very often found in business, banking, construction, the military, and politics, as well as many other areas where hands-on efficiency, analysis, and responsible action are required.

ESTJs are usually quite matter-of-fact in their interactions with others. They are confident, direct, and typically tough-minded. Because they want clarity, and because their dominant thinking gives them a sense of certainty in their reasoning and conclusions, ESTJs are usually quite comfortable issuing directives to get something done. This style can work well in business but can backfire in one's personal life. ESTJs consider it essential to treat people fairly, but paradoxically their certainty about what is correct can lead to their making decisions for others. Since they may also have difficulty listening to perspectives and observations that oppose their own, they may at times be seen as autocratic.

Without development of introverted sensing, ESTJs may rush to closure, making decisions too quickly without pausing to gather enough factual information. As a result they can appear inflexible, closed to input, and all too willing to make decisions just for the sake of getting things settled. Development of sensing will help them stay open to new information and avoid these traps. Also, development of intuition will help them see the longer term consequences of some of the decisions they make. With their task orientation and drive to increase efficiency, ESTJs can miss the human factor in getting things done. Thus, they may be seen as critical and impatient. Development of feeling will help them see the importance of attending not only to what they themselves care about, but to others' feelings and needs for appreciation.

Under stress ESTJs may become hypercritical, both of themselves and of others. They may feel unappreciated or may hear innocent comments as personal attacks. Under great stress, ESTJs may also become angry and controlling, issuing directives with out attention to the consequences to other people. In the extreme, and in contrast to their usual outgoing and tough-minded style, they may feel trapped and alone, and even have out-of-proportion explosions of emotion.

---

**Keywords**

active organizer ■ logical ■ facts ■ analytical

manage ■ pragmatic ■ productive ■ responsible ■ tough-minded

## ESFJ

## Extraverted Feeling with Introverted Sensing

For ESFJs the dominant quality in their lives is an active and intense caring about people and a strong desire to bring harmony into their relationships. ESFJs bring an aura of warmth to all that they do, and they naturally move into action to help others, to organize the world around them, and to get things done. Sensing orients their feeling to current facts and realities, and thus gives their feeling a hands-on pragmatic quality. ESFJs take their work seriously and believe others should do so as well.

ESFJs are decisive because they are clear about what they value; they are clear about what is right and wrong, and what is good or bad. ESFJs want and expect the world to function harmoniously and in accord with the values and standards they feel are inherent in the natural order of things. Thus, they are comfortable using their dominant feeling to bring order to the outer world of people, events, and things. They are organizers who naturally move into action to give structure and to get things done.

ESFJs have an aura of warmth and friendliness that is easily felt by those around them. Openly expressive, they wear their hearts on their sleeves. They want to know others, and they want others to know them; above all else, they are sociable. ESFJs are concerned and compassionate, and their caring is not only intense, but *active* as well. They reach out to nurture others because they understand that helping is one of the highest goods in life. Their empathy cannot sit quietly. It translates immediately into energetic support and generous attention to the welfare of others.

ESFJs strive to develop harmony in their relationships. Harmony is *essential* to their well-being, and one way it is evident is in their appreciation of cooperation. ESFJs are not only cooperative themselves but with the cooperation of others through their enthusiastic warmth and helpfulness. Since relationships are of great importance to them, confrontations that may lead to hard feelings can be difficult for them to initiate. Their concern for harmony may also show itself as an avoidance of conflict, which can lead to a painful trap for ESFJs. They want harmony, but they also want above all else to do the right thing, two goals which are not always compatible. Sometimes doing the right thing means others may feel hurt, a conflict ESFJs eventually face as they mature.

Sensing orients ESFJs to the present and to the facts, and thus their style is both caring and pragmatic. Their preference for sensing gives them a hands-on approach to life, and they look for what *works*. They are typically not great lovers of theory preferring rather to be actively involved in real life and to have the actual experience. Sensing gives ESFJs a realistic down-to-earth quality, and makes them look precise in their structuring of their lives. Sensing also provides support to the dominant feeling by keeping them open to new facts, but the dominant force for them is still their desire to actively bring the outer world into harmony with their intensely felt people-values.

ESFJs are responsible and dependable; they take their jobs seriously. They have a strong sense of duty and are thorough in their follow-through. They will do what needs to be done. This ethic arises out of a concern for carrying their fair share of the group's work. ESFJs feel accountable to the group, because they appreciate the need for people to be able to work together well.

Traditions are of great importance to ESFJs, who guard and protect customs and celebrations great and small. Anniversaries, birthdays, and holidays are enthusiastically observed and regarded. Stability and continuity are appreciated by ESFJs, who know that social structures help ease the chaos that exists in society. Often upholders of the customs and standards of the culture or community, they strive to create and preserve structure, both at home and at work. As hosts, hostesses, and caretakers, ESFJs help smooth the bumps of everyday life by ensuring the necessities are taken care of and people's needs are attended to in very practical ways. They are skilled at providing a warm, safe, and nurturing environment. Needless to say, family is very important to them.

The ESFJs' outgoing warmth can also find expression in the careers they often choose, careers where they can actively work with people, particularly in a hands-on or pragmatic way. ESFJs are often found in business, hands-on health care, education (particularly K–12), religious, and service careers. They can be comfortable in the leadership role and will delegate as necessary.

Relationships are very important to ESFJs. They seek active involvement with others, and they like to feel a sense of belonging. They readily express appreciation and they themselves like to be appreciated. Because feedback and affirmation are important to them, they may be easily hurt by criticism or indifference. With good development, ESFJs can be exquisitely sensitive to others; they have good communication skills and are usually quite tactful. Though they are usually seen as caring, ESFJs may at times be seen as intolerant and unwilling to listen to others, behavior that can arise from their strong sense of right and wrong. They may even make decisions for others that they feel are in that person's best interest and become impatient if others don't see the correctness of the action taken. Of course, others may be offended by this presumption, and as a result ESFJs can be seen as controlling or overbearing.

Without development of introverted sensing, ESFJs may rush to closure, jumping to conclusions too quickly without pausing to gather enough factual information. Development of sensing will help them stay open to new information, particularly about people. ESFJs can have too many "shoulds," which may lead to excessive amounts of guilt or to their being perceived as inflexible. Alternatively, in their desire to maintain harmony, their own personal needs may sometimes go unmet, as they respond too readily to what others think or feel. Development of intuition and thinking will help them address the worst of these difficulties. Thinking will help them learn to acknowledge both positives and negatives about themselves and others. Development of thinking can also help them solve rather than ignore or feel trapped by problems. Intuition and thinking will also help ESFJs see the longer range consequences of their actions, and to be open to new ways of doing things.

Under stress ESFJs can become overindulgent and excessively emotional. They may also have difficulty thinking clearly and thus see or imagine only the negative possibilities in a situation. In addition, they may become excessively sensitive and overly personalize comments made by others. Under extreme stress, ESFJs may become exceptionally critical of both themselves and of others.

---

**Keywords**

warm ■ concerned ■ caring ■ enthusiastic
empathic ■ harmony ■ responsible ■ energetic ■ pragmatic ■ organize

## ENFJ

## Extraverted Feeling with Introverted Intuition

For ENFJs the dominant quality in their lives is an active and intense caring about people and a strong desire to bring harmony into their relationships. ENFJs are openly expressive and empathic people who bring an aura of warmth to all that they do. Intuition orients their feeling to the new and to the possible, thus they often enjoy working to manifest a humanitarian vision, or helping others develop their potential. ENFJs naturally and conscientiously move into action to care for others, to organize the world around them, and to get things done.

ENFJs love opportunities to talk with and learn from others, and derive great joy and energy from diving right into the sea of relationships that make up our world. To ENFJs, people are what the world is about. They are warm, enthusiastic, and optimistic people who have a wide range of friends and an active social life. Their sociability is not quiet, but very expressive and fun-loving, and they wear their hearts on their sleeves.

ENFJs tend also to have exceptional people skills. At their best, they are compassionate and exquisitely sensitive to the feelings and needs of others, and they energetically respond to those needs. ENFJs strive to establish harmony in their relationships, one expression of which is their bias toward cooperation. They are not only cooperative themselves, but win cooperation from others through their empathy and warm caring. Their concern with harmony may at times, however, manifest itself as an avoidance of conflict.

ENFJs make decisions based on personal values and on their very clear sense of right and wrong, which they usually share openly. Conclusions about people are often drawn quickly and with certainty. When an ENFJ decides a person is trustworthy and good, it is a difficult conclusion to dispel; ENFJs prize and embody loyalty.

However, it is equally difficult for them to dispel negative conclusions they may draw. They can also at times be frustrated by those who are not as quick to decide and to act as are they.

Intuition orients ENFJs to the future, to possibilities, and to patterns, thus their style is both caring and imaginative. They are creative folks who enjoy planning, and they are especially excited by "possibilities for people." Their preference for intuition also gives them a more conceptual and global approach to life. Intuition provides support to dominant feeling by keeping them open to new information, but the dominant force for ENFJs is still their desire to actively bring the outer world into harmony with their intensely felt people-values.

As a rule, ENFJs are responsible people who like to get things settled and who are conscientious in following through on commitments. They like to be involved in many things at once and often pull it off because they are organized. ENFJs can be particularly skillful in energizing people and orchestrating activities to achieve a vision. They are most deeply moved by causes that feed, nurture, and support people, and they have endless energy for work that fulfills their humanitarian values.

ENFJs are skilled communicators; they are often masters of the spoken word, but they may be quite skilled writers as well. Their thought is symbolic and metaphorical, and they look for meaning in everything. They revel in accounts of human events and relationships, as found in the theater, in cinema, and in writing, perhaps enjoying the active forms more so than the written. In their curiosity about ideas, they often enjoy school, particularly the humanities and arts. Since ENFJs value creativity, and they often have strong needs for freedom of expression, they are commonly found in careers in the performing and fine arts.

ENFJs are idealists who want and need active people contact in their careers. They orient naturally to the positive in people, and they want to help others manifest their potential. Often deeply concerned with the emotional and spiritual life, they are frequently found in careers where they can attend to issues of growth and human development. Since they look for meanings in words, actions, and events, ENFJs can have acute insight into people. They are often group catalysts and may be inspiring and persuasive healers, teachers, motivators, and leaders. ENFJs issue directives naturally, which they see as a way of facilitating group process; with business interests and with their orientation to the future, they can be insightful marketers and natural planners.

In relationships, ENFJs are friendly, energetic, and emotionally expressive. They exude charm, but may also overwhelm others through too much enthusiasm. Typically generous and hospitable folks, they also value genuineness in their relationships. Though ENFJs can be very tactful, they may at times be experienced as manipulative. They certainly do not intend to be, but their clear perception of "the good" can lead them to make decisions for others and to push others toward what the ENFJ perceives to be the best for that person.

Another danger for ENFJs is that they may inadvertently take on the concerns and responsibilities of others, and in their desire for harmony their own needs may not get met. They express appreciation naturally, and they thrive on both recognition and appreciation; as a result ENFJs tend to be hurt by indifference. They are very much turned off by criticism and cool logic.

For ENFJs, there is often a certainty in their conclusions about what is the good and right action. Development of introverted intuition will help them stay open to new information, particularly about people, and also help them avoid some of the pitfalls of this certainty. With their idealism, ENFJs can have unrealistic expectations about relationships, and they may have too many "shoulds." Development of intuition will keep them open to others' ideas, and help them listen to what others have to say. Development of sensing will help them see things as they are, and ways to work out their dreams in the practical world. ENFJs can also grow from learning to acknowledge unpleasant facts about themselves and others, and from learning to solve rather than ignore problems, a skill that will come with development of their thinking.

Under stress, ENFJs can become rigidly narrow in their perceptions, and become extremely emotional and generally irritable. They may doubt themselves and their abilities, and indiscriminately seek help or advice from others. Under great stress, ENFJs can become exceptionally critical of themselves and in contrast to their usual concern for appreciation and harmony, they can become decidedly critical of others.

**Keywords**

warmth ■ enthusiasm ■ harmony
vision ■ active ■ cooperation ■ ideals ■ catalyst ■ communicate

# ENTJ

## Extraverted Thinking with Introverted Intuition

For ENTJs the driving force in their lives is their need to analyze and bring into logical order the outer world of events, people, and things. ENTJs are natural leaders who build conceptual models that serve as plans for strategic action. Intuition orients their thinking to the future, and gives their thinking an abstract quality. ENTJs will actively pursue and direct others in the pursuit of goals they have set, and they prefer a world that is structured and organized.

For ENTJs logic and analysis are paramount. They believe the outer world should and will make sense, and they strive to bring that world into logical order. Energetic and decisive, ENTJs literally drive toward closure in the outer world, and they naturally push organizations and the people in them to be more effective. They abhor disorganized activity and live for decisions; it feels good to them to settle things and move onward. ENTJs would rather be certain and be wrong than be uncertain.

ENTJs have very clear standards about what constitutes right and wrong, correct and incorrect behavior, and they are usually open in their critique of what goes on around them. They are natural skeptics and will spontaneously question anything that comes into their purview. With their sense of certainty, ENTJs are decidedly willing to take on responsibility and will quickly take the initiative to bring order out of chaos. They are movers and shakers, becoming excited by an idea and enthusiastically working to find an application for it.

Intuition orients ENTJs to meanings, patterns, and the big picture, and thus their thinking is both logical and abstract. Intuition's orientation to possibilities also makes their thinking creative and futuristic. Intuition provides support to dominant thinking by keeping ENTJs open to new information and new possibilities, but the dominant force for them is still a drive to analyze and to make logical sense of things.

ENTJs are energetic planners and builders, projecting themselves into the future with ease. As complex and critical thinkers, they naturally find logical flaws and inconsistencies in what is said or done, and are at home analyzing what will or won't work in a plan. Since ENTJs strategically analyze alternatives and possible outcomes, they believe, and easily convince others, that they have the wherewithal to make the future happen now. The truth is that they usually *will* make it happen; they will set a goal and achieve it at all costs. As a result, ENTJs are often found in leadership positions.

ENTJs are intellectually curious and love exploring new ideas. They like to exercise their ingenuity in solving problems and in addressing challenges. In spite of their love of mental models, their drive for closure in the outer world does tend to make them pragmatic. Above all, ENTJs want to be "effective" and like to demonstrate it. They want the world to run efficiently and planfully, but may themselves be intolerant of routine and may prefer to leave follow-through on plans and projects to others.

ENTJs deeply value competence and intelligence, both in themselves and in others. They set high goals, and continually hold themselves to an exceptionally high (possibly too high at times) standard of accomplishment. ENTJs value achievement and want to be recognized for what they have done. They are strong believers in the power of the will, assuming that with the correct application of willpower, anything can be accomplished. ENTJs also deeply value autonomy, and they are often acutely aware of status and power issues.

ENTJs are often found in the fields of science and technology, but are also found in teaching, law, business, and the military. Typically, they are found in executive, administrative, and leadership positions, whatever their field.

ENTJs are usually quite frank and straightforward in

their interactions with others. They are confident and assertive, and can take a clear stand and maintain it in the face of dissent. ENTJs will not be bound by rules or expectations imposed by others. Interestingly, they may be or appear to be all too willing to make decisions for others. Though rules may be seen as practical necessities, their inherent skepticism won't let them follow structures without question. If they see a better way, and they often do, ENTJs will drive their way to the top in order to redefine the rules. If they appear to hold themselves in high regard at times, it is only because they are certain of the correctness of their logic and insightful analyses, and are willing to outwardly express their certainty.

ENTJs deeply value justice, and they consider it essential to treat others fairly. Paradoxically, in their drive to be fair, they may come across as cool and impersonal. In the extreme, they can appear arrogant, critical, and argumentative. They may even overwhelm others with their drive and decisiveness. ENTJs may indeed be insensitive at times to interpersonal issues and the needs of others, particularly others' needs for appreciation or recognition.

Without development of introverted intuition, ENTJs can rush to closure, making decisions without pausing to gather enough information and without exploring possible alternatives. Thus, they may appear rigid and closed to input. Development of intuition will help them stay open to new information. Since ENTJs can be bored with the literal working out of plans, development of sensing will help them have a healthy respect for the details necessary to turn plans into realities. Development of feeling will benefit ENTJs in a number of ways, including helping them be more tolerant of the perceived incompetence or inefficiency of others, and of themselves. Such development would also help them give greater attention to the human aspects of situations, including how others and they themselves feel.

Under stress ENTJs may become hypercritical of themselves and of others. They may also become angry and controlling, issuing directives without attention to the consequences or the impact of their behavior on other people. Under extreme stress, and in contrast to their usually active and logical style, they may feel trapped, overemotional, and alone, or may even hear innocent comments as personal attacks.

---

**Keywords**
driving ■ leader ■ planner ■ vision ■ organizer
strategic ■ systems ■ tough-minded ■ logic ■ analysis ■ patterns ■ competence

Gordon D. Lawrence, Ph.D.

**Gordon Lawrence,** Ph.D., has been developing practical uses of the Myers-Briggs Type Indicator since the early 1970s. He helped to organize the first-ever conference of MBTI users in 1975, and helped to found the Association for Psychological Type four years later. When his book, *People Types and Tiger Stripes,* appeared in 1979 it was the first book about uses of the MBTI other than the MBTI Manual. Through workshops and college teaching, he has introduced the MBTI and its concepts to thousands of people. *People Types and Tiger Stripes,* now much expanded and in its third edition (1993), continues to be widely read. Among numerous publications he has authored are, *Looking at Type and Learning Styles* (1997), and *Descriptions of the 16 Types* (1995, 1998).

Gordon was the third president of the Association for Psychological Type, and directed the development of its MBTI training program to qualify people to purchase and use the MBTI. He used the MBTI extensively in research, teaching and consulting during the twenty years that he was professor of instructional leadership at the University of Florida. He has served on the training faculty and the board of directors of CAPT since its founding in 1975 by Mary McCaulley and Isabel Myers, the author of the MBTI.

Charles R. Martin, Ph.D.

**Charles R. Martin,** Ph.D., is a licensed psychologist whose background includes work in personality assessment, the psychology of peak experiences, and integral (mind-body-spirit) approaches to individual development and optimum performance. Charles' work with individuals and organizations focuses on executive coaching, leadership development, career planning and personal coaching. He has provided services in business, government, healthcare, military and educational settings, and his clients include Fortune 50 companies. All of Charles' work has a developmental focus, with the intent of building organizational talent and empowering individuals to live and work with balance and effectiveness.

Charles is the author of *Looking at Type: The Fundamentals* and *Looking at Type and Careers,* and has co-authored *Out-of-the-Box Exercises: Using the Power of Type to Build Effective Teams.*

In his coaching work with individuals, Charles' emphasis is on promoting self-mastery and enhanced effectiveness through the development of personal and professional skills. In both consulting and coaching, he draws on his background to use a variety of models and assessment tools. Charles was the architect of, and a major contributor in the development of CAPT's qualifying program, and consults and delivers MBTI training workshops nationally and internationally.

## W

## Z